Letters on the Equality of the Sexes and Other Essays

LETTERS

ON THE

EQUALITY OF THE SEXES,

AND THE

CONDITION OF WOMAN.

ADDRESSED TO

MARY S. PARKER,

PRESIDENT OF THE

Boston Female Anti-Slavery Society.

By Sarah M. Grimke

BOSTON:
PUBLISHED BY ISAAC KNAPP,
25, CORNHILL.

1838.

Sarah Grimké

Letters on the Equality of the Sexes and Other Essays

Edited and with an Introduction by
Elizabeth Ann Bartlett

Yale University Press
New Haven and London

Designed by Sujata Keshavan Guha and set in Sabon type by
Brevis Press, Bethany, Connecticut.
Printed in the United States of America by Vail-Ballou Press,
Binghamton, New York.

Library of Congress Cataloging-in-Publication Data

Grimké, Sarah Moore, 1792–1873.
Letters on the equality of the sexes, and other essays / Sarah
  Grimké: edited and with an introduction by Elizabeth
  Ann Bartlett.
    p. cm.
Bibliography: p.
Includes index.
Contents: Letters on the equality of the sexes—The education of
women—Condition of women—Essay on the laws respecting
women—Marriage—Sisters of charity.
    ISBN 0-300-04113-6 (alk. paper)
    1. Women—United States—Social conditions. 2. Women's
rights—United States. I. Bartlett, Elizabeth Ann. II. Title.
HQ1423.G79 1988
305.4'2'0973—do19   87-23940
                                                   CIP

10 9 8 7 6 5 4 3 2 1

For my mother

Contents

Note on the Editing Process

It is not clear whether Sarah Grimké ever intended to publish the manuscripts contained herein. Certainly she edited and revised some of them many times; but none is in a finished, polished form. They are rough, with many additions and deletions, quotations sometimes randomly thrown in, sometimes without clear beginning and concluding paragraphs, often with long run-on sentences or without any sentence structure at all.

The purist would have me retain every misspelled word and crossed-out sentence. My intent, however, has been to make the manuscripts as readable as possible, while taking great care to preserve Grimké's meanings and ideas in the form in which she originally presented them. To this end I have retained such spellings as were popular at the time, such as "thro'" and "Hindoo," but have corrected any obvious misspellings. I have punctuated her sentences for readability. I have at times deleted a phrase or a paragraph; these are noted with ellipses. I have sometimes inserted a word for greater clarity; this is denoted by brackets. And I have occasionally moved a paragraph to a place in the text where it made more sense; this is footnoted. Grimké included several extensive quotations. Where possible, the source has been noted, but most are simply included without citations.

It is possible that all of the manuscripts, with the exception of "Marriage," were draft sections of one essay. "Sisters of Charity" is also entitled "Condition of Women" and contains many of the arguments found in "Condition of Women." A manuscript not included here, entitled "Education of Women Number Two Section Two," duplicates many of the same arguments and much of the wording found in both "The Education of Women" and "Condition of Women." "Essay on the Laws Respecting Women" contains points similar to those raised in "Sisters of Charity." With the exception of "Education of Women Number Two Section Two," however, each essay had enough integrity to stand on its own, so I have included each one as a separate entity.

All the manuscripts are located in the Theodore Dwight Weld Collection in the Clements Library at the University of Michigan. No dates are given, but it has been estimated by Gerda Lerner and others that they were written largely between 1848 and 1855. Thus there is no strict chronological order to these essays, which are arranged as they are here because this is how they seemed to flow best. I placed "Sisters of Charity" last because it is the strongest statement of Grimké's feminism.

Acknowledgments

I would like to thank the many people who helped in the writing, editing, and publication of this book. First, many thanks to my Ph.D. advisor, Mulford Q. Sibley, for suggesting Sarah Grimké to me as someone I might include in my research, and for his continual support and enduring friendship.

I am grateful to the political science department and the College of Liberal Arts of the University of Minnesota-Duluth and to the University of Minnesota for their financial assistance.

I wish to thank the Clements Library at the University of Michigan for permission to publish the essays, and the staff of the Clements Library for all their helpfulness. Special thanks go to Galen Wilson, Manuscript Curator at the Clements Library, for his help in deciphering Sarah Grimké's often illegible handwriting and for making the project so enjoyable.

Thanks go as well to the many librarians at the University of Minnesota-Duluth, especially Mara Hart, who joined in the treasure hunt and helped me track down obscure sources.

I am especially grateful to Sandy Cochran for all her efforts in transforming the original handwritten manuscripts into typewritten copy and researching Sarah Grimké's references. Special thanks as well to Amy Ollendorf for her invaluable assistance in researching and typing the final version of the manuscript.

Barb Williams gave invaluable help with the computer; and special thanks to Bonnie Turk for her help, encouragement, and support in typing, printing, xeroxing, mailing, and generally getting the book out. Thanks also to Judy Trolander for reviewing the manuscript, and for all her comments and suggestions. The anonymous reader for Yale University Press also provided many useful comments.

I would especially like to thank Craig Grau for his comments, criticisms, and suggestions; for his efforts in securing funds and research assistance; for listening; for caring enough to keep pushing me; for always believing in me; for being a friend.

I would like to thank the editors at Yale: Barbara Folsom, for her fine job in editing the manuscript, Stephanie Jones, and Chuck Grench for his enthusiastic support, patience, kind words, and immense cooperation and assistance.

This book could not have been started or completed without the enthusiasm and support of many students, especially those in women's studies; to them my sincere thanks.

Finally, I would like to express my gratitude to my family and friends for their encouragement, love, and celebration.

*Letters on the Equality of the Sexes
and Other Essays*

1.

Introduction

When the leaders of the early women's movement in America are named, Sarah Grimké usually goes unmentioned. Yet several years before Elizabeth Cady Stanton and Lucretia Mott organized the first women's rights convention, Sarah and her sister, Angelina, were paving the way, speaking out for the rights of slaves and women on the abolitionist platform. And six years before Margaret Fuller wrote *Woman in the Nineteenth Century,* Sarah published the first book-length philosophical statement by an American woman on "the woman question," *Letters on the Equality of the Sexes.*

Sarah and Angelina Grimké (1792–1873 and 1805–79, respectively) were pioneering figures in both the abolitionist and the women's rights movements. Of the two, it is generally acknowledged that Sarah was the more ardent feminist. For Angelina, the "woman question" was a side issue to abolition. But Angelina did make an important contribution to feminist literature in portions of her abolitionist tracts, *Appeal to the Christian Women of the Southern States* and *Appeal to the Women of the Nominally Free States.* In these she suggests the parallel between the oppression of slaves and that of women, and she urges women to political action. Nevertheless, these are primarily abolitionist rather than feminist treatises. For Sarah, on the other hand, the "woman question" became central to her life. This is reflected in her writings, and for this reason I have chosen to include only her writings in this volume.

Sarah and Angelina Grimké were the first female abolitionist agents—the only women among Theodore Weld's band of seventy who toured New England in the late 1830s, speaking out against the ills of slavery. Their prominence on the lecture circuit quickly brought the Grimké sisters to the forefront of the abolitionist movement. They stirred souls and controversy wherever they spoke. Women, and occasionally men, would walk six, eight, ten miles to hear the sisters speak. Their large following was due in part to their reputation—especially Angelina's—as eloquent speakers, and in part to their background, unique among the abolitionist speakers, as former slaveowners. In fact, however, their notoriety stemmed in large part from the fact that they were engaged in an activity forbidden to women by the mores of the day—speaking in public. This in and of itself made their cause not only that of the slave but of women.

So the sisters were both acclaimed and condemned. The most vicious attack came in the form of a Pastoral Letter from the Council of Congregationalist Ministers of Massachusetts, which denounced their behavior as unwomanly and unChristian. It read in part:

> We invite your attention to the dangers which at present seem to threaten the female character with widespread and permanent injury. The appropriate duties and influence of women are clearly stated in the New Testament. . . . We appreciate the unostentatious prayers of women in advancing the cause of religion at home and abroad; in Sabbath-schools; in leading religious inquirers to the pastor for instruction; and in all such associated efforts as become the modesty of her sex. . . . But when she assumes the place and tone of man as a public reformer . . . she yields the power which God has given her for her protection, and her character becomes unnatural. (Stanton, Anthony, Gage, 1881: 1:61)

While the attacks certainly raised concern and doubt for Sarah and Angelina (when Angelina, many years later, could not nurse her first child, she wondered if it was because of her earlier unwomanly behavior), they continued their work. Sarah confronted the attacks head-on in a series of letters to Mary Parker, president of the Boston Female Anti-Slavery Society, in the *New England Spectator,* on "The Province of Woman." In these letters she responded specifically to the charges raised against her and her sister in the Pastoral Letter, arguing:

> In contemplating the great moral reformation of the day, and the part which they [women] are bound to take in them, instead of puzzling themselves with the harassing, because unnecessary inquiry, how far they may go without overstepping the bounds of propriety, which separate male and female duties, they will only inquire, "Lord, what wilt thou have me do?" They will be enabled to see the simple truth, that God had made no distinction between men and women as moral beings . . . whatsoever it is morally

right for a man to do, it is morally right for a woman to do.
(Grimké, 1838:9–10)

Sarah went on to chronicle the condition of women in the United States, Europe, Asia, and Africa; to analyze the laws affecting women; to examine the inequities women faced in education and employment; to address the specific injuries suffered by female slaves; and, perhaps most significantly, to provide a biblical justification for the moral autonomy and equality of women. William Lloyd Garrison printed these letters in his abolitionist newspaper, *The Liberator,* and eventually Sarah published them in a single tract, the main text of which is included in this volume, *Letters on the Equality of the Sexes.*

After the Pastoral Letter, both Sarah and Angelina, but especially Sarah, took up the cause of women with more fervor in their speeches on abolition. They raised the issue of the specific sufferings of female slaves and boldly addressed their sexual victimization. They also likened the plight of all women to that of slaves and continually defended the rights and duties of women as moral and intelligent beings.

Bringing "the woman question" into the abolitionist arena sparked much controversy, not only among the audiences and the press, but also within the abolitionist movement itself. In fact, this was one of the issues that eventually divided the movement.

For a few years, the Grimké sisters were the acknowledged leaders of the female antislavery movement. It was they who were chosen to present an antislavery petition with twenty thousand women's signatures to a committee of the Legislature of the State of Massachusetts—the first time a woman had ever addressed such a body in this country. Though their activity and prominence waned after their retirement into domesticity following Angelina's marriage to Theodore Weld in 1838, the sisters continued to play a role in both abolitionist and feminist politics for the remainder of their lives. In the 1850s, Sarah wrote fragments of manuscripts regarding women and the law, education, marriage, employment—all contained in this volume. She also compiled the laws regarding women's status in different states. She occasionally wrote articles anonymously for the *New York Tribune, The Independent,* and *The Woman's Journal,* though these are unaccounted for and unavailable (Lerner, 1971:355).

Throughout her life, Sarah continued to pursue her interest in the conditions of working women. Toward the end of her life she developed more of an interest in suffrage. She and Angelina shared the vice-presidency of the Massachusetts Woman Suffrage Association from 1870 until their deaths. And in 1870, at the ages of seventy-eight and sixty-five, Sarah and Angelina led forty-two women in a suffrage demonstration, marching through a snowstorm to cast their ballots in an election despite the restrictions against them doing so. Each woman dropped her ballot into a special container that the election officials had prepared, and then all marched back as they had come. While this did not win them the right to vote, it did gain significant amounts of publicity for their cause.

The impact of the Grimké sisters on both the abolition and women's rights movements was significant. In their speaking tour alone, it is estimated that they were heard by forty thousand people (Lerner, 1971:226). Their very presence as women forced people to question their own attitudes toward women's roles and rights. And, as Lerner has said, "at the very least, as Weld had pointed out, they won the right for respectable, religious women to speak in public" (Lerner, 1971:228).

Sarah and Angelina were also role models for younger women who later became leaders in the feminist movement—Abby Kelley, Elizabeth Cady Stanton, Lucy Stone, Susan B. Anthony—all were inspired by the words and deeds of the Grimké sisters (Lerner, 1971:12). Sarah and Angelina are two of the eighteen women to whom the *History of Woman Suffrage* (Stanton, Anthony, and Gage's massive account of the woman suffrage movement in the United States) is dedicated. The references to the Grimkés in that book indicate their pioneering role and the deep respect their contemporaries felt for them.

Of particular interest here is the impact Sarah's *Letters on the Equality of the Sexes* had on her contemporaries. Certainly they aroused controversy. Although many churches shut their doors to both sisters following the publication of the *Letters,* it seems that their impact on feminists was significant and lasting. Lucy Stone traced her involvement in the women's movement to the Pastoral Letter and Sarah's response to it. Lucy wrote to her brother, "I tell you they [Sarah's articles on women in *The Spectator*] are first-rate and only help to confirm the resolution I had made before, to call no man master" (Nies, 1977:23). Lucretia Mott described the *Letters* as "the most important work since Mary Wollstonecraft's *Rights of Women* [*sic*]" (Nies, 1977:24). Apparently, when Elizabeth Cady Stanton and Lucretia Mott visited England in 1840, they found the *Letters* well known there (Flexner, 1959:344). Many decades after their publication, Stanton turned to Grimké's biblical analysis of women's rights before writing her own *Woman's Bible* in 1898 (Nies, 1977:24).

Though significant to Sarah's contemporaries, her *Letters on the Equality of the Sexes* have largely been forgotten until fairly recently. From the time of their original publication in 1838 there had been no reprintings until 1970, when there were two (by Burt Franklin, and Source Book Press, both of New York). In addition, Gerda Lerner has edited and published two of the previously unpublished manuscripts contained in this volume: "Sisters of Charity" (*Signs,* 1, no. 1 [Autumn 1975]:246–56); and "Marriage" (in Lerner's *The Female Experience: An American Documentary* [Indianapolis: Bobbs-Merrill Co., 1977], 87–98). These have served to make Sarah Grimké's works more visible to current feminists and historians. Nancy

Cott's book on women in the nineteenth century, *The Bonds of Womanhood,* is significant in this regard. The title is taken directly from the closing of Sarah's letters in *Letters on the Equality of the Sexes*—"thine in the bonds of womanhood" (Cott, 1977).

This volume differs from the other publications of Sarah Grimké's work in being the only complete collection of her feminist writings. It also includes some essays—"The Education of Women," "Condition of Women," and "Essay on the Laws Respecting Women"—which have never before seen the light of day, thus enabling the reader to trace the development of Sarah's feminist thought over time in a way that has not been possible before.

Grimké's *Letters on the Equality of the Sexes* and other writings have not received the recognition they deserve. As Eleanor Flexner has argued, "Six years before the far more widely known *Woman in the Nineteenth Century* by Margaret Fuller, this pamphlet [*Letters on the Equality of the Sexes*] deserves the honor usually bestowed on the later work, of being known as the first serious discussion of woman's rights by an American woman" (Flexner, 1959:344). This volume was compiled in recognition of that deserved place of the *Letters* and of Sarah Grimké in the history of feminism.

But Sarah Grimké's writings are not only significant for their place in the history of feminism but also for the insights they provide into issues of contemporary feminism. One hundred and fifty years ago Grimké addressed problems such as "comparable worth" and the "superwoman syndrome," problems still being encountered by liberal feminists today. She presented a feminist critique of religion while maintaining a religious base to her feminism. She found a way to invalidate patriarchal religion's subjugation of women while clearly affirming women as spiritual beings. In this she prepared the way for the work of contemporary feminist theologians such as Carol Ochs and Mary Daly (Ochs, 1983; Daly, 1978 and 1985). Also, in her argument that women's moral natures are uniquely shaped by their experience as mothers, Grimké anticipated the thinking of contemporary maternalists such as Adrienne Rich and Jean Bethke Elshtain (Rich, 1976; Elshtain, 1981) and thus sheds light on the current feminist debate regarding the significance to be placed on women's maternal qualities.[1] Perhaps most important, Grimké's own shift from a male-centered to a female-centered feminism offers us intriguing insights into the current minimalist/maximalist debate (that is, between those feminists who seek to minimize the differences between the sexes and those who would maximize them).

I will explore how Sarah Grimké's work relates to this debate in contemporary feminism in more depth at the end of this introduction. My

1. For a better understanding of the issues, see Joyce Trebilcot, ed., *Mothering: Essays in Feminist Theory* (Totowa, N.J.: Rowman and Allanheld, 1983), and Mary G. Dietz, "Citizenship and Maternal Thinking: Citizenship with a Feminist Face: The Problem with Maternal Thinking," *Political Theory* (February 1985), 19–37.

main purpose here, however, is to examine the nature and development of her feminist thought in its own right. Fully to appreciate that thought, it is essential to place it in the contexts of her life and times. To that end, I will examine, first, the intellectual and social origins of nineteenth-century feminism and, then, the origins of Grimké's personal feminism in her own life story.

Intellectual and Social Origins

Sarah Grimké's feminism was born out of an intellectual and social context that fostered the questioning of women's status. Liberal political ideas of equality and natural rights, Quakerism, abolitionism, and even the cult of domesticity all contributed to the developing feminist movement of which Grimké was a part.

Though often characterized as being merely an offshoot of Enlightenment thought (Rossi, 1973), nineteenth-century feminist ideology in fact drew upon several different intellectual traditions—primarily, the Enlightenment, romanticism, utopian socialism, and Anglo-American radical sectarianism. Certainly, with their emphasis on liberty, equality, natural rights, and the importance of education and environment in shaping individual character, Enlightenment philosophies provided much fertile ground for feminist arguments. A fundamental tenet of the Enlightenment was the idea that the universe is understandable and orderly, and that universal truths are discoverable through reason and observation. Though religion and its "superstitions" were the main targets of the Enlightenment's critical attitude, they were certainly not the sole target. Religion, history, language, and the political and social orders were equally subjected to criticism (Gay, 1966:150). Recognizing no single set of convictions and no single culture as providing absolute standards, the Enlightenment ushered in an era of critical inquiry, at the same time clearing the way for feminism's critique of the position of women in society.

Enlightenment philosophers questioned the whole notion of a "human nature." Rather, they argued that human beings enter society as tabulae rasae, and that our characters are shaped by our experiences, education, and general environment. Opening this nature-versus-nurture debate had significant implications for feminists, who extended it to question the concept of a "female nature." Early feminists such as Mary Wollstonecraft and Frances Wright stressed the importance of education and socialization in shaping female character and behavior, and argued vigorously for the equal education of the sexes (Wollstonecraft, 1965; Wright, 1834).

Liberalism, the political philosophy that evolved from the Enlightenment, was articulated in the first half of the Enlightenment by natural law theorists such as John Locke and Thomas Jefferson, and in the second half by utilitarians such as Jeremy Bentham and John Stuart Mill (Gay, 1966:18).

Many of the early feminist writings were extensions of the arguments of natural law liberalism to include women. Whereas natural law theorists sought to guarantee the natural rights to life, liberty, and property equally to all men, feminists sought to guarantee these rights equally to all men and women. The principles and rhetoric of the Enlightenment theory of natural rights are evident, for example, in Mary Wollstonecraft's pioneering work, *A Vindication of the Rights of Women,* and in the 1848 women's rights manifesto "A Declaration of Sentiments," which merely includes women in the language of the classic natural law document, Jefferson's Declaration of Independence.

By the nineteenth century, the liberal political tradition, though still emphasizing liberty, moved away from the standard of natural rights to the principle of utilitarianism. Simply put, the utilitarian maxim for good government was what both Jeremy Bentham and John Stuart Mill called the greatest happiness principle—namely, the greatest good for the greatest number. Generally speaking, the utilitarian justification for any political principle or action was the amount of happiness and improvement it brought to the community. Feminists used this utilitarian standard to justify the free and equal status of women. Many feminists, Frances Wright and John Stuart Mill foremost among them, argued that, through the improvement of women's status, men and society in general would reap the benefits of increased civility, intelligence, and happiness.

While many tenets of feminist ideology are drawn from Enlightenment liberalism, nineteenth-century romanticism also spawned much feminist thinking. Indeed, Susan Phinney Conrad has gone so far as to argue that romanticism and feminism are one and the same (Conrad, 1976:78). As intellectuals and artists, romantics rejected Enlightenment ideas of rationality, atomistic individualism, and the scientific method. Theirs was a philosophy based on the assumption of the metaphysical union of all of creation, a transcendent unity and truth that could be discovered through the contemplation of nature and beauty and the development of one's spiritual and intuitive faculties.

This romantic concept of a universal transcendent harmony had significant implications for a developing feminist ideology. For Margaret Fuller, the nineteenth-century feminist and author of *Woman in the Nineteenth Century,* this implied the interweaving not only of individuals in a divine harmony, but also of male and female, masculine and feminine, in divine harmony. It led to her early notions of androgyny.

The universal whole also implies a fundamental equality of women and men. Every soul is an expression of the universal soul: no one has "better connections" than another. A soul knows no distinction of race or sex, intellect or strength, wealth or status. All—male and female alike—are equal, for each is an equal expression of the universal soul.

The most important political and moral value of romanticism, and the feminism that draws upon it, is the freedom for individuals to be self-determining—that is, to become more and more themselves. This theme of women's self-determination and discovery, both of themselves and of the nature of womanhood, is reiterated throughout the writings of nineteenth-century feminists.

In its valuing of intuitive knowledge, spirituality, poetic imagination, reverence for the earth and its wisdom, beauty, and creativity—all qualities most often associated with female nature—romanticism at its core affirmed "the feminine" and "femaleness." Certainly this provided an intellectual context in which romantic feminists such as Sarah Grimké's contemporary Margaret Fuller were able to articulate their beliefs and gain acceptance for them. (The significance of this for feminism as a whole has been lasting and is evident in the woman-centered visions of such contemporary feminists as Susan Griffin, Adrienne Rich, and Audre Lorde.)

Nineteenth-century feminist ideology also had roots in a third intellectual and political tradition: utopian socialism. Utopian socialists such as Robert Owen and Charles Fourier were critical of the existing social and economic order. They especially objected to the exploitation of an economic underclass that resulted from the prevailing system of economic individualism and competition, and sought to replace this system with "cooperation" and "association."

Utopian socialists shared the Enlightenment view that human character is shaped by one's environment. Believing that evil conditions and bad training create evil individuals, not vice versa, the utopian socialists argued that the social ills of the day could be cured by creating new social institutions and by teaching principles of "brotherhood." This they set about doing in small-scale experimental communities throughout Europe and the United States.

Utopian socialists advocated the full equality of condition of all individuals in the society, females as well as males. They advocated the economic, educational, and political liberty and equality of women. Moreover, they were among the first to extend the argument for women's freedom and equality to the private sphere. Many sought reform of the marriage relationship, and some advocated abolishing the institution of marriage altogether. In the utopian communities, many domestic tasks, such as laundry, cooking, and child care, were the collective responsibility of both women and men in the community, freeing women to follow other pursuits.

Thus, utopian socialism was fertile ground for feminist arguments. In particular, feminist insights into the necessary links between women's domestic role and their economic, social, and spiritual oppression can be traced back to the socialist tradition. For example, socialist feminist Frances Wright was arguing in the 1830s that women largely made up the economic underclass in this society. Unable to earn a wage sufficient to support themselves, and thus forced to depend upon men and their larger incomes for survival, women retreated into domesticity (or prostitution) (Wright, Nov. 9, 1830:39). Feminists recognized that the demands of domestic chores and child-rearing perpetuated women's oppression, and some sought socialist solutions. Margaret Fuller, for example, championed community laundries and child care as prerequisites to women finding sufficient time and solitude for self-discovery and growth (Fuller, 1978:58; Ossoli, 1856:187–88). Many, including the Grimké sisters, lived for a time in utopian socialist communities in which all domestic chores were performed communally.

Finally, the other major intellectual tradition in which feminism finds its roots is what has been called Anglo-American radical sectarianism (Cooper and Cooper, 1973). This was not a single body of thought, but rather a term encompassing a variety of dissenting sects, including Quakerism, abolitionism, nonresistance, "come-outerism," "perfectionism," and spiritualism. The sects were linked in part by overlapping memberships, but more importantly by a common belief in the moral supremacy of individual conscience. Individuals were ultimately held accountable to God's will, but only as they discovered it through conscience, "inner light," or spiritual revelation. For many of the sectarians, especially "come-outers," perfectionists, and nonresistance abolitionists, this moral supremacy of conscience implied an opposition to any form of government that attempted to mediate between the individual and God (Perry, 1973:36, 57, 66, 92, and 95). They rejected political activity because it is tainted by the laws of men, a theme which carried over into American feminism.

Feminists also picked up on the sectarian notion of human perfectibility. The followers of John Humphrey Noyes—"perfectionists"—believed that if individuals were to follow the dictates of their consciences, they would be able to achieve perfect holiness. As Hersh has pointed out, this belief in human perfectibility underlies the feminist idea that women and men not only could but *should* change in a way that would minimize sex differences (Hersh, 1978:206).

Of all the sects, Quakerism had perhaps the strongest influence on American feminism. Many of the nineteenth-century American feminist leaders, Lucretia Mott foremost among them, were Quakers.[2] Along with Elizabeth Cady Stanton, Mott and three other Quaker women—Mary Ann McClintoch, Jane Hunt, and Martha Wright—organized the first women's rights convention in Seneca Falls, New York, in 1848. At least one-fourth of the one hundred signers of the Declaration of Sentiments, drafted at the convention, were Quaker women (Hewitt, 1986:29).

Three aspects of Quaker doctrine and practice were particularly conducive to the development of American feminism: (1) the doctrine of

2. Blanche Glassman Hersh made a study of feminist abolitionist leaders. Of the fifty-one studied, twenty-one grew up in Quaker, Unitarian, or Universalist families. Of the twenty-seven raised in evangelist or orthodox religious traditions, nine rejected their faith to become Unitarians, Universalists, or Quakers (Hersh, 1978).

"inner light"; (2) the faith and practice of marriage; and (3) the roles of women in the ministry and governance of the church. First, as with the other sects, according to Quaker doctrine, all persons, male and female alike, are to be guided in their moral actions by their "inner light" of conscience. This promoted an autonomy and independent spirit in Quaker women. The doctrine of inner light also established a principle of the moral equality of the sexes, a belief central to the views of feminist Friends. The Quaker beliefs in the moral autonomy and moral equality of women are at the very core of Grimké's arguments in *Letters on the Equality of the Sexes*.

Second, Quakers believed in the spiritual equality of partners in marriage. Husband and wife exchanged reciprocal vows in the marriage ceremony and were expected to be "companion" and "friend" to each other (Hersh, 1978:200; Hewitt, 1986:31). In practice, especially among the agrarian Quakers who predominated among Quaker feminists, Quaker husbands and wives were more likely than their contemporaries to share their labors, though gender divisions did not altogether disappear (Hewitt, 1986:29–32). Quaker women ministers often traveled in their ministry, and it was not uncommon for their husbands to take care of the children at these times (Hersh, 1978:222). Quakers raised their children with a strong sense of community awareness and conscience, and believed in educating their daughters as well as their sons. With its emphasis on equality and self-reliance, the Quaker family was an early training ground for many feminists.

Finally, to a certain extent, Quakerism provided women with a voice equal to men's in the ministry and governance of the Society of Friends. The fact that women could be ministers in the Society gave some of them the experience of speaking in mixed groups—a rare opportunity in a time when women were not "supposed" to speak in public at all, let alone to "promiscuous" (mixed-sex) audiences. In addition, female ministers served as role models to other women, presenting them with the example of females acting in a capacity equal to males.

However, the role of women in the Society of Friends was also one source of division in the Society in the 1820s and 1840s.[3] Though as ministers and speakers women and men were regarded as equals, according to the official *Rules of Discipline*, women and men were to sit in separate meetings, and each meeting had responsibility for the members of its own sex. As Quakerism grew, most of the policies and programs of the Society came to be implemented by a core group of ministers and elders. While women could and did serve in this group, men tended to dominate (Hewitt, 1986:36).

Concerned over the growing bureaucratization of the Society of Friends, as well as disagreeing over interpretation of texts, a dissenting group

3. Other sources of division included concerns about the increasing bureaucratization of the Society, its role in worldly reform, and the proper interpretation of Quaker texts (Hewitt, 1986:36).

known as the Hicksites (so called because they followed the teachings of Elias Hicks) split off from orthodox Quakers. Hicksites rejected churchly structure and placed more emphasis on simple democratic forms of worship. They asserted the full equality of women and, over time, grew increasingly radical and vocal regarding women's rights. Hicksite women called their own meetings; trained themselves as speakers, healers, and ministers; and claimed the right to equality with men in decision-making bodies (Hewitt, 1986:38). Hicksite Quakerism was the seedbed for both Quaker feminism and the larger American feminist movement. Many of the Hicksites' views regarding women's autonomy and equality, and many of their leaders, filtered into the women's rights movement of the 1840s and 1850s.

One of the few points agreed upon by the major feminist thinkers of the 1830s and 1840s was that priests and "religious superstition" seemed to have a hold on women. Wright, Fuller, Grimké, and others were unanimous in their denunciation of clerics and clerical control over women's lives and beliefs. Feminists recognized that breaking with orthodox religious tradition was an essential step toward the development of a feminist consciousness. Indeed, Hersh has argued that "emancipation from religious orthodoxy was a crucial element in the development of a feminist leadership" (Hersh, 1978:ix). Radical sectarianism provided an avenue of dissent from orthodox religion that stressed women's ability, indeed duty, to think and act according to the dictates of their own moral authority. It supported women's moral autonomy and equality. And, doctrine aside, it provided a practical "guide to survival as a righteous but unpopular minority" (Hersh, 1978:253), invaluable training for those who sought to survive as feminists.

Though it is true that these traditions—Enlightenment liberalism, romanticism, utopian socialism, and Anglo-American radical sectarianism— comprised some of the intellectual roots of American feminism, the movement grew from social roots as well. These roots tap into three different, though related, sources: (1) the deprivation in status experienced by middle-class women; (2) the cult of domesticity; and (3) other social reform movements.

In the Jacksonian era of the 1820s and 1830s, the mood in the country was one of limitless opportunity and optimism for the "common man." Industrialization and urbanization were expanding the options and horizons of the average middle-class man. Just the opposite was the case, however, for middle-class women: while men's roles and opportunities were expanding, women's were contracting. More and more, women's traditional functions—spinning, weaving, soap-making, and so forth—were being performed outside the home in factories. Woman's sphere narrowed to what has been called "domesticity"—housekeeping, child care, entertaining. Finding their own roles to be no longer vital to the household economy, at the same time that their husbands' and brothers' roles were gaining even more importance, women suffered from deprivation in their relative status. They simply were not valued as their mothers before them had been, or as their husbands and brothers were valued now. Most women adapted and passively accepted their new roles and status. However, for those women who did not accept the justifying myth of "the cult of true womanhood" (Welter, 1966:151–74), this relative loss of status catalyzed them into feminist awareness and action (Freeman, 1975:14–17; Rossi, 1973:241–51).

According to the status deprivation theory, only those women who rejected the cult of true womanhood joined the feminist ranks, but Cott has successfully argued that the cult of domesticity itself was fertile ground for feminism (Cott, 1977). On the surface, it would appear that the roles and vision of womanhood cultivated by the cult of domesticity would negate those of feminism. The cult of domesticity supported the view of women's subordination to men: women's role was to serve men, in their work and in their home life. All their wages and property belonged to their husbands. Insofar as women were to be educated, it was to make them better companions to men and better mothers of sons. Women were expected to make of their homes a refuge from the competitive world and salve men's wounds and weariness. Women were to find self-fulfillment in self-denial.

It is clear how rebellion against the cult of domesticity would foster feminist self-assertion and self-worth in women, but how was immersion in domesticity conducive to feminism? In many ways, the cult of domesticity set women apart from men; and in matters of morality, it set women above men. Men were caught up in the cruel and competitive world of work and the marketplace, whereas women's world was that of church and home. Because of their unique links to religious sentimentality and to affectional relationships, especially that between mother and child, women were widely regarded as morally superior to men. Their vocation was to redeem men and the world. Feminists appropriated this claim to women's moral superiority and made it central to much of nineteenth-century feminism. They used the notion of women's moral superiority to justify their involvement in government, the church, education, medicine, and law. These institutions could only benefit from women's influence. Women were not inferior to men; indeed, they were superior. All the more reason why they should have a voice in shaping the character of the nation. Women's roles as wives and mothers did not disqualify them from public life, feminists argued, but rather better prepared them for it. This maternalistic vision is still echoed among contemporary feminists such as Rich and Elshtain.

Perhaps most significant for feminism was the way in which the cult of domesticity fostered a collective consciousness among women (Cott, 1977:passim). The canon of domesticity classed all women together and gave them all the same vocation (Cott, 1977:98). Women were educated together for purposes of fulfilling that common vocation. In their homes, women shared housekeeping and child-care tasks. As part of their domestic function, women increasingly became active in moral reform societies, through which they gained a sense of common purpose and identity. And perhaps of greatest consequence for feminism was the developing "female world of love and ritual" (Smith-Rosenberg, 1975)—the experience of female friendship that lay the foundation for feminist sisterhood.

As men's lives and work increasingly took them away from home and as women's lives and work increasingly narrowed their focus to the home, a specifically female world developed—a world of mother-daughter, sister-sister, aunt-niece, and female friend bonding. Rigid role definitions separated women and men from each other not only physically but emotionally. The notion of female "purity" made social intercourse between women and men nearly impossible (Taylor and Lasch, 1963:35). Men, corrupted and hardened by the competitive world of work and politics, could not be expected to respond to women's feelings. The identification of women, but not men, with matters of the heart, implied that women could find truly reciprocal relationships only with each other (Cott, 1984:168). And indeed, women turned to each other for the emotional support, understanding, and affection they needed and could find only with each other.

The implications of this "sisterhood of sensitivity" (Taylor and Lasch, 1963:34) went far beyond the meeting of affectional needs, however. Women turning to each other for affirmation and support fostered the type of group consciousness necessary for the development of a political consciousness of sex-class (Cott, 1977:194). Feminism only emerged as women came to regard themselves as a discrete class in society (Eisenstein, 1981). So, ironically, by fostering the development of female bonding and group identity, the cult of domesticity made conditions ripe for an incipient feminist movement.

Finally, nineteenth-century feminism found its roots in other social reform movements of the day. Historians have noted that women's rights only seem to make headway in a general environment of reform and in conjunction with other reform movements.[4] Endowed with their mission to regenerate the moral character of the society, women became crusaders in many different though interwoven reform movements—"moral reform," health reform, temperance, and antislavery.

The cult of domesticity was taking hold in women's lives at a time when religious revivalism was sweeping the country. The church was one arena in which women could find purpose and fulfillment outside the home, and women flocked to it. Female converts to the Second Great Awakening (1798–1826) outnumbered males three to two. Clergy called on women to use their unique moral natures to reform the world. Women formed prayer groups, missionary societies, and moral reform societies.

---

4. For a good discussion of this, see Sara Evans, *Personal Politics: The Roots of Women's Liberation in the Civil Rights Movement and the New Left* (New York: Random House, 1980).

The cult of domesticity also contributed to increasingly negative views toward sexuality (Rossi, 1973:272). Religious revivalism added to this the perspective of sexuality as sinful—men practiced licentiousness and women endured it (Cott, 1977:152). Women formed moral reform societies to oppose the existing double standard of sexual behavior, to eliminate prostitution, and to promote chastity and sexual purity in men as well as women.

These moral reform societies were intimately linked with the budding health reform movement. Begun in the 1820s, health reform was in large part a response to women's vulnerability to sexual disease and unwanted pregnancies. It stressed preventive hygiene—pure air, loose dress, exercise, and careful "regulation of the passions" (Leach, 1980:25). It sought to achieve marital success and social order through emotional, intellectual, and physical harmony. Both the moral reform and the health reform movements urged women to acquaint themselves with human anatomy, physiology, and sexuality. In so doing, they empowered women to take responsibility for their own health and sexuality.

Moral reform was also directly linked to the temperance movement. One way to control men's licentiousness was to temper their consumption of alcohol. The women of the temperance movement were not speaking out against the "evil of liquor" per se, but rather were combating the emotional, physical, and sexual abuse of women that so often accompanied men's drinking. Temperance movement women were strong female advocates. It should also be said, however, that some women were drawn to the women's rights movement because of their ill-treatment by men in the temperance movement. Susan B. Anthony, for example, began as a temperance reformer but converted to women's rights when she was not allowed to speak on the floor of a temperance convention.

Many women's rights advocates started in the abolition movement. For one thing, the movement taught them the political tactics of speaking, organizing, and strategizing. The antislavery petition campaign of 1834–43 gave women firsthand experience in practical politics, as they went door to door collecting signatures on antislavery petitions. Also, feminist leaders modeled some of their techniques after those of abolitionist leaders. Sarah Grimké, for example, used Theodore Weld as a role model. Other women's rights advocates drew on the precepts and strategies of abolitionist William Lloyd Garrison in pursuit of their goals for women (DuBois, 1979:251).

Not only did the antislavery movement teach women political skills, it also raised their awareness of their own subordinate status. Many, including Grimké, came to see parallels between their own position and that of slaves. Like women temperance reformers, women abolitionists became aware of their subordination to men in the movement. It was while being denied the right to speak because of their sex at the World Antislavery Convention in London in 1840 that Lucretia Mott and Elizabeth Cady Stanton hatched the idea for the first women's rights convention, held in Seneca

Falls, New York, eight years later. And, as stated previously, it was the clergy's attack on the propriety of women (meaning, specifically, the Grimké sisters) speaking out publicly against slavery that prompted Sarah Grimké to write *Letters on the Equality of the Sexes.*

Women's active involvement in reform movements and benevolent societies gave rise to feminism in a variety of ways. It provided women with social, political, and organizational skills. It gave them a sense of purposefulness, which increased their self-esteem. It raised their awareness of their common plight: all women—prostitutes, prisoners, slaves, working-class, and middle class—shared a subordinate status to men and all were victims of male dominance. Finally, the very definition of *sorority* is women working together with other women for a common purpose. Working side by side for social reform created bonds of sisterhood essential to feminist theory and practice.

Sarah Grimké: A Biographical Sketch

Sarah Grimké grew up in a slaveholding patriarchal family in Charleston, South Carolina. Her mother's family was part of the wealthy governing plutocracy of South Carolina; her father was chief judge of the South Carolina Supreme Court.

Her early years were ones of affluent material comfort, yet it was in these years that she experienced violations of her very being to which she would bear witness the rest of her life. The first of these was her witnessing the whipping of a slave. Repelled by the sight, Sarah at that moment became an opponent of slavery.

Another personal degradation was more diffuse: the general experience of growing up female in a household dominated by males. Sarah was a bright child, and her father and brother Thomas encouraged her intellectual development—to a point. Thomas taught her Latin, Greek, mathematics, geography. Yet as she grew older, she found her aspirations toward the higher education pursued by her brothers discouraged and her schooling changed to the more typical fare for a young woman of her day—French, watercolors, harspichord, and embroidery.

Sarah's mind and spirit were stifled. She felt that her calling was to be a lawyer, and she studied law secretly on her own. Her father is said to have told Sarah that she would have made the greatest jurist in the land— had she not been a woman. She learned very early what it meant to be denied something because of her sex, a lesson that was to shape the course of her life, both in what she did not become and in her life's testimony to the liberty and equality of women.

Well into her sixties this experience was still vivid to her. She wrote in "The Education of Women," "Had I received the education I wanted and been bred to the profession of the law, a dignity to which I secretly aspired,

I might have been a useful member of society, and instead of myself and my property being taken care of I might have been a protector of the helpless and the unfortunate, a pleader for the poor and the drunk" (Grimké, "Education of Women").

After her disappointment, she plunged into the life of the stereotypical Southern belle, spending her time frivolously at balls, parties, and picnics. Looking back on that period, she called it the "prostitution of my womanhood . . . the utter perversion of the ends of my being" (Grimké, "Education of Women").

Her years of gaiety were followed by years of somber solitude and meditation. Under the influence of the Reverend Dr. Henry Kollock, a Presbyterian minister, who warned her that her frivolity would lead to everlasting punishment, she tried to atone through good works and self-deprecation. Her diaries of the time are filled with despair of ever achieving salvation (Grimké diary, Theodore Weld MSS). The one bright spot in all of this was her sister, Angelina. When Angelina was born, Sarah, then twelve, requested that she be allowed to take care of the child. She became part sister, part mother to Angelina, forging the most important relationship of her life.

In 1819, Sarah accompanied her father to Philadelphia, where he had traveled for medical care. There she attended him in his final illness. This was a turning point for her, as she encountered the frailty of the person who had heretofore been the single most important source of order and authority in her life (Nies, 1977:13–14).

Sarah's time in Philadelphia was made more significant by the fact that it was there that she first became acquainted with the Society of Friends. She was impressed by the Quaker idea that women and men are equal through inner light and felt a calling from God to go north and become a Quaker minister. Thus began a fifteen-year period in Philadelphia (where she was joined by Angelina in 1829) of personal growth, intellectual development, and theological study with the Society of Friends. She read and reread John Woolman's works, in which she found great insight and inspiration. (Indeed, Woolman's journals read much as do Grimké's, including an early period of vanity and frivolity, followed by deep despair and spiritual distress, followed by spiritual enlightenment and comfort; Woolman, 1962:249–73). Both she and Woolman found a common source of support and inspiration in Quaker doctrine. She became for a time completely absorbed in Quakerism, her only source of current information being *The Friend,* a weekly newspaper of the Society of Friends (Birney, 1885:91; Lerner, 1971:65). Grimké was to spend many years with the Society of Friends, and its influence on her thought was deep. This is evident, for example, in her denunciation of vanity and concern with appearances, in her principle of nonresistance to violence, and in her emphasis on good acts.

But life with the Society was not easy for Grimké. She was constantly opposed by elder Jonathan Evans. Thus intimidated and condemned, she spoke in meetings only with intense suffering. She became increasingly dissatisfied with the Society's theological doctrines and particularly its racial prejudice and opposition to abolition. In a "Letter on the Subject of Prejudice Amongst the Society of Friends in the United States" (1839, Sarah Grimké, Letters, Boston Public Library MSS), she described in detail her disappointment with the blatant prejudice existent in the Society of Friends. She related that Friends were unwilling to associate with blacks and had even set up a separate bench for them in the meeting (on which Sarah and Angelina joined the blacks in protest). She went on to cite numerous examples of prejudice among the Friends, for example, that many were engaged in the cotton trade, and so on. She also expressed her sadness over the fact that to become an abolitionist was to lose caste in the Society.

Quakerism was perhaps most significant as Sarah's first introduction to the more general Puritan idea that each person must read and interpret the Bible for him- or herself and take responsibility for his or her own soul. This provided her with the justification for the primary source of her feminism, her own interpretation of the Bible.

During this time Grimké also became acquainted with the perfectionism of John Humphrey Noyes. In his writings, Noyes gave expression to much that Sarah believed regarding civil government, public worship, ministry, and the sabbath. She found in his work a wonderful release from the *duty* of public worship. She also found his no-government arguments of nonresistance and perfectionism to be compelling. Noyes argued that civil government is based on physical force and physical force is forbidden by the Law of Love. If we have no right to resist evil ourselves, then we have no right to call upon another to resist it for us. If we have no right to call on a magistrate for aid, then they have no right to render us aid. This gave support to Grimké's belief that God is the only true lawgiver and judge. Perfectionist thought runs throughout her feminist works, especially in her concern that no man be an intermediary between God and woman, as well as in her conviction of her right to interpret the Bible for herself.

Grimké's thought evolved away from the perfectionist stands against government, however, and she eventually sought full political rights and privileges for women. Hersh argues that the source of this feminist tenet was the Enlightenment ideology of human rights (Hersh, 1978:191). But one must be careful to distinguish the idea of having rights from the governing rules or moral principles that define the substance of those rights. Certainly the rhetoric of rights emerged from the Enlightenment, and Grimké borrowed the idea and its terminology, but it is not so clear that the rules upon which her concept of rights is based come from the Enlightenment. The source of Grimké's concept of rights is to be found not in the term "rights" but rather in the governing rules and principles. During the period in which she wrote *Letters on the Equality of the Sexes,* her principles were from quite a different source. Whereas for the Enlightenment the governing principle of human rights was a natural law discoverable only through our senses and our reason, Grimké's governing principle of human rights was a divine law discernible in the immutable truths of the Bible.

Twenty years later, Grimké did come to distinguish from divine will a natural law discernible through reason, which served as the basis of human conduct. This is clarified in the following passage:

> the will of *any being* ought not to be assigned as a rule of conduct for a rational creature. Truth should be the only standard of Right, and Truth stands alone, independent even of the will of Jehovah. . . . God never designed to make his arbitrary will the standard of our actions, he endowed us with reason and in these oracles received as his revelation to man, he says, "come now let us reason together saith the Lord." ("Essay on the Laws Respecting Women")

Yet even in justifying the use of reason, she relied upon revelation. The difference between Grimké's governing principles and those of the Enlightenment is that Grimké's are inextricably bound to the notion of a Creator and must find their ultimate justification not in reasoned principles but in the divine revelation of scripture. The basis for her concept of human rights remains fundamentally scriptural.

The other major influence on Sarah's thought at this time was her involvement in the abolitionist movement. The story of that involvement—her being one of Weld's seventy agents; the furor caused by Sarah and Angelina overstepping the bounds of propriety by speaking in public; the Pastoral Letter condemning their unwomanly behavior; Sarah's subsequent publication of her *Letters on the Equality of the Sexes*—has previously been told. But it is important here to trace the impact of her abolition work upon her feminism.

For several reasons, Sarah's work as an abolitionist deepened her concern for women's plight and propelled her into the women's rights movement. First of these was the above-mentioned controversy, both in and out of abolitionist circles, over women speaking in public before "promiscuous" audiences. They were constantly criticized and harassed for speaking in public simply because they were female. Wherever they went, they were asked what right women had to hold public meetings (Sarah Grimké to Elizabeth Pease, 1837). Finding their rights as women denied, they were forced to assert them even more vigorously.

As she wrote in *Letters on the Equality of the Sexes,* Sarah saw a strong parallel between the condition of the slaves whom she defended as an abolitionist and the condition of women. Both groups were treated as inferior beings and deprived of basic human liberties. The plight of the slavewoman was especially grave, since she was called upon to gratify the brutal appetites of her male masters. Sarah could not plead the cause of the slave without also pleading the cause of woman.

Finally, Sarah confronted the subordination of women among the women she encountered in her abolition work. In her manuscript on the "Education of Women" she reflected, "It was when my soul was deeply moved at the wrongs of the slave that I first perceived distinctly the subject condition of women" (Grimké, "Condition of Woman"). She was referring to her frequent experience in the antislavery petition campaign of seeing women who wanted to sign the petitions but were forbidden to do so by their husbands. Until that time, Sarah had not realized the extent to which women sacrificed their consciences to the opinions of husbands, brothers, and fathers in order to preserve domestic tranquillity (Grimké, "Condition of Woman").

For Sarah, the "woman question" was second to none in importance (Birney, 1885:172). She was an active speaker and writer on women's behalf. But Sarah's feminist activity came a decade before any organized movement for women's rights. By the time of the Seneca Falls Convention (1848), she had retired into domesticity with her sister and her sister's family. In 1838, Angelina had married fellow abolitionist Theodore Weld, and Sarah, who deliberately chose not to marry, lived with them, helping Angelina with the tasks of housekeeping and child rearing.[5] The enormity of this task increased greatly during the five years (1840–54) in which Sarah and the Welds ran a boarding school for more than twenty children in their own home.

In 1853, the Welds joined Raritan Bay Union, a cooperative community based on the principles of utopian socialist Charles Fourier. Largely at the urgings of Angelina, Sarah did not accompany them. It appears that over the years, Angelina had come to resent Sarah's mothering of herself and of her children, as well as her dependence on Angelina for any domestic life of her own. At the age of sixty, then, Sarah found herself on her own for the first time. It is most likely during this period that she wrote the manuscripts contained in this volume (Lerner, 1971:320).

Uneasy in her aloneness, Sarah rejoined the Welds six months later and remained with their household the rest of her life. Her retreat into domesticity was not, however, a withdrawal from her active concern for women's rights. She kept in touch with the women's movement, subscribing to the early papers, *The Una* and *The Lily*. She translated Lamartine's biography of Joan of Arc into English. She even wore the bloomer costume for a while. And in her eighties until her death in 1873, she went door to door selling copies of J. S. Mill's *The Subjection of Women*. The irony and the pity is that it was not her own work that she was peddling.

---

5. Sarah received two proposals of marriage, one at the age of nineteen and one, much later in life, from Israel Morris, which she rejected because of her fears of being deprived of her rights and autonomy.

Letters on the Equality of the Sexes and the Manuscripts

One can speculate as to why Sarah Grimké did not republish and widely circulate her *Letters on the Equality of the Sexes* during her lifetime, and why she did not finish and then publish the fragments of manuscripts contained in this volume. Theodore Weld had been able to accomplish what none of the New England clergy had—convince Sarah to remove herself from the abolitionist lectern. He did so not by questioning her rights or her propriety but her capabilities and her effectiveness as a speaker. Certainly, if Weld's criticism was sufficient to silence Sarah in the cause of abolition, enough self-doubt may have lingered to make her question the wisdom of expressing herself publicly in any form. Her lack of confidence regarding her intellectual abilities surfaced in a letter to Harriot Hunt written around the time Sarah would have been working on the manuscripts:

> I have for so long been cooking, sweeping and teaching the abc of French and the angles and curves of drawing that I seem to have lost the mental activity I once had. Besides the poweres [*sic*] of my mind have never been allowed expansion; in childhood they were repressed by the false idea that a girl need not have the education I coveted. In early youth by wrong views of God and religion, then I was fairly ground to powder in the Quaker Society. . . . Now, after all, what can I expect in old age? (Sarah Grimké to Harriot Kezia Hunt, Dec. 31, 1852)

Whatever the reason, she chose to keep her thoughts to herself, to the loss of the feminist movement. Though it is true that the manuscripts are incomplete and at times incoherent and poorly organized, they nonetheless provide insight into the lives and struggles of nineteenth-century women. Further, they represent significant growth and change in Grimké, giving us a much fuller picture of her development as a woman and a feminist than we could derive from her early *Letters on the Equality of the Sexes* alone. Ten years after she published the *Letters,* she confided to Harriot Hunt that if she were to rewrite them, they would be so different that she would need a new copyright (Sarah Grimké to Harriot Kezia Hunt, Aug. 22, 1848).

Much of Grimké's argument in the *Letters* is devoted to demonstrating a scriptural basis for the equality of the sexes. She made a vital contribution to feminist thought in taking as the basis for her concept of equality the same text which for hundreds of years had been used to demonstrate the inequality of the sexes. She provided new interpretations of those scriptural verses to show that they support the essential equality of women and men. Her argument, briefly stated, is as follows.

According to Grimké, the first account of creation demonstrates the equality of the sexes in two ways. First, both male and female were created in the image of God. If this is so, then there can be no difference between them. Second, God gave man and woman dominion over all other creatures, but not over each other. Men and women were created in perfect equality, neither one intended to be subservient to the other. The second account of creation provides a third justification for the equality of man and woman. According to this narrative, God created woman to be a companion to man. Grimké argued that the only way woman can be a true companion of man in all his endeavors is to be his equal in all respects. The translation of the word *helpmeet* means a helper *like unto himself*. Thus it is impossible for woman to fill this function assigned to her by God unless man treats her as an equal moral being.

Perhaps most important, Grimké took the Genesis story of Eve first tasting the forbidden fruit and thus bringing sin and evil into the world, which has been used to condemn women for centuries, and turned it around. She accepted the fact that Eve had sinned but asserted that Adam had too. He also ate of the fruit, though both had been commanded not to do so. The difference between their sins is that, whereas Eve was beguiled through a supernatural agent and was easily fooled by a satanic influence of which she was ignorant, Adam sinned through the instrumentality of his equal—a free agent, like himself, able to transgress the divine command. If Adam had tried to make Eve repent rather than sharing her guilt, we could accord man the moral superiority he claims; but Adam was as weak as Eve. Both were equally guilty. Grimké summarized: "They both fell from innocence, and consequently from happiness, *but not from equality*" (Grimké, 1838:7).

Grimké found evidence of the equality of the sexes in the New Testament as well. Taking the verse, "There is neither Jew nor Greek, there is neither *male* nor *female;* for ye are all one in Jesus Christ" (Grimké, 1838:24), she argued that there are no distinctions among persons as Christians. All are equal because all are brought together in unity. All are one. Moreover, God regards all individuals as souls and all souls as alike, in that all are capable of receiving the influence of the Holy Spirit.

Grimké found the principal "scriptural" support for the dogma of woman's inferiority in Paul's letters, but she had no particular respect for these, not regarding them as revealed Scripture. Rather, she felt that Paul had written his letters under the influence of the Jewish culture's prejudice against women.

Grimké found much more scriptural evidence for the assumption of the equality of the sexes, but her main arguments were these: God created men and women equally in his image; God gave dominion to *both* over other creatures but not over each other; God created woman as a helpmeet for man, which implies her moral and intellectual equality with him; Adam sinned equally with Eve; all, including male and female, are one in Christ, and all souls are alike in the eyes of God.

Over the years, Grimké moved away from scriptural bases of truth. In her spirituality she became more mystical—though, paradoxically, in her feminism she placed greater emphasis upon reason. As she stated in the manuscript on "The Laws Respecting Woman," God endowed us with reason, and with this reason we can discover truth, which provides us with a rule of conduct independent of God's will. This change of emphasis is expressed in her later feminism in several ways. First, unlike her early writings, in which she expresses the moral outrage of the radical sectarian she was, her later arguments take on the moderate, reasonable tone of other Enlightenment feminists, urging that the values of liberty, equality, and rights be extended to women. In this, she loses some of her originality.

Second, like other Enlightenment feminists, in her later writings Grimké places much more emphasis upon education and law as means by which women will gain freedom and equality. Although the education of women had always been important to her, she stressed it more in her later writings, particularly because education enabled women to develop their powers of reason. However, Grimké's later emphasis on women's involvement in goverment and law is in stark contrast to her views in the *Letters*. In these early writings, she regarded the political arena as completely immoral and corrupt. For women to enter it was to endanger the integrity of their moral beings. "I had rather," she wrote, "we should suffer any injustice or oppression, than that my sex should have any voice in the political affairs of the nation" (Grimké, 1838:81). Twenty years later, she shared the sentiments of many of her feminist contemporaries, that women's moral superiority particularly equips them for a role in government. She argued not only that advances made in women's condition must come through changes in the law *and* that women should have a voice in these changes, but also that women, more than men, are "peculiarly fit to select those who are to represent and watch over the interests and legislate for a Christian community" (Grimké, "Condition of Woman").

Finally, the moral autonomy of women for which Grimké so ardently argued in the *Letters* was their autonomy to pursue, discover, and fulfill God's design for them. It was the ability to act on God's purpose. In her later writings, Grimké still stressed women's moral autonomy, but instead of urging them to discover and fulfill God's plan, she urged women to discover their own natures and purposes.

Another sphere which Grimké addressed well and at length both in the *Letters* and in her later writings is that of marriage. She found that more often than not women were debased in marriage, and a good part of the *Letters* is devoted to an examination of the reasons for this suffering. According to her, the problems with marriage start long before a woman marries. They date from the moment a woman regards marriage as not only necessary, and the one avenue to distinction, but also as the sine qua non of her existence, the ultimate fulfullment of her being. When a woman defines her future solely in terms of marriage, the chief business of her life becomes attracting men. She focuses on those traits in herself which she thinks men will find alluring rather than those which fulfill her as a moral and autonomous being. ·

This situation is only aggravated after marriage. The main problem, as Grimké saw it, was that in marriage a woman loses all her individuality, her independent character, and her responsibility as a moral being. She becomes absorbed by her husband. Thus the crime of marriage in Grimké's eyes was that it denied woman's autonomy as a moral and intelligent being accountable only to God, not to her husband.

Grimké singled out two other elements of marriage that support this denial of woman's personhood and moral responsibility: (1) the marriage laws and (2) the husband's functionalist attitude toward his wife. She regarded the laws concerning married women to be an "outrage." Like those regarding the slave, they completely consigned the woman—her rights and her possessions—to the master. Grimké argued that the laws deprived woman of her autonomy in two respects: financial and moral.

For example, a woman lost all rights to property in marriage. All her personal property and earnings during marriage were the husband's, and he could do with them as he wished—even will them away. Thus a wife would become totally dependent on the good will of her husband for her material needs. This financial dependence served to underscore and guarantee the wife's moral dependence. How could she realistically go against her husband's wishes when he controlled her material well-being?

The laws assured this moral dependence. By the law of coverture, the woman, upon marriage, ceased to exist. All acts performed, all contracts entered into by a woman during marriage were considered to be null and void. She could not even be found guilty of a criminal offense if she had been commanded to commit it by her husband. She was not regarded as capable of independent thought and action, and was entrusted to her husband as though he were her legal and moral guardian. Indeed, the law gave the husband the right to restrain, judge, and punish the actions of his wife. No wonder the effect of the laws was to render wives completely dependent on their husbands. The insidious effect of the marriage laws was to destroy not only woman's autonomy but also her sense of self-worth.

The husband's functionalist attitude toward his wife furthered this destruction. As Grimké observed, husbands regarded their wives, not as moral and intellectual companions, but as instruments for their domestic comfort and physical pleasure. Other feminist writers had mentioned this attitude, but Grimké was one of the first to regard it as a central problem for women. She argued that woman's inferior status was in large part a result of man's disregard for her as a human being. Man thought of woman as an ornament, a tool, a toy—a means rather than an end in herself.

The sad thing about all this, in Grimké's eyes, was that women had been taught to expect such treatment. They had been trained to regard themselves as instruments. They thought themselves inferior to men, and this notion was the real cause of women's suffering and degradation in marriage.

Grimké's concern for the subjugation of women in marriage continued into her later writings. In these she is much more frank in raising the issues of the abuse women endured in marriage, particularly sexual abuse. She wrote ardently about the sufferings of women who were forced into motherhood against their will; who were burdened by the cares of ever multiplying children; or, who, unable to care for more, were broken in body and spirit by abortions. In this, she joined her feminist contemporaries.

Nineteenth-century feminists recognized women's double bind— that motherhood was the source of both their revered status in society and the very real dangers associated with pregnancy, childbirth, abortion, and venereal disease. The solution advocated by Grimké and her contemporaries was that of "voluntary motherhood," birth control by means of abstinence. For nineteenth-century feminists did not approve of contraceptive devices: to do so would be to sanction male promiscuity and affirm women's sexuality (Gordon, 1973:6–8). At a time when feminists were arguing for women's rights on the basis of their uniquely pure moral nature, to approve of contraception would have been to deny them the power of their own argument. Instead, feminists called for self-restraint and for the right of wives to refuse their husbands sex. This served the dual purpose of safeguarding women's lives, health, and autonomy while preserving the notion of their "sexual purity."

Despite her real concern for the condition of women in marriage and her strong belief that women need not marry in order to fulfill their duties as women, Grimké did support marriage. She regarded it as a divinely sanctioned union and argued that, when a husband and wife had taken their vows, they were honor-bound to them. Though well aware of the horror of a bad marriage, she felt divorce could only be worse. Nor did Grimké condone male-female relationships outside of marriage. At the time she was writing, supporters of women's rights were often associated in people's minds with "Free Lovers"—remnants of utopian socialism who did oppose the institution of marriage. Like some present-day opponents, critics of the women's movement accused it of destroying the marriage relationship. Grimké's later writings reflect these accusations, and her defensiveness seems, if anything, to bolster her views on the virtue and indissolubility of marriage. Like her feminist contemporaries, she argued strongly that, far from destroying the marriage relationship, the women's movement would strengthen it by placing both partners on an equal footing and thus allowing women to exist as independent moral beings within marriage. As Gordon has pointed out, to reject marriage and motherhood as women's primary vocations and measures of worth at a time when there were no viable alternatives would be to deny women all sources of purpose and esteem in society.

Without these options, feminists needed to strengthen rather than reject their position in traditional marriage (Gordon, 1973:19).

Grimké did seek to open a wide variety of vocational options to women. She was a pioneer in advocating woman's pursuit of any and every vocation. She did not believe that any sphere should be closed to women on account of their sex. Furthermore, she was a hundred and fifty years ahead of her time in arguing for comparable worth—that a laundress who works as long and as hard as a wood sawyer should be paid equally with him. She was also well aware of and expressed her concern for the exceedingly hard labors of working-class women. Nevertheless, Grimké was firmly entrenched in the nineteenth-century cult of domesticity and consistently maintained that women must not abandon their special responsibilities in the home.

Feminist historians have been divided over the meaning of the cult of domesticity for women's lives and for feminism. Those who have regarded women as victims of the ideology of domesticity tend to see feminism springing up in opposition to and rejection of this restrictive notion of woman's sphere. Others have noted the way in which women linked the ideology of domesticity to the notion of their moral superiority, and used this to advance their status in society. These have attributed the development of nineteenth-century feminism directly *to* the cult of domesticity. Finally, others have regarded women's domesticity as providing the basis for a female subculture in which women discovered their unique psychic and social resources, a phenomenon that supported feminists' notions of sisterhood (Cott, 1977:197–98).

Grimké has elements of all three of these positions in her thought. She regarded women as victims of domesticity, abhorring the fact that men valued women not for their personhood but rather for their usefulness in providing domestic services. As mentioned above, she rejected any narrow definition of women's roles. Grimké wanted to define what a woman *is,* not what a woman *is for.* Yet, at the same time, she regarded the domestic sphere as woman's special province. Though she did challenge the notion of dual spheres—man's as the public world of work and woman's the private world of home and family—by striving to include women in the public sphere, she did not think of extending men's opportunities and responsibilities into the private. She felt that women's claims to an enlarged sphere and to equality could only be legitimated by scrupulous attention to their domestic duties.

Grimké believed that women should be able to perform all the functions and roles of men, *in addition* to being solely responsible for all domestic functions. The result was that she essentially advocated what we know today as the "superwoman." She took upon herself, and upon all women, the burden of two spheres—"let her fulfill in the circle of home all the obligations that rest upon her," Grimké proclaimed, "but let her not waste her powers on inferior objects when higher and holier responsibilities demand her attention" (Grimké, "Education of Women"). Women had to succeed in both spheres.

So Grimké both rejected and accepted women's domesticity. This paradox points up a problem in her thought. By isolating the domestic as "woman's sphere," she was doing precisely what she deplored in men—treating women as domestic instruments rather than as persons. She regarded her own retirement into domesticity as proof to the world that women can be successful in both their public and private functions. She was in effect arguing that women must first justify themselves (to men) as women, and perform the functions equated with that view of them, before they can be accepted as human beings.

Grimké's later writings show a marked ambivalence about women's special domesticity. She was reluctant to give up that one province that was considered woman's, and yet she readily acknowledged and wished to relieve women of the burden of the drudgery involved. She was caught in the middle—between her entrenched sense of female obligation to men and her ever-increasing sense of obligation to women; between maintaining at least one sphere as woman's own and opening up all spheres; between her respect for conservatism and her impulse toward radical change. Though she did over the years expand her notion of women's appropriate sphere to include not only home and work but also the political arena, and she did come to question more and more women's role in the home, in her lifetime Grimké never resolved this ambivalence.

The viewpoint that domesticity led to the development of a female subculture which strengthened feminism is apparent in a final theme in Grimké's feminism—"sorority"—an expression of her sisterhood among women. Central to this theme is her rejection of the notion of the inferiority of women and her affirmation of the dignity of women as moral and responsible beings, as creatures of God, as immortal souls—and as women. She respected women, and felt strongly the bond and unity of all women in sisterhood.

In many ways, Sarah's affirmations were angry, rebellious protests against the indignities and oppressions that women suffered at the hands of men. By denying women access to education, to law, to positions of power in church, state, and business, men prevented women's intellectual growth and moral autonomy. Far from protecting women, men used and abused them for their own purposes, advancement, and comfort.

Grimké believed that it is this common plight which binds women together in a sisterhood. The unity of womanhood, expressed so passionately in her thought, is primarily the unity of common suffering. Though she certainly experienced the positive bonding of women with her sister and other close friends, the emphasis, especially in the *Letters,* is on women unified by their oppression, rather than by a positive feeling of womanhood. Grimké referred not to "the *bond* of womanhood," an expression of positive unity and solidarity, but to "the *bonds* of womanhood"—an expression of their common bondage. We receive the impression of women being bound together by the same rope rather than bound in a common embrace.

This impression may be due in part to the fact that in Grimké's writing there is no consistent, strong recognition of or appreciation for the unique nature and qualities of woman and womanhood. For the most part, her notion of womanhood is either male-defined or a reaction against that male definition. Her notion of equality was an equality *to man* rather than an equality of men and women together. She knew that women lacked what men had, and she sought to obtain it for them, but she had little idea of what women lacked *as women*. Similarly, her conception of sex roles is based on a societal definition, imposed from without, rather than a woman's definition. Instead of defining woman's identity from an inner notion of the nature of womanhood, Grimké appropriated society's definition of both men's and women's identities (men as public; women as domestic) to define the nature of womanhood. The very notion of sisterhood in her concept of sorority focuses on women's common oppression *by men,* rather than the common experiences and unity of womanhood.

Yet, in her later years, Grimké more vigorously rejected male-defined notions of femininity and urged women to explore their own natures. As she wrote in "Sisters of Charity":

> The debasing and unsatisfying babble of representation through another, of the beauty of feminine delicacy and dependence, has had time to echo and reecho itself . . . she has listened to it, paid homage to it—she is weary of it. She feels its emptiness with reference to that inward life which is not yet extinguished. . . . She can no longer receive the superstitions whose death warrant her reason has signed but she is awakening to higher and clearer ideas of her own nature and capacities and responsibilities. (Grimké, "Sisters of Charity")

Early in her writings, Grimké had appealed to men to lift the burden of oppression from women. "All I ask of our brethren," she wrote, "is that they will take their feet from off our necks, and permit us to stand on that ground which God has designed us to occupy" (Grimké, 1838:10). She had long believed that women could gain equality through the equal and just legislations of men. But as she grew older, she became more and more disenchanted with the nature and motivations of men, finally coming to believe that because of their different nature and experiences, men were not even capable of recognizing and affirming women's place in society.

Grimké came to believe that women must rely only on themselves for their own elevation. They cannot expect men to come to their aid. In "Sisters of Charity" she wrote eloquently of women's need for self-reliance: "Woman by surrendering herself to the tutelage of man may in many cases live at her ease, but she will live the life of a slave, by asserting and claiming her natural Rights she assumes the prerogative which every free intelligence ought to assume that she is the arbiter of her own destiny. . . . Self-reliance only can create true and exalted women" (Grimké, "Sisters of Charity").

Grimké had hinted at the potential of womanhood, especially in her discussion of freedom, in which she sought after the freedom of woman to fulfill God's duty for her as a woman and, later, to fulfill her potential as a woman. In time she came to realize that this nature of womanhood was not something that could be defined by men, but only by women, on their own.

Grimké's Feminism and the Contemporary Minimalist/Maximalist Debate

The transition in Grimké's feminism from a male-centered vision to a gynocentric vision reflects the current minimalist/maximalist debate in contemporary feminist theory.[6] Feminists at the forefront of the most recent wave of feminism, like Kate Millett and Shulamith Firestone, argued that the emphasis upon sex difference was the source of women's oppression. The roots of liberation thus lay in minimizing the differences between the sexes. The implications of this ranged from abolishing male/female distinctions in employment, education, political, and legal rights to eradicating all psychosocial conceptions and roles of gender. Firestone went so far as to suggest the elimination not only of gender differences but of reproductive differences as well, through the use of artificial reproduction technologies (Firestone, 1971).

The reaction to these views was immediate, and there followed a "woman-centered" writing which celebrated the unique nature and experiences of women. Feminists such as Adrienne Rich and Jean Bethke Elshtain specifically affirmed the unique values and perspectives of nurturing, compassion, and maternal care that arise from women's experiences as mothers (Rich, 1976; Elshtain, 1981). "Cultural feminists"—Judy Chicago, Holly Near, Chris Williamson, Margie Adam, and Marge Piercy, to name only a few—celebrated the strength of women in their art, music, and poetry. Others, such as Susan Griffin and Rosemary Reuther, have addressed women's unique connection with the earth and have linked our sensitivities and creativity with our link to all of creation (Griffin, 1978; Reuther, 1975). More recently, feminists like Audre Lorde, Nancy Hartsock, and Starhawk have been examining the distinctive nature of male-defined power and providing alternative woman-centered visions of power (Lorde, 1984; Hartsock, 1986; Starhawk, 1982).

6. I first heard these terms used in an address by Catherine Stimpson to the Northwest Women's Studies Association Meeting in Bellingham, Washington, in April 1984. The best discussion I have found of the debate is Maggie McFadden's in her "Anatomy of Difference: Toward a Classification of Feminist Theory" (*Women's Studies International Forum*, 1984 7[6]: 495–504).

Taking this woman-centered vision to its extreme, Mary Daly and others have argued not only for the affirmation of "femaleness," but for the separation of the sexes and the supremacy of the female sex (Daly, 1978). These visions have raised concern, if not alarm, among some feminists who see the potential danger of the reactionary nature of such visions. Adopted by feminists, they could be the source of some type of "feminist fascism"; adopted by the conservative right, they could be used against women to relegate them once again to particular spheres (McFadden, 1984; Eisenstein, 1983; Bartlett, 1986).

The concern reflected in the current debate is how to find a balance among these perspectives—how to appreciate and affirm the qualities of woman without binding her to a predetermined role. Grimké struggled with this question over the course of her lifetime, and the questions and issues she raised may prove valuable to feminists today. What I believe to be most instructive in this regard is a movement in Grimké's feminism from resentment to rebellion[7]—from a potentially self-destructive envy of what women do not have to a creative affirmation of who women are.

While the affirmation of the dignity of women as moral and responsible human beings is clear throughout Grimké's feminism, her earlier writings are also filled with resentment toward men. Men had what she wanted and was denied—education, vocational outlets for their talents and abilities, respect for their intelligence and ambitions, freedom of movement in the world, power; and it was men who denied these rights to women. Grimké's earlier writings are angry and often hostile claims for women to share equally in those powers and privileges.

In her later writings, Grimké is still angry, but this anger takes the form not so much of a resentful envy as of a rebellious affirmation of the dignity of womanhood. As she grew, Grimké came to focus more and more on who women are and of what they are capable, rather than on what they lack and are denied. As it evolved, her feminism became increasingly a statement of the strength and beauty and bond of women.

Sarah Grimké was a rebel. She cared passionately and compassionately for women. Her writings are the legacy of that caring. Although her voice was silenced during her lifetime, this volume seeks to give her recognition as one of the foremothers whose labor and love gave birth to feminism.

---

7. Albert Camus made the distinction between resentment and rebellion, resentment being envy of what one does not have, and rebellion, an affirmation of who one is. Albert Camus, *The Rebel: An Essay on Man in Revolt,* trans. Anthony Bower, with a foreword by Sir Herbert Read (New York: Vintage Books, 1956), pp. 17–18.

2.

Letters on the Equality of the Sexes, and the Condition of Woman.

Addressed to Mary S. Parker, President of the Boston Female Anti-Slavery Society

LETTER I

The Original Equality of Woman

Amesbury, 7th Mo. 11th, 1837

My Dear Friend,

In attempting to comply with thy request to give my views on the Province of Woman, I feel that I am venturing on nearly untrodden ground, and that I shall advance arguments in opposition to a corrupt public opinion, and to the perverted interpretation of Holy Writ, which has so universally obtained. But I am in search of truth; and no obstacle shall prevent my prosecuting that search, because I believe the welfare of the world will be materially advanced by every new discovery we make of the designs of Jehovah in the creation of woman. It is impossible that we can answer the purpose of our being, unless we understand that purpose. It is impossible that we should fulfil our duties, unless we comprehend them; or live up to our privileges, unless we know what they are.

In examining this important subject, I shall depend solely on the Bible to designate the sphere of woman, because I believe almost every thing that has been written on this subject, has been the result of a misconception of the simple truths revealed in the Scriptures, in consequence of the false translation of many passages of Holy Writ. My mind is entirely delivered from the superstitious reverence which is attached to the English version of the Bible. King James's translators certainly were not inspired. I therefore claim the original as my standard, *believing that to have been inspired,* and I also claim to judge for myself what is the meaning of the inspired writers, because I believe it to be the solemn duty of every individual to search the Scriptures for themselves, with the aid of the Holy Spirit, and not be governed by the views of any man, or set of men.

We must first view woman at the period of her creation. "And God said, Let us make man in our own image, after our likeness; and let them have dominion over the fish of the sea, and over the fowl of the air, and over the cattle, and over all the earth, and over every creeping thing that creepeth upon the earth. So God created man in his own image, in the image of God created he him, male and female created he them" [Gen. 1:26–27]. In all this sublime description of the creation of man, (which is a generic term including man and woman), there is not one particle of difference intimated as existing between them. They were both made in the image of God; dominion was given to both over every other creature, but not over each other. Created in perfect equality, they were expected to exercise the vicegerence intrusted to them by their Maker, in harmony and love.

Let us pass on now to the recapitulation of the creation of man— "The Lord God formed man of the dust of the ground, and breathed into his nostrils the breath of life; and man became a living soul. And the Lord God said, it is not good that man should be alone, I will make him an help meet for him" [Gen. 2:7–18]. All creation swarmed with animated beings capable of natural affection, as we know they still are; it was not, therefore, merely to give man a creature susceptible of loving, obeying, and looking up to him, for all that the animals could do and did do. It was to give him a companion, *in all respects* his equal; one who was like himself *a free agent,* gifted with intellect and endowed with immortality; not a partaker merely of his animal gratifications, but able to enter into all his feelings as a moral and responsible being. If this had not been the case, how could she have been an help meet for him? I understand this as applying not only to the parties entering into the marriage contract, but to all men and women, because I believe God designed woman to be an help meet for man in every good and perfect work. She was a part of himself, as if Jehovah designed to make the oneness and identity of man and woman perfect and complete; and when the glorious work of their creation was finished, "the morning stars sang together, and all the sons of God shouted for joy" [Job 38:7].

This blissful condition was not long enjoyed by our first parents. Eve, it would seem from the history, was wandering alone amid the bowers of Paradise, when the serpent met with her. From her reply to Satan, it is evident that the command not to eat "of the tree that is in the midst of the garden," was given to both, although the term man was used when the prohibition was issued by God. "And the woman said unto the serpent, WE may eat of the fruit of the trees of the garden, but of the fruit of the tree which is in the midst of the garden, God hath said, YE shall not eat of it, neither shall YE touch it, lest YE die" [Gen. 3:3]. Here the woman was exposed to temptation from a being with whom she was unacquainted. She had been accustomed to associate with her beloved partner, and to hold communion with God and with angels; but of satanic intelligence, she was in all probability entirely ignorant. Through the subtlety of the serpent, she was beguiled. And "when she saw that the tree was good for food, and that it was pleasant to the eyes, and a tree to be desired to make one wise, she took of the fruit thereof and did eat" [Gen. 3:6].

We next find Adam involved in the same sin, not through the instrumentality of a supernatural agent, but through that of his equal, a being whom he must have known was liable to transgress the divine command, because he must have felt that he was himself a free agent, and that he was restrained from disobedience only by the exercise of faith and love towards his Creator. Had Adam tenderly reproved his wife, and endeavored to lead her to repentance instead of sharing in her guilt, I should be much more ready to accord to man that superiority which he claims; but as the facts stand disclosed by the sacred historian, it appears to me that to say the least, there was as much weakness exhibited by Adam as by Eve. They both fell from innocence, and consequently from happiness, *but not from equality.*

Let us next examine the conduct of this fallen pair, when Jehovah interrogated them respecting their fault. They both frankly confessed their guilt. "The man said, the woman whom thou gavest to be with me, she gave me of the tree and I did eat. And the woman said, the serpent beguiled me and I did eat" [Gen. 3:12]. And the Lord God said unto the woman, "Thou wilt be subject unto thy husband, and he will rule over thee" [Gen. 3:16]. That this did not allude to the subjection of woman to man is manifest, because the same mode of expression is used in speaking to Cain of Abel [Gen. 4:10–12]. The truth is that the curse, as it is termed, which was pronounced by Jehovah upon woman, is a simple prophecy. The Hebrew, like the French language, uses the same word to express shall and will. Our translators having been accustomed to exercise lordship over their wives, and seeing only through the medium of a perverted judgment, very naturally, though I think not very learnedly or very kindly, translated it *shall* instead of *will,* and thus converted a prediction to Eve into a command to Adam; for observe, it is addressed to the woman and not to the man. The consequence of the fall was an immediate struggle for dominion, and Jehovah foretold which would gain the ascendency; but as he created them in his image, as that image manifestly was not lost by the fall, because it is urged in Gen. 9:6, as an argument why the life of man should not be taken by his fellow man, there is no reason to suppose that sin produced any distinction between them as moral, intellectual and responsible beings. Man might just as well have endeavored by hard labor to fulfil the prophecy, thorns and thistles will the earth bring forth to thee, as to pretend to accomplish the other, "he will rule over thee," by asserting dominion over his wife.

> Authority usurped from God, not given.
> He gave him only over beast, flesh, fowl,
> Dominion absolute: that right he holds
> By God's donation: but man o'er woman
> He made not Lord, such title to himself
> Reserving, human left from human free.

Here then I plant myself. God created us equal;—he created us free agents;—he is our Lawgiver, our King and our Judge, and to him alone is woman bound to be in subjection, and to him alone is she accountable for the use of those talents with which her Heavenly Father has entrusted her. One is her Master even Christ.

Thine for the oppressed in the bonds of womanhood,

Sarah M. Grimké

LETTER II

Woman Subject Only To God

Newburyport, 7th mo. 17, 1837

My Dear Sister,

In my last, I traced the creation and the fall of man and woman from that state of purity and happiness which their beneficent Creator designed them to enjoy. As they were one in transgression, their chastisement was the same. "So God drove out *the man,* and he placed at the East of the garden of Eden a cherubim and a flaming sword, which turned every way to keep the way of the tree of life" [Gen. 3:24]. We now behold them expelled from Paradise, fallen from their original loveliness, but still bearing on their foreheads the image and superscription of Jehovah; still invested with high moral responsibilities, intellectual powers, and immortal souls. They had incurred the penalty of sin, they were shorn of their innocence, but they stood on the same platform side by side, acknowledging *no superior* but their God. Notwithstanding what has been urged, woman I am aware stands charged to the present day with having brought sin into the world. I shall not repel the charge by any counter assertions, although, as was before hinted, Adam's ready acquiescence with his wife's proposal, does not savor much of that superiority *in strength of mind,* which is arrogated by man. Even admitting that Eve was the greater sinner, it seems to me man might be satisfied with the dominion he has claimed and exercised for nearly six thousand years, and that more true nobility would be manifested by endeavoring to raise the fallen and invigorate the weak, than by keeping woman in subjection. But I ask no favors for my sex. I surrender not our claim to equality. All I ask of our brethren is, that they will take their feet from off our necks, and permit us to stand upright on that ground which God designed us to occupy. If he has not given us the rights which have, as I conceive, been wrested from us, we shall soon give evidence of our inferiority, and shrink back into that obscurity, which the high souled magnanimity of man has assigned us as our appropriate sphere.

As I am unable to learn from sacred writ when woman was deprived by God of her equality with man, I shall touch upon a few points in the Scriptures, which demonstrate that no supremacy was granted to man. When God had destroyed the world, except Noah and his family, by the deluge, he renewed the grant formerly made to man, and again gave him dominion over every beast of the earth, every fowl of the air, over all that moveth upon the earth, and over all the fishes of the sea; into his hands they were delivered. But was woman, bearing the image of her God, placed under the dominion of her fellow man? Never! Jehovah could not surrender his authority to govern his own immortal creatures into the hands of a being, whom he knew, and whom his whole history proved, to be unworthy of a trust so sacred and important. God could not do it, because it is a direct contravention of his law, "Thou shalt worship the Lord thy God, and *him only* shalt thou serve" [Mt. 4:10]. If Jehovah had appointed man as the guardian, or teacher of woman, he would certainly have given some intimation of this surrender of his own prerogative. But so far from it, we find the commands of God invariably the same to man and woman; and not the slightest intimation is given in a single passage of the Bible, that God designed to point woman to man as her instructor. The tenor of his language always is, "Look unto ME, and be ye saved, all the ends of the earth, for I am God, and there is none else" [Isa. 45:22].

The lust of dominion was probably the first effect of the fall; and as there was no other intelligent being over whom to exercise it, woman was the first victim of this unhallowed passion. We afterwards see it exhibited by Cain in the murder of his brother, by Nimrod in his becoming a mighty hunter of men, and setting up a kingdom over which to reign.[1] Here we see the origin of that Upas of slavery, which sprang up immediately after the fall, and has spread its pestilential branches over the whole face of the known world. All history attests that man has subjected woman to his will, used her as a means to promote his selfish gratification, to minister to his sensual pleasures, to be instrumental in promoting his comfort; but never has he desired to elevate her to that rank she was created to fill. He has done all he

---

1. Nimrod (ca. 2450 B.C.), according to Mosaic scripture, was the founder of the Babylonian monarchy and was considered a mighty hunter.

could to debase and enslave her mind; and now he looks triumphantly on the ruin he has wrought, and says, the being he has thus deeply injured is his inferior.

Woman has been placed by John Quincy Adams, side by side with the slave, whilst he was contending for the right side of petition.[2] I thank him for ranking us with the oppressed; for I shall not find it difficult to show, that in all ages and countries, not even excepting enlightened republican America, woman has more or less been made a *means* to promote the welfare of man, without due regard to her own happiness, and the glory of God as the end of her creation.

During the *patriarchal* ages, we find men and women engaged in the same employments. Abraham and Sarah both assisted in preparing the food which was to be set before the three men, who visited them in the plains of Mamre [Gen. 18]; but although their occupations were similar, Sarah was not permitted to enjoy the society of the holy visitant; and as we learn from Peter, that she "obeyed Abraham, calling him Lord" [I Peter 3:6], we may presume he exercised dominion over her. We shall pass on now to Rebecca [Gen. 24]. In her history, we find another striking illustration of the low estimation in which woman was held. Eleazur is sent to seek a wife for Isaac. He finds Rebecca going down to the well to fill her pitcher. He accosts her; and she replies with all humility, "Drink, my lord." How does he endeavor to gain her favor and confidence? Does he approach her as a dignified creature, whom he was about to invite to fill an important station in his master's family, as the wife of his only son? No. He offered incense to her vanity, and "he took a golden ear-ring of half a shekel weight, and two bracelets for her hands of ten shekels weight of gold," and gave them to Rebecca.

The cupidity of man soon led him to regard woman as property, and hence we find them sold to those, who wished to marry them, as far as appears, without any regard to those sacred rights which belong to woman, as well as to man in the choice of a companion. That women were a profitable kind of property, we may gather from the description of a virtuous woman in the last chapter of Proverbs [Prov. 31:10–31]. To work willingly with her hands, to open her hands to the poor, to clothe herself with silk and purple, to look well to her household, to make fine linen and sell it, to deliver girdles to the merchant, and not to eat the bread of idleness, seems to have constituted in the view of Solomon, the perfection of a woman's character and achievements. "The spirit of that age was not favorable to intellectual improvement; but as there were wise men who formed exceptions to the general ignorance, and were destined to guide the world into more advanced states, so there was a corresponding proportion of wise women; and among the

2. John Quincy Adams (1767–1848) was a member of Congress following his term as president and argued against the slavery petition.

Jews, as well as other nations, we find a strong tendency to believe that women were in more immediate connection with heaven than men."—L. M. Child's Con. of Woman.[3] If there be any truth in this tradition, I am at a loss to imagine in what the superiority of man consists.

Thine in the bonds of womanhood,

Sarah M. Grimké.

LETTER III

The Pastoral Letter of the General Association of Congregational Ministers of Massachusetts

Haverhill, 7th Mo. 1837

Dear Friend,

When I last addressed thee, I had not seen the Pastoral Letter of the General Association.[4] It has since fallen into my hands, and I must digress from my intention of exhibiting the condition of women in different parts of the world, in order to make some remarks on this extraordinary document. I am persuaded that when the minds of men and women become emancipated from the thraldom of superstition and "traditions of men," the sentiments contained in the Pastoral Letter will be recurred to with as much astonishment as the opinions of Cotton Mather and other distinguished men of his day, on the subject of witchcraft;[5] nor will it be deemed less wonderful, that a body of divines should gravely assemble and endeavor to prove that woman has no right to "open her mouth for the dumb," than it now is that judges should have sat on the trials of witches, and solemnly condemned nineteen persons and one dog to death for witchcraft.

But to the letter. It says, "We invite your attention to the dangers which at present seem to threaten the FEMALE CHARACTER with wide-spread and permanent injury." I rejoice that they have called the attention of my sex to this subject, because I believe if woman investigates it, she will soon discover that danger is impending, though from a totally different source

3. Lydia Maria Child (1802–80) was an abolitionist, author, and early supporter of the women's rights movement.

4. The "Pastoral Letter of the General Association of Massachusetts to the Congregational Churches under their care," July 28, 1837, issued a condemnation of William Lloyd Garrison and the Grimké sisters, though it did not name names. The association particularly condemned the practice of women speaking out publicly for the abolitionist cause.

5. Cotton Mather (1663–1728), clergyman, theologian, and author, is reputed to be the fomenter of the witchcraft hysteria in New England in the late seventeenth century.

from that which the Association apprehends,—danger from those who, having long held the reins of *usurped* authority, are unwilling to permit us to fill that sphere which God created us to move in, and who have entered into league to crush the immortal mind of woman. I rejoice, because I am persuaded that the rights of woman, like the rights of slaves, need only be examined to be understood and asserted, even by some of those, who are now endeavoring to smother the irrepressible desire for mental and spiritual freedom which glows in the breast of many, who hardly dare to speak their sentiments.

"The appropriate duties and influence of women are clearly stated in the New Testament. Those duties are unobtrusive and private, but the sources of *mighty power.* When the mild, *dependent,* softening influence of woman upon the sternness of man's opinions is fully exercised, society feels the effects of it in a thousand ways." No one can desire more earnestly than I do, that woman may move exactly in the sphere which her Creator has assigned her; and I believe her having been displaced from that sphere has introduced confusion into the world. It is, therefore, of vast importance to herself and to all the rational creation, that she should ascertain what are her duties and her privileges as a responsible and immortal being. The New Testament has been referred to, and I am willing to abide by its decisions, but must enter my protest against the false translation of some passages by the MEN who did that work, and against the perverted interpretation by the MEN who undertook to write commentaries thereon. I am inclined to think, when we are admitted to the honor of studying Greek and Hebrew, we shall produce some various readings of the Bible a little different from those we now have.

The Lord Jesus defines the duties of his followers in his Sermon on the Mount. He lays down grand principles by which they should be governed, without any reference to sex or condition.—"Ye are the light of the world. A city that is set on a hill cannot be hid. Neither do men light a candle and put it under a bushel, but on a candlestick, and it giveth light unto all that are in the house. Let your light so shine before men, that they may see your good works, and glorify your Father which is in Heaven" [Matt. 5:14–16]. I follow him through all his precepts, and find him giving the same directions to women as to men, never even referring to the distinction now so strenuously insisted upon between masculine and feminine virtues: this is one of the anti-christian "traditions of men" which are taught instead of the "commandments of God." Men and women were CREATED EQUAL; they are both moral and accountable beings, and whatever is *right* for man to do, is *right* for woman.

But the influence of woman, says the Association, is to be private and unobtrusive; her light is not to shine before man like that of her brethren; but she is passively to let the lords of the creation, as they call themselves, put the bushel over it, lest peradventure it might appear that the world has been benefitted by the rays of *her* candle. So that her quenched light, according to their judgment, will be of more use than if it were set on the candlestick. "Her influence is the source of mighty power." This has ever been the flattering language of man since he laid aside the whip as a means to keep woman in subjection. He spares her body; but the war he has waged against her mind, her heart, and her soul, has been no less destructive to her as a moral being. How monstrous, how anti-christian, is the doctrine that woman is to be dependent on man! Where, in all the sacred Scriptures, is this taught? Alas! she has too well learned the lesson, which MAN has labored to teach her. She has surrendered her dearest RIGHTS, and been satisfied with the privileges which man has assumed to grant her; she has been amused with the show of power, whilst man has absorbed all the reality into himself. He has adorned the creature whom God gave him as a companion, with baubles and gewgaws, turned her attention to personal attractions, offered incense to her vanity, and made her the instrument of his selfish gratification, a plaything to please his eye and amuse his hours of leisure. "Rule by obedience and by submission sway," or in other words, study to be a hypocrite, pretend to submit, but gain your point, has been the code of household morality which woman has been taught. The poet has sung, in sickly strains, the loveliness of woman's dependence upon man, and now we find it reechoed by those who profess to teach the religion of the Bible. God says, "Cease ye from man whose breath is in his nostrils, for wherein is he to be accounted of?" Man says, depend upon me. God says, "HE will teach us of his ways." Man says, believe it not, I am to be your teacher. This doctrine of dependence upon man is utterly at variance with the doctrine of the Bible. In that book I find nothing like the softness of woman, nor the sternness of man: both are equally commanded to bring forth the fruits of the Spirit, love, meekness, gentleness, &c.

But we are told, "the power of woman is in her dependence, flowing from a consciousness of that weakness which God has given her for her protection." If physical weakness is alluded to, I cheerfully concede the superiority; if brute force is what my brethren are claiming, I am willing to let them have all the honor they desire; but if they mean to intimate, that mental or moral weakness belongs to woman, more than to man, I utterly disclaim the charge. Our powers of mind have been crushed, as far as man could do it, our sense of morality has been impaired by his interpretation of our duties; but no where does God say that he made any distinction between us, as moral and intelligent beings.

"We appreciate," say the Association, "the *unostentatious* prayers and efforts of woman in advancing the cause of religion at home and abroad, in leading religious inquirers TO THE PASTOR for instruction." Several points here demand attention. If public prayers and public efforts are necessarily ostentatious, then "Anna the prophetess, (or preacher,) who departed not from the temple, but served God with fastings and prayers night and day," "and spake of Christ to all them that looked for redemption in Israel," was ostentatious in her efforts.[6] Then, the apostle Paul encourages women to be ostentatious in their efforts to spread the gospel, when he gives them directions how they should appear, when engaged in praying, or preaching in the public assemblies. Then, the whole association of Congregational ministers are ostentatious, in the efforts they are making in preaching and praying to convert souls.

But woman may be permitted to lead religious inquirers to the PASTORS for instruction. Now this is assuming that all pastors are better qualified to give instruction than woman. This I utterly deny. I have suffered too keenly from the teaching of man, to lead any one to him for instruction. The Lord Jesus says,—"Come unto me and learn of me" [Matt. 11:29]. He points his followers to no man; and when woman is made the favored instrument of rousing a sinner to his lost and helpless condition, she has no right to substitute any teacher for Christ; all she has to do is, to turn the contrite inquirer to the "Lamb of God which taketh away the sins of the world" [John 1:29]. More souls have probably been lost by going down to Egypt for help, and by trusting in man in the early stages of religious experience, than by any other error. Instead of the petition being offered to God,—"Lead me in thy truth, and TEACH me, for thou art the God of my salvation" [Ps. 25:5],—instead of relying on the precious promises—"What man is he that feareth the Lord? him shall HE TEACH in the way that he shall choose" [Ps. 25:12]—"I will instruct thee and TEACH thee in the way which thou shalt go—I will guide thee with mine eye" [Ps. 27:11]—the young convert is directed to go to man, as if he were in the place of God, and his instructions essential to an advancement in the path of righteousness. That woman can have but a poor conception of the privilege of being taught of God, what he alone can teach, who would turn the "religious inquirer aside" from the fountain of living waters, where he might slake his thirst for spiritual instruction, to those broken cisterns which can hold no water, and therefore cannot satisfy the panting spirit. The business of men and women, who are ORDAINED OF GOD to preach the unsearchable riches of Christ to a lost and perishing world, is to lead souls to Christ, and not to Pastors for instruction.

The General Association say, that "when woman assumes the place and tone of man as a public reformer, our care and protection of her seem unnecessary; we put ourselves in self-defence against her, and her character becomes unnatural." Here again the unscriptural notion is held up, that there is a distinction between the duties of men and women as moral beings; that what is virtue in man, is vice in woman; and women who dare to obey the

---

6. Anna was an aged widow and woman of faith who lived in the Temple at Jerusalem. Seeing Jesus as an infant at the ceremonial service of his mother's repurification, she was the first to proclaim him the Christ. She was likened to Miriam, Deborah, and Huldah in her prophetic powers (Luke 2:36–38).

command of Jehovah, "Cry aloud, spare not, lift up thy voice like a trumpet, and show my people their transgression" [Isa. 58:1], are threatened with having the protection of the brethren withdrawn. If this is all they do, we shall not even know the time when our chastisement is inflicted; our trust is in the Lord Jehovah, and in him is everlasting strength. The motto of woman, when she is engaged in the great work of public reformation should be,—"The Lord is my light and my salvation; whom shall I fear? The Lord is the strength of my life; of whom shall I be afraid?" [Ps. 27:1]. She must feel, if she feels rightly, that she is fulfilling one of the important duties laid upon her as an accountable being, and that her character, instead of being "unnatural," is in exact accordance with the will of Him to whom, and to no other, she is responsible for the talents and the gifts confided to her. As to the pretty simile, introduced into the "Pastoral Letter," "If the vine whose strength and beauty is to lean upon the trellis work, and half conceal its clusters, thinks to assume the independence and the overshadowing nature of the elm," &c. I shall only remark that it might well suit the poet's fancy, who sings of sparkling eyes and coral lips, and knights in armor clad; but it seems to me utterly inconsistent with the dignity of a Christian body, to endeavor to draw such an anti-scriptural distinction between men and women. Ah! how many of my sex feel in the dominion, thus unrighteously exercised over them, under the gentle appellation of *protection,* that what they have leaned upon has proved a broken reed at best, and oft a spear.

Thine in the bonds of womanhood,

Sarah M. Grimké

LETTER IV

Social Intercourse of the Sexes

Andover, 7th Mo. 27th, 1837

My Dear Friend,

Before I proceed with the account of that oppression which woman has suffered in every age and country from her *protector,* man, permit me to offer for your consideration, some views relative to the social intercourse of the sexes. Nearly the whole of this intercourse is, in my apprehension, derogatory to man and woman, as moral and intellectual beings. We approach each other, and mingle with each other, under the constant pressure of a feeling that we are of different sexes; and, instead of regarding each other only in the light of immortal creatures, the mind is fettered by the idea which is early and industriously infused into it, that we must never forget the distinction between male and female. Hence our intercourse, instead of being elevated and refined, is generally calculated to excite and keep alive the lowest propensities of our nature. Nothing, I believe, has tended more to destroy the true dignity of woman, than the fact that she is approached by man in the character of a female. The idea that she is sought as an intelligent and heaven-born creature, whose society will cheer, refine and elevate her companion, and that she will receive the same blessings she confers, is rarely held up to her view. On the contrary, man almost always addresses himself to the weakness of woman. By flattery, by an appeal to her passions, he seeks access to her heart; and when he has gained her affections, he uses her as the instrument of his pleasure—the minister of his temporal comfort. He furnishes himself with a housekeeper, whose chief business is in the kitchen, or the nursery. And whilst he goes abroad and enjoys the means of improvement afforded by collision of intellect with cultivated minds, his wife is condemned to draw nearly all her instruction from books, if she has time to peruse them; and if not, from her meditations, whilst engaged in those domestic duties which are necessary for the comfort of her lord and master.

Surely no one who contemplates, with the eye of a Christian philosopher, the design of God in the creation of woman, can believe that she is now fulfilling that design. The literal translation of the word "help-meet" is a helper like unto himself; it is so rendered in the Septuagint,[7] and manifestly signifies a companion. Now I believe it will be impossible for woman to fill the station assigned her by God, until her brethren mingle with her as an equal, as a moral being; and lose, in the dignity of her immortal nature, and in the fact of her bearing like himself the image and superscription of her God, the idea of her being a female. The apostle beautifully remarks, "As many of you as have been baptized into Christ, have put on Christ. There is neither Jew nor Greek, there is neither bond nor free, there is neither *male* nor *female;* for ye are all one in Christ Jesus" [Gal. 3:28]. Until our intercourse is purified by the forgetfulness of sex,—until we rise above the present low and sordid views which entwine themselves around our social and domestic interchange of sentiment and feelings, we never can derive that benefit from each other's society which it is the design of our Creator that we should. Man has inflicted an unspeakable injury upon woman, by holding up to her view her animal nature, and placing in the back ground her moral and intellectual being. Woman has inflicted an injury upon herself by submitting to be thus regarded; and she is now called upon to rise from the station where *man,* not God, has placed her, and claim those sacred and inalienable rights, as a moral and responsible being, with which her Creator has invested her.

What but these views, so derogatory to the character of woman, could have called forth the remark contained in the Pastoral Letter? "We

---

7. The Septuagint is the oldest Greek version of the Bible.

especially deplore the intimate acquaintance and promiscuous conversation of *females* with regard to things 'which ought not to be named,' by which that modesty and delicacy, which is the charm of domestic life, and which constitutes the true influence of woman, is consumed." How wonderful that the conceptions of man relative to woman are so low, that he cannot perceive that she may converse on any subject connected with the improvement of her species, without swerving in the least from that modesty which is one of her greatest virtues! Is it designed to insinuate that woman should possess a greater degree of modesty than man? This idea I utterly reprobate. Or is it supposed that woman cannot go into scenes of misery, the necessary result of those very things, which the Pastoral Letter says ought not to be named, for the purpose of moral reform, without becoming contaminated by those with whom she thus mingles?

This is a false position; and I presume has grown out of the never-forgotten distinction of male and female. The woman who goes forth, clad in the panoply of God, to stem the tide of iniquity and misery, which she beholds rolling through our land, goes not forth to her labor of love as a female. She goes as the dignified messenger of Jehovah, and all she does and says must be done and said irrespective of sex. She is in duty bound to communicate with all, who are able and willing to aid her in saving her fellow creatures, both men and women, from that destruction which awaits them.

So far from woman losing any thing of the purity of her mind, by visiting the wretched victims of vice in their miserable abodes, by talking with them, or of them, she becomes more and more elevated and refined in her feelings and views. While laboring to cleanse the minds of others from the malaria of moral pollution, her own heart becomes purified, and her soul rises to nearer communion with her God. Such a woman is infinitely better qualified to fulfil the duties of a wife and a mother, than the woman whose *false delicacy* leads her to shun her fallen sister and brother, and shrink from *naming those sins* which she knows exist, but which she is too fastidious to labor by deed and by word to exterminate. Such a woman feels, when she enters upon the marriage relation, that God designed that relation not to debase her to a level with the animal creation, but to increase the happiness and dignity of his creatures. Such a woman comes to the important task of training her children in the nurture and admonition of the Lord, with a soul filled with the greatness of the beings committed to her charge. She sees in her children, creatures bearing the image of God; and she approaches them with reverence, and treats them at all times as moral and accountable beings. Her own mind being purified and elevated, she instils into her children that genuine religion which induces them to keep the commandments of God. Instead of ministering with ceaseless care to their sensual appetites, she teaches them to be temperate in all things. She can converse with her children on any subject relating to their duty to God, can point their attention to those vices which degrade and brutify human nature, without in the least defiling her own mind or theirs. She views herself, and teaches her children to regard themselves as moral beings; and in all their intercourse with their fellow men, to lose the animal nature of man and woman, in the recognition of that immortal mind wherewith Jehovah has blessed and enriched them.

Thine in the bonds of womanhood,

Sarah M. Grimké

LETTER V

Condition in Asia and Africa

Groton, 8th Mo. 4th, 1837

My Dear Sister,

I design to devote this letter to a brief examination of the condition of women in Asia and Africa. I believe it will be found that men, in the exercise of their usurped dominion over woman, have almost invariably done one of two things. They have either made slaves of the creatures whom God designed to be their companions and their coadjutors in every moral and intellectual improvement, or they have dressed them like dolls, and used them as toys to amuse their hours of recreation.

I shall commence by stating the degrading practice of SELLING WOMEN, which we find prevalent in almost all the Eastern nations.

Among the Jews,—

> Whoever wished for a wife must pay the parents for her, or perform a stipulated period of service; sometimes the parties were solemnly betrothed in childhood, and the price of the bride stipulated.

> In Babylon, they had a yearly custom of a peculiar kind.

> In every district, three men, respectable for their virtue, were chosen to conduct all the marriageable girls to the public assembly. Here they were put up at auction by the public crier, while the magistrate presided over the sales. The most beautiful were sold first, and the rich contended eagerly for a choice. The most ugly, or deformed girl was sold next in succession to the handsomest, and assigned to any person who would take her with the least sum of money. The price given for the beautiful was divided into dowries for the homely.

Two things may here be noticed; first, the value set upon personal charms, just as a handsome horse commands a high price; and second, the utter disregard which is manifested towards the feelings of woman.

In no part of the world does the condition of women appear more dreary than in Hindostan. The arbitrary power of a father disposes of them in childhood. When they are married, their husbands have despotic control over them; if unable to support them, they can lend or sell them to a neighbor, and in the Hindoo rage for gambling, wives and children are frequently staked and lost. If they survive their husbands, they must pay implicit obedience to the oldest son; if they have no sons, the nearest male relation holds them in subjection; and if there happen to be no kinsmen, they must be dependent on the chief of the tribe.

Even the English, who are numerous in Hindostan, have traded in women.

India has been a great marriage market, on account of the emigration of young enterprising Englishmen, without a corresponding number of women. Some persons actually imported women to the British settlements, in order to sell them to rich Europeans, or nabobs, who would give a good price for them. How the importers acquired a right thus to dispose of them is not mentioned; it is probable that the women themselves, from extreme poverty, or some other cause, consented to become articles of speculation, upon consideration of receiving a certain remuneration. In September, 1818, the following advertisement appeared in the Calcutta Advertiser:

FEMALES RAFFLED FOR.

Be it known, that six fair pretty young ladies, with two sweet engaging children, lately imported from Europe, having the roses of health blooming on their cheeks, and joy sparkling in their eyes, possessing amiable tempers and highly accomplished, whom the most indifferent cannot behold without rapture, are to be raffled for next door to the British gallery.

The enemy of all good could not have devised a better means of debasing an immortal creature, than by turning her into a saleable commodity; and hence we find that wherever this custom prevails, woman is regarded as a mere machine to answer the purposes of domestic combat or sensual indulgence, or to gratify the taste of her oppressor by a display of personal attractions.

Weighed in the balance with a tyrant's gold,
Though nature cast her in a heavenly mould.

I shall now take a brief survey of the EMPLOYMENTS of women in Asia and Africa. In doing this, I have two objects in view; first to show, that women are capable of acquiring as great physical power as men, and secondly to show, that they have been more or less the victims of oppression and contempt.

The occupations of the ancient Jewish women were laborious. They spent their time in spinning and weaving cloth for garments, and for the covering of the tents, in cooking the food, tending the flocks, grinding the corn, and drawing water from the wells.

Of Trojan women we know little, but we find that—"Andromache, though a princess and well beloved by her husband, fed and took care of the horses of Hector."[8]

So in Persia, women of the middling class see that proper care is taken of the horses. They likewise do all the laborious part of the house work.

The Hindoo women are engaged in every variety of occupation, according to the caste of their husbands. They cultivate the land, make baskets and mats, bring water in jars, carry manure and various other articles to market in baskets on their heads, cook food, tend children, weave cloth, reel thread and wind cocoons.

The Thibetian women of the laboring classes are inured to a great deal of toil. They plant, weed, reap, and thresh grain, and are exposed to the roughest weather, while their indolent husbands are perhaps living at their ease.

Females of the lower classes among the Chinese endure as much labor and fatigue as the men. A wife sometimes drags the plough in rice fields with an infant tied upon her back, while her husband performs the less arduous task of holding the plough.

The Tartar women in general perform a greater share of labor than the men; for it is a prevalent opinion that they were sent into the world for no other purpose, but to be useful and convenient SLAVES to the stronger sex. Among some of the Tartar tribes of the present day, females manage a horse, hurl a javelin, hunt wild animals, and fight an enemy as well as the men.

In the island of Sumatra, the women do all the work, while their

8. According to Greek legend, Andromache was the wife of Hector, reputed to be the most valiant of the Trojan chiefs in the war against the Greeks. She was noted for her affection for her husband and son and for her nobility.

husbands lounge in idleness, playing on the flute, with wreaths of globe amaranth on their heads, or racing with each other, without saddle or stirrup, or hunting deer, or gambling away their wives, their children, or themselves. The Battas consider their wives and children as slaves, and sell them whenever they choose.

The Moors are indolent to excess. They lie whole days upon their mats, sleeping and smoking, while the women and slaves perform all the labor. Owing to their uncleanly habits, they are much infested with vermin; and as they consider it beneath their dignity to remove this annoyance, the task is imposed on the women. They are very impatient and tyrannical, and for the slightest offence beat their wives most cruelly.

In looking over the condition of women as delineated in this letter, how amply do we find the prophecy of Jehovah to Eve fulfilled, "Thy husband will rule over thee" [Gen. 3:16]. And yet we perceive that where the physical strength of woman is called into exercise, there is no inferiority even in this respect; she performs the labor, while man enjoys what are termed the pleasures of life.

I have thought it necessary to adduce various proofs of my assertion, that men have always in some way regarded women as mere instruments of selfish gratification; and hope this sorrowful detail of the wrongs of woman will not be tedious to thee.

Thine in the bonds of womanhood,

Sarah M. Grimké

LETTER VI

Women in Asia and Africa

Groton, 8th Mo. 15th, 1837

Dear Friend,

In pursuing the history of woman in different ages and countries, it will be necessary to exhibit her in all the various situations in which she has been placed.

We find her sometimes *filling the throne,* and exercising the functions of royalty. The name of Semiramis is familiar to every reader of ancient history.[9] She succeeded Ninus in the government of the Assyrian empire; and to render her name immortal, built the city of Babylon. Two millions of men were constantly employed upon it. Certain dykes built by order of this queen, to defend the city from inundations, are spoken of as admirable.

Nicotris, wife of Nabonadius, the Evil-Merodach of Scripture, was a woman of great endowments.[10] While her husband indulged in a life of ease and pleasure, she managed the affairs of state with wisdom and prudence.

> Zenobia queen of Palmyra and the East, is the most remarkable among Asiatic women.[11] Her genius struggled with and overcame all the obstacles presented by oriental laws and customs. She knew the Latin, Greek, Syriac, and Egyptian languages; and had drawn up for her own use an abridgement of oriental history. She was the companion and friend of her husband, and accompanied him on his hunting excursions with eagerness and courage equal to his own. She despised the effeminacy of a covered carriage, and often appeared on horseback in military costume. Sometimes she marched several miles on foot, at the head of the troops. Having revenged the murder of her husband, she ascended the throne, and for five years governed Palmyra, Syria, and the East, with wonderful steadiness and wisdom.
>
> Previous to the introduction of Mohammedism into Java, women often held the highest offices of government; and when the chief of a district dies, it is even now not uncommon for the widow to retain the authority that belonged to her deceased husband.

Other instances might be adduced to prove that there is no natural inferiority in woman. Not that I approve of woman's holding the reins of government over man. I maintain that they are equal, and that God never invested fallen man with unlimited power over his fellow man; and I rejoice that circumstances have prevented woman from being more deeply involved in the guilt which appears to be inseparable from political affairs. The few instances which I have mentioned prove that intellect is not sexed; and doubtless if woman had not almost universally been depressed and degraded, the page of history would have exhibited as many eminent statesmen and politicians among women as men. We are much in the situation of the slave.

9. Semiramis is considered the most important of the Assyrian queens. She was the wife of King Shamshi-Adad V (r. 823–811 B.C.) and the mother of Adadnirari III (r. 810–783 B.C.), and was the queen regent from 810 to 806 B.C., during which time she was responsible for large irrigation projects and the development of a great army.
10. Nicotris was the wife of Nabonidus, the last king of Babylon (555–539 B.C.).
11. Zenobia reigned as queen of Palmyra from 267 to 272 B.C., following the death of her husband, Odenathus. Much of Palmyra's conquest of the Near East and Asia Minor is attributed to her, though she was eventually conquered by the Roman emperor Aurelian.

Man has asserted and assumed authority over us. He has, by virtue of his power, deprived us of the advantages of improvement which he has lavishly bestowed upon himself, and then, after having done all he can to take from us the means of proving our equality, and our capability of mental cultivation, he throws upon us the burden of proof that God created man and woman equal, and endowed them, without any reference to sex, with intelligence and responsibilities, as rational and accountable beings. Hence in Hindostan, even women of the higher classes are forbidden to read or write; because the Hindoos think it would inevitably spoil them for domestic life, and assuredly bring some great misfortune upon them. May we not trace to the same feeling, the disadvantages under which women labor even in this country, for want of an education, which would call into exercise the powers of her mind, and fortify her soul with those great moral principles by which she would be qualified to fill *every* department in *social, domestic* and *religious* life with dignity?

In Hindostan, the evidence of women is not received in a court of justice.

In Burmah, their testimony is not deemed equal to that of a man, and they are not allowed to ascend the steps of a court of justice, but are obliged to give their testimony outside of the building.

In Siberia, women are not allowed to step across the foot-prints of men, or reindeer; they are not allowed to eat with men, or to partake of particular dainties. Among many tribes, they seem to be regarded as impure, unholy beings.

> The Mohammedan law forbids pigs, dogs, women and other impure animals to enter a mosque; and the hour of prayers must not be proclaimed by a female, a madman, a drunkard, or a decrepit person.

Here I am reminded of the resemblance between the situation of women in heathen and Mohammedan countries, and our brethren and sisters of color in this Christian land, where they are despised and cast out as though they were unclean. And on precisely the same ground, because they are said to be inferior.

The treatment of women as wives is almost uniformly the same in all heathen countries.

The ancient Lydians[12] are the only exception that I have met with, and the origin of their peculiar customs is so much obscured by fable, that it is difficult to ascertain the truth. Probably they arose from some great benefit conferred on the state by women.

12. Lydia was the main trade route between the Aegean Sea and the territory of Anatolia in ca. 700 B.C. It became part of Persia in ca. 500; Greece, ca. 300; and Rome, ca. 180.

Among the Druses[13] who reside in the mountains of the Anti Libanus, a wife is often divorced on the slightest pretext. If she ask her husband's permission to go out, and he says,—"Go," without adding "but come back again," she is divorced.

In Siberia, it is considered a wife's duty to obey the most capricious and unreasonable demands of her husband, without one word of expostulation or inquiry. If her master be dissatisfied with the most trifling particular in her conduct, he tears the cap or veil from her head, and this constitutes a divorce.

A Persian woman, under the dominion of the kindest master, is treated much in the same manner as a favorite animal. To vary her personal graces for his pleasure, is the sole end and aim of her existence. As moral or intellectual beings, it would be better for them to be among the dead than the living. The mother instructs her daughter in all the voluptuous coquetry, by which she herself acquired precarious ascendency over her absolute master; but all that is truly estimable in female character is utterly neglected.

Hence we find women extravagantly fond of adorning their persons. Regarded as instruments of pleasure, they have been degraded into mere animals, and have found their own gratification principally in the indulgence of personal vanity, because their external charms procured for them, at least a temporary ascendency over those, who held in their hands the reins of government. A few instances must suffice, or I shall exceed the limits I have prescribed to myself in this letter.

During the magnificent prosperity of Israel, marriages were conducted with great pomp; and with the progress of luxury and refinement, women became expensive, rather than profitable in a pecuniary point of view. Hence probably arose the custom of wealthy parents giving a handsome dowry with their daughters. On the day of the nuptials, the bride was conducted by her female relations to the bath, where she was anointed with the choicest perfumes, her hair perfumed and braided, her eyebrows deepened with black powder, and the tips of her fingers tinged with rose color. She was then arrayed in a marriage robe of brilliant color; the girdle and bracelets were more or less costly.

Notwithstanding the Chinese women have no opportunity to rival each other in the conquest of hearts, they are nevertheless very fond of ornaments. Bunches of silver or gilt flowers are always interspersed among their ringlets, and sometimes they wear the Chinese phœnix made of silver gilt. It moves with the slightest motion of the wearer, and the spreading tail forms a glittering aigrette on the middle of the head, and the wings wave over the front. Yet a Chinese ballad says,—The pearls and precious stones, the silk and gold with which a coquette so studiously bedecks herself, are a transparent varnish which makes all her defects the more apparent.

13. The Druses (Druze) are a religious sect begun by al-Hahim, the sixth imam of the Fatamid dynasty in A.D. 996–1021.

The Moorish women have generally a great passion for ornament. They decorate their persons with heavy gold ear-rings, necklaces of amber, coral and gold; gold bracelets; gold chains and silver bells for the ankles; rings on the fingers, &c. &c. The poorer class wear glass beads around the head, and curl the hair in large ringlets. Men are proud of having their wives handsomely dressed.

The Moors are not peculiar in this fancy. Christian men still admire women who adorn their persons to gratify the lust of the eye and the pride of life. Women, says a Brahminical expositor, are characterized by an inordinate love of jewels, fine clothes, &c. &c. I cannot deny this charge, but it is only one among many instances, wherein men have reproached us with those very faults and vices which their own treatment has engendered. Is it any matter of surprise that women, when unnaturally deprived of the means of cultivating their minds, of objects which would elevate and refine their passions and affections, should seek gratification in the toys and the trifles which now too generally engage their attention?

I cannot close this, without acknowledging the assistance and information I have derived and shall continue to derive on this part of my subject, from a valuable work entitled "Condition of Women, by Lydia M. Child." It is worth the perusal of every one who is interested in the subject.

Thine in the bonds of womanhood,

Sarah M. Grimké

LETTER VII

Condition in Some Parts of Europe and America

Brookline, 8th Mo., 22d, 1837

Dear Sister,

I now come to the consideration of the condition of woman in Europe.—In this portion of the world, she does not appear to have been as uniformly or as deeply debased, as in Eastern countries; yet we shall find little in her history which can yield us satisfaction, when we regard the high station she was designed to occupy as a *moral and intellectual* being.

In Greece, if we may judge from what Eustathius says, "women should keep within doors, and there talk,"—we may conclude, that in general their occupations were chiefly domestic. Thucydides also declares, that "she was the best woman, of whom the least was said, either of good or of harm."[14] The heathen philosophers doubtless wished to keep woman in her

14. Thucydides (460?–401? B.C.) was the author of *The History of the Peloponnesian Wars*.

"appropriate sphere"; and we find our clerical brethren of the present day re-echoing these pagan sentiments, and endeavoring to drive woman from the field of moral labor and intellectual culture, to occupy her talents in the pursuit of those employments which will enable her to regale the palate of her lord with the delicacies of the table, and in every possible way minister to his animal comfort and gratification. In my humble opinion, woman has long enough subserved the interests of man; and in the spirit of self-sacrifice, submitted almost without remonstrance to his oppression; and now that her attention is solicited to the subject of her rights, her privileges and her duties, I would entreat her to double her diligence in the performance of all her obligations as a *wife,* a *mother,* a *sister,* and a *daughter.* Let us remember that our claim to stand on perfect equality with our brethren, can only be substantiated by a scrupulous attention to our domestic duties, as well as by aiding in the great work of moral reformation—a work which is now calling for the energies and consecrated powers of every man and woman who desires to see the Redeemer's kingdom established on earth. That man must indeed be narrow minded, and can have but a poor conception of the power of moral truth on the female heart, who supposes that a correct view of her own rights can make woman *less solicitous to fill up every department of duty.* If it should have this effect, it must be because she has not taken a comprehensive view of the whole subject.

In the history of Rome, we find a little spot of sunshine in the valley where woman has been destined to live, unable from her lowly situation to take an expansive view of that field of moral and mental improvement, which she should have been busy in cultivating.

> In the earliest and best days of Rome, the first magistrates and generals of armies ploughed their own fields, and threshed their own grain. Integrity, industry and simplicity, were the prevailing virtues of the times; and the character of woman was, as it always must be, graduated in a degree by that of man. Columella says, Roman husbands, having completed the labors of the day, entered their houses free from all care, and there enjoyed perfect repose. There reigned union and concord and industry, supported by mutual affections. The most beautiful woman depended for distinction on her economy and endeavors to assist in crowning her husband's diligence with prosperity. All was in common between them; nothing was thought to belong more to one than another. The wife by her assiduity and activity within doors, equalled and seconded the industry and labor of her husband.

In the then state of the world, we may conclude from this description, that woman enjoyed as much happiness as was consistent with that comparatively unimproved condition of our species; but now a new and vast sphere of usefulness is opened to her, and she is pressed by surrounding circumstances to come up to the help of the Lord against the giant sins which desolate our beloved country. Shall woman shrink from duty in this exigency, and retiring within her own domestic circle, delight herself in the abundance of her own selfish enjoyments? Shall she rejoice in her home, her husband, her children, and forget her brethren and sisters in bondage, who know not what it is to call a spot of earth their own, whose husbands and wives are torn from them by relentless tyrants, and whose children are snatched from their arms by their unfeeling task-masters, whenever interest, or convenience, tempts them to this sacrilegious act? Shall woman disregard the situation of thousands of her fellow creatures, who are the victims of intemperance and licentiousness, and retreating to the privacy of her own comfortable home, be satisfied that her whole duty is performed, when she can exhibit "her children well clad and smiling, and her table neatly spread with wholesome provisions?" Shall she, because "her house is her *home*," refuse her aid and her sympathy to the down trodden slave, to the poor unhappy outcasts who are deprived of those blessings which she so highly prizes? Did God give her those blessings to steel her heart to the sufferings of her fellow creatures? Did he grant her the possession of husband and children, to dry up the fountains of feeling for those who know not the consolations of tenderness and reciprocal affection? Ah no! for every such blessing, God demands a grateful heart; and woman must be recreant to her duty, if she can quietly sit down in the enjoyments of her own domestic circle, and not exert herself to procure the same happiness for others.

But it is said woman has a mighty weapon in secret prayer. She has, I acknowledge, *in common with man;* but the woman who prays in sincerity for the regeneration of this guilty world, will accompany her prayers by her labors. A friend of mine remarked—"I was sitting in my chamber, weeping over the miseries of the slave, and putting up my petitions for his deliverance from bondage; when in the midst of my meditations, it occurred to me that my tears, unaided by effort, could never melt the chain of the slave. I must be up and doing." She is now an active abolitionist—her prayers and her works go hand in hand.

I am here reminded of what a slave once said to his master, a Methodist minister. The slaveholder inquired, "How did you like my sermon today?" "Very good, master, but it did not preach me free."

Oh, my sisters, suffer me to entreat you to assert your privileges, and to perform your duties as moral beings. Be not dismayed at the ridicule of man; it is a weapon worthy only of little minds, and is employed by those who feel that they cannot convince our judgment. Be not alarmed at contumely, or scorn; we must expect this. I pray that we may meet it with forbearance and love; and that nothing may drive us from the performance of our high and holy duties. Let us "cease from man, whose breath is in his nostrils, for wherein is he to be accounted of?" and press forward in all the great moral enterprises of the age, leaning *only* on the arm of our Beloved.

But I must return to the subject I commenced with, viz. the condition of woman in Europe.

The northern nations bore a general resemblance to each other. War and hunting were considered the only honorable occupations for men, and all other employments were left to women and slaves. Even the Visigoths, on the coasts of Spain, left their fields and flocks to the care of women. The people who inhabit the vast extent of country between the Black sea and the North sea, are divided into various distinct races. The women are generally very industrious; even in their walks, they carry a portable distaff, and spin every step of the way. Both Croatian and Walachian women perform all the agricultural operations in addition to their own domestic concerns.

Speaking of the Morlachian women, M. Fortis says, "Being treated like beasts of burden, and expected to endure submissively every species of hardship, they naturally become very dirty and careless in their habits."

The Cossack women afford a contrast to this disgusting picture. They are very cleanly and industrious, and in the absence of their husbands, supply their places by taking charge of all their usual occupations, in addition to their own. It is rare for a Cossack woman not to know some trade, such as dyeing cloth, tanning leather, &c.

The condition of Polish and Russian serfs in modern times is about the same. The Polish women have scarcely clothing enough for decency, and they are subjected to great hardships and privations. "In Russia, women have been seen paving the streets, and performing other similar drudgery. In Finland, they work like beasts of burden, and may be seen for hours in snow water, up to the middle, tugging at boats and sledges."

In Flanders and in France, women are engaged in performing laborious tasks; and even in England, it is not unusual to see them scraping up manure from the streets with their hands, and gathering it into baskets.

In Greece, even now the women plough and carry heavy burdens, while the lordly master of the family may be seen walking before them without any incumbrance.*

*Since the preceding letters were in type, I have met with the following account in a French work entitled "De l'education des mères de famille on de la civilization du Genre Humain par les femines," printed in Brussels in 1837. The periodicals have lately published the following circumstance from the journal of an English physician, who travelled in the East. He visited a slave market, where he saw about twenty Greek women half naked, lying on the ground waiting for a purchaser. One of them attracted the attention of an old Turk. The barbarian examined her shoulders, her legs, her ears, her mouth, her neck, with the minutest care, just as a horse is examined, and during the inspection, the merchant praised the beauty of her eyes, the elegance of her shape, and other perfections; he protested that the poor girl was but thirteen years of age, &c. After a severe scrutiny and some dispute about the price, she was sold body and soul for 1375 francs. The soul, it is true, was accounted of little value in the bargain. The unfortunate

Generally speaking, however, there is much more comparative equality of labor between the sexes in Europe than among the Orientals.

I shall close this letter with a brief survey of the condition of women among the Aborigines of America.

Before America was settled by Europeans, it was inhabited by Indian tribes, which greatly resembled each other in the treatment of their women. Every thing, except war and hunting, was considered beneath the dignity of man.—During long and wearisome marches, women were obliged to carry children, provisions and hammocks on their shoulders; they had the sole care of the horses and dogs, cut wood, pitched the tents, raised the corn, and made the clothing. When the husband killed game, he left it by a tree in the forest, returned home, and sent his wife several miles in search of it. In most of the tribes, women were not allowed to eat and drink with men, but stood and served them, and then ate what they left.

The following affecting anecdote may give some idea of the sufferings of these women:

Father Joseph reproved a female savage for destroying her infant daughter. She replied, "I wish my mother had thus prevented the manifold sufferings I have endured. Consider, father, our deplorable situation. Our husbands go out to hunt; we are dragged along with one infant at our breast, and another in a basket. Though tired with long walking, we are not allowed to sleep when we return, but must labor all night in grinding maize and making chica for them.—They get drunk and beat us, draw us by the hair of the head, and tread us under foot. Would to God my mother had put me under ground the moment I was born."

In Greenland, the situation of woman is equally deplorable. The men hunt bears and catch seals; but when they have towed their booty to land, they would consider it a disgrace to help the women drag it home, or skin and dress it. The often stand and look idly on, while their wives are staggering beneath the load that almost bends them to the earth. The women are cooks, butchers, masons, curriers, shoemakers and tailors. They will manage a boat in the roughest seas, and will often push off from the shore in the midst of a storm, that would make the hardiest European sailor tremble.

The page of history teems with woman's wrongs, and it is wet with

creature, half fainting in the arms of her mother, implored help in the most touching accents, but it availed nothing—This infernal scene passed in Europe in 1829, only 600 leagues from Paris and London, the two capitals of the human species, and at the time in which I write, it is the living history of two thirds of the inhabitants of the earth" [Grimké's note].

woman's tears.—For the sake of my degraded sex every where, and for the sake of my brethren, who suffer just in proportion as they place woman lower in the scale of creation than man, lower than her Creator placed her, I entreat my sisters to arise in all the majesty of moral power, in all the dignity of immortal beings, and plant themselves, side by side, on the platform of human rights, with man, to whom they were designed to the companions, equals and helpers in every good word and work.

Thine in the bonds of womanhood,

Sarah M. Grimké

LETTER VIII

On the Condition of Women in the United States

Brookline, 1837

My Dear Sister,

I have now taken a brief survey of the condition of woman in various parts of the world. I regret that my time has been so much occupied by other things, that I have been unable to bestow that attention upon the subject which it merits, and that my constant change of place has prevented me from having access to books, which might probably have assisted me in this part of my work. I hope that the principles I have asserted will claim the attention of some of my sex, who may be able to bring into view, more thoroughly than I have done, the situation and degradation of woman. I shall now proceed to make a few remarks on the condition of women in my own country.

During the early part of my life, my lot was cast among the butterflies of the *fashionable* world; and of this class of women, I am constrained to say, both from experience and observation, that their education is miserably deficient; that they are taught to regard marriage as the one thing needful, the only avenue to distinction; hence to attract the notice and win the attentions of men, by their external charms, is the chief business of fashionable girls. They seldom think that men will be allured by intellectual acquirements, because they find, that where any mental superiority exists, a woman is generally shunned and regarded as stepping out of her "appropriate sphere," which, in their view, is to dress, to dance, to set out to the best possible advantage her person, to read the novels which inundate the press, and which do more to destroy her character as a rational creature, than any thing else. Fashionable women regard themselves, and are regarded by men, as pretty toys or as mere instruments of pleasure; and the vacuity of mind, the heartlessness, the frivolity which is the necessary result of this false and debasing estimate of women, can only be fully understood by those who have mingled in the folly and wickedness of fashionable life; and who have been called from such pursuits by the voice of the Lord Jesus, inviting their weary and heavy laden souls to come unto Him and learn of Him, that they may find something worthy of their immortal spirit, and their intellectual powers; that they may learn the high and holy purposes of their creation, and consecrate themselves unto the service of God; and not, as is now the case, to the pleasure of man.

There is another and much more numerous class in this country, who are withdrawn by education or circumstances from the circle of fashionable amusements, but who are brought up with the dangerous and absurd idea, that *marriage* is a kind of preferment; and that to be able to keep their husband's house, and render his situation comfortable, is the end of her being. Much that she does and says and thinks is done in reference to this situation; and to be married is too often held up to the view of girls as the sine qua non of human happiness and human existence. For this purpose more than for any other, I verily believe the majority of girls are trained. This is demonstrated by the imperfect education which is bestowed upon them, and the little pains taken to cultivate their minds, after they leave school, by the little time allowed them for reading, and by the idea being constantly inculcated, that although all household concerns should be attended to with scrupulous punctuality at particular seasons, the improvement of their intellectual capacities is only a secondary consideration, and may serve as an occupation to fill up the odds and ends of time. In most families, it is considered a matter of far more consequence to call a girl off from making a pie, or a pudding, than to interrupt her whilst engaged in her studies. This mode of training necessarily exalts, in their view, the animal above the intellectual and spiritual nature, and teaches women to regard themselves as a kind of machinery, necessary to keep the domestic engine in order, but of little value as the *intelligent* companions of men.

Let no one think, from these remarks, that I regard a knowledge of housewifery as beneath the acquisition of women. Far from it: I believe that a complete knowledge of household affairs is an indispensable requisite in a woman's education,—that by the mistress of a family, whether married or single, doing her duty thoroughly and *understandingly,* the happiness of the family is increased to an incalculable degree, as well as a vast amount of time and money saved. All I complain of is, that our education consists so almost exclusively in culinary and other manual operations. I do long to see the time, when it will no longer be necessary for women to expend so many precious hours in furnishing "a well spread table," but that their husbands will forego some of their accustomed indulgences in this way, and encourage their wives to devote some portion of their time to mental cultivation, even at the expense of having to dine sometimes on baked potatoes, or bread and butter.

I believe the sentiment expressed by the author of "Live and let Live,"[15] is true:

> Other things being equal, a woman of the highest mental endowments will always be the best housekeeper, for domestic economy, is a science that brings into action the qualities of the mind, as well as the graces of the heart. A quick perception, judgment, discrimination, decision and order are high attributes of mind, and are all in daily exercise in the well ordering of a family. If a sensible woman, an intellectual woman, a woman of genius, is not a good housewife, it is not because she is either, or all of those, but because there is some deficiency in her character, or some omission of duty which should make her very humble, instead of her indulging in any secret self-complacency on account of a certain superiority, which only aggravates her fault.

The influence of women over the minds and character of *children* of both sexes, is allowed to be far greater than that of men. This being the case by the very ordering of nature, women should be prepared by education for the performance of their sacred duties as mothers and as sisters. A late American writer,* speaking on this subject, says in reference to an article in the Westminster Review:

> I agree entirely with the writer in the high estimate which he places on female education, and have long since been satisfied, that the subject not only merits, but *imperiously demands* a thorough reconsideration. The whole scheme must, in my opinion, be reconstructed. The great elements of usefulness and duty are too little attended to. Women ought, in my view of the subject, to approach to the best education now given to men, (I except mathematics and the classics,) far more I believe than has ever yet been attempted. Give me a host of educated, pious mothers and sisters, and I will do more to revolutionize a country, in moral and religious taste, in manners and in social virtues and intellectual cultivation, than I can possibly do in double or treble the time, with a similar host of educated men. I cannot but think that the miserable condition of the great body of the people in all ancient com-

15. Catherine Maria Sedgewick, *Live and Let Live: or Domestic Service Illustrated* (New York: Harper, 1837).
*Thomas S. Grimké.[16]
16. Thomas S. Grimké (1786–1834) was a leader of educational and moral reform. He was Sarah Grimké's older brother and encouraged her education as a child.

munities, is to be ascribed in a very great degree to the degradation of women.

There is another way in which the general opinion, that women are inferior to men, is manifested, that bears with tremendous effect on the laboring class, and indeed on almost all who are obliged to earn a subsistence, whether it be by mental or physical exertion—I allude to the disproportionate value set on the time and labor of men and of women. A man who is engaged in teaching, can always, I believe, command a higher price for tuition than a woman—even when he teaches the same branches, and is not in any respect superior to the woman. This I know is the case in boarding and other schools with which I have been acquainted, and it is so in every occupation in which the sexes engage indiscriminately. As for example, in tailoring, a man has twice, or three times as much for making a waistcoat or pantaloons as a woman, although the work done by each may be equally good. In those employments which are peculiar to women, their time is estimated at only half the value of that of men. A woman who goes out to wash, works as hard in proportion as a wood sawyer, or a coal heaver, but she is not generally able to make more than half as much by a day's work. The low remuneration which women receive for their work, has claimed the attention of a few philanthropists, and I hope it will continue to do so until some remedy is applied for this enormous evil. I have known a widow, left with four or five children, to provide for, unable to leave home because her helpless babes demand her attention, compelled to earn a scanty subsistence, by making coarse shirts at 12½ cents a piece, or by taking in washing, for which she was paid by some wealthy persons 12½ cents per dozen. All these things evince the low estimation in which woman is held. There is yet another and more disastrous consequence arising from this unscriptural notion— women being educated, from earliest childhood, to regard themselves as inferior creatures, have not that self-respect which conscious equality would engender, and hence when their virtue is assailed, they yield to temptation with facility, under the idea that it rather exalts than debases them, to be connected with a superior being.

There is another class of women in this country, to whom I cannot refer, without feelings of the deepest shame and sorrow. I allude to our female slaves. Our southern cities are whelmed beneath a tide of pollution; the virtue of female slaves is wholly at the mercy of irresponsible tyrants, and women are bought and sold in our slave markets, to gratify the brutal lust of those who bear the name of Christians. In our slave States, if amid all her degradation and ignorance, a woman desires to preserve her virtue unsullied, she is either bribed or whipped into compliance, or if she dares resist her seducer, her life by the laws of some of the slave States may be, and has actually been sacrificed to the fury of disappointed passion. Where such laws do not exist, the power which is necessarily vested in the master over his property, leaves the defenceless slave entirely at his mercy, and the sufferings of some females on this account, both physical and mental, are intense. Mr. Gholson,[17] in the House of Delegates of Virginia, in 1832, said, "He really had been under the impression that he owned his slaves. He had lately purchased four women and ten children, in whom he thought he had obtained a great bargain; for he supposed they were his own property, *as were his brood mares*." But even if any laws existed in the United States, as in Athens formerly, for the protection of female slaves, they would be null and void, because the evidence of a colored person is not admitted against a white, in any of our Courts of Justice in the slave States. "In Athens, if a female slave had cause to complain of any want of respect to the laws of modesty, she could seek the protection of the temple, and demand a change of owners; and such appeals were never discountenanced, or neglected by the magistrate." In Christian America, the slave has no refuge from unbridled cruelty and lust.

S. A. Forrall, speaking of the state of morals at the South, says, "Negresses when young and likely, are often employed by the planter, or his friends, to administer to their sensual desires. This frequently is a matter of speculation, for if the offspring, a mulatto, be a handsome female, 800 or 1000 dollars may be obtained for her in the New Orleans market. It is an occurrence of no uncommon nature to see a Christian father sell his own daughter, and the brother his own sister." The following is copied by the N.Y. Evening Star from the Picayune, a paper published in New Orleans. "A very beautiful girl, belonging to the estate of John French, a deceased gambler at New Orleans, was sold a few days since for the round sum of $7,000. An ugly-looking bachelor named Gouch, a member of the Council of one of the Principalities, was the purchaser. The girl is a brunette; remarkable for her beauty and intelligence, and there was considerable contention, who should be the purchaser. She was, however, persuaded to accept Gouch, he having made her princely promises." I will add but one more from the numerous testimonies respecting the degradation of female slaves, and the licentiousness of the South. It is from the Circular of the Kentucky Union, for the moral and religious improvement of the colored race. "To the female character among our black population, we cannot allude but with feelings of the bitterest shame. A similar condition of moral pollution and utter disregard of a pure and virtuous reputation, is to be found *only without the pale of Christendom*. That such a state of society should exist in a Christian nation, claiming to be the most enlightened upon earth, without calling forth any *particular attention* to its existence, though ever before our eyes and *in our families*, is a moral phenomenon at once unaccountable and disgraceful." Nor does the colored woman suffer alone: the moral purity of the white woman is deeply contaminated. In the daily habit of seeing the virtue of her

17. James Herbert Gholson (1798–1848) was a member of the House of Delegates in Virginia from 1824 to 1828, and again from 1830 to 1838.

enslaved sister sacrificed without hesitancy or remorse, she looks upon the crimes of seduction and illicit intercourse without horror, and although not personally involved in the guilt, she loses that value for innocence in her own, as well as the other sex, which is one of the strongest safeguards to virtue. She lives in habitual intercourse with men, whom she knows to be polluted by licentiousness, and often is she compelled to witness in her own domestic circle, those disgusting and heart-sickening jealousies and strifes which disgraced and distracted the family of Abraham. In addition to all this, the female slaves suffer every species of degradation and cruelty, which the most wanton barbarity can inflict; they are indecently divested of their clothing, sometimes tied up and severely whipped, sometimes prostrated on the earth, while their naked bodies are torn by the scorpion lash.

> The whip on WOMAN's shrinking flesh!
> Our soil yet reddening with the stains
> Caught from her scourging warm and fresh.

Can any American woman look at these scenes of shocking licentiousness and cruelty, and fold her hands in apathy and say, "I have nothing to do with slavery"? *She cannot and be guiltless.*

I cannot close this letter, without saying a few words on the benefits to be derived by men, as well as women, from the opinions I advocate relative to the equality of the sexes. Many women are now supported, in idleness and extravagance, by the industry of their husbands, fathers, or brothers, who are compelled to toil out their existence, at the counting house, or in the printing office, or some other laborious occupation, while the wife and daughters and sisters take no part in the support of the family, and appear to think that their sole business is to spend the hard bought earnings of their male friends. I deeply regret such a state of things, because I believe that if women felt their responsibility, for the support of themselves, or their families it would add strength and dignity to their characters, and teach them more true sympathy for their husbands, than is now generally manifested,— a sympathy which would be exhibited by actions as well as words. Our brethren may reject my doctrine, because it runs counter to common opinions, and because it wounds their pride; but I believe they would be "partakers of the benefit" resulting from the Equality of the Sexes, and would find that woman, as their equal, was unspeakably more valuable than woman as their inferior, both as a moral and an intellectual being.

Thine in the bonds of womanhood,

Sarah M. Grimké

LETTER IX·

Heroism of Women—Women in Authority

Brookline, 8th Mo., 25th, 1837

My Dear Sister,

It seems necessary to glance at the conduct of women under circumstances which place them in juxtaposition with men, although I regard it as entirely unimportant in proving the moral equality of the sexes; because I condemn, in both, the exercise of that brute force which is as contrary to the law of God in men as in women; still, as a part of our history, I shall notice some instances of courage exhibited by females.

"Philippa, wife of Edward III., was the principal cause of the victory gained over the Scots at Neville Cross.[18] In the absence of her husband, she rode among the troops, and exhorted them to 'be of good courage.'" Jane, Countess of Mountfort, and a contemporary of Philippa, likewise possessed a great share of physical courage. The history of Joan of Arc is too familiar to need repetition.[19] During the reign of James II. [1633–1701], a singular instance of female intrepidity occurred in Scotland. Sir John Cochrane being condemned to be hung, his daughter twice disguised herself, and robbed the mail that brought his death warrant. In the mean time, his pardon was obtained from the King. Instances might be multiplied, but it is unnecessary. I shall therefore close these proofs of female courage with one more fact. "During the revolutionary war, the women shared in the patriotism and bravery of the men. Several individuals carried their enthusiasm so far as to enter the army, where they faced all the perils and fatigues of the camp, until the close of the war.

When I view my countrywomen in the character of soldiers, or even behold them loading fire arms and moulding bullets for their brethren to destroy men's lives, I cannot refrain a sigh. I cannot but contrast their conduct at that solemn crisis with the conduct of those women who followed their Lord and Master, with unresisting submission, to Calvary's Mount. With the precepts and example of a crucified Redeemer, who, in that sublime precept, "Resist not evil," has interdicted to his disciples all war and all violence, and taught us that the spirit of retaliation for injuries, whether in the camp, or at the fire-side, is wholly at variance with the peaceful religion he came to promulgate. How little do we comprehend that simple truth, "By this shall all men know that ye are my disciples, if ye have *love one to another*" [John 13:25].

Women have sometimes distinguished themselves in a way more

18. Philippa of Haincault (1312–69), married to Edward III, is considered responsible for repelling the Scottish invasion of England in 1346.
19. Joan of Arc (ca. 1412–31), a French saint, was a heroine during the Hundred Years' War.

consistent with their duties as moral beings. During the war between the Romans and the Sabines [290 B.C.], the Sabine women who had been carried off by the Romans, repaired to the Sabine camp, dressed in deep mourning, with their little ones in their arms, to soften, if possible, the feelings of their parents. They knelt at the feet of their relatives; and when Hersilia,[20] the wife of Romulus, described the kindness of their husbands, and their unwillingness to be separated from them, their fathers yielded to their entreaties, and an alliance was soon agreed upon. In consequence of this important service, peculiar privileges were conferred on women by the Romans. Brutus said of his wife,[21] I must not answer Portia in the words of Hector, "Mind your wheel, and to your maids give law," for in courage, activity and concern for her country's freedom, she is inferior to none of us." After the fatal battle of Cannæ [216 B.C.], the Roman women consecrated all their ornaments to the service of the state. But when the triumvirs attempted to tax them for the expenses of carrying on a civil war, they resisted the innovation. They chose Hortensia for their speaker, and went in a body to the market-place to expostulate with the magistrates. The triumvirs wished to drive them away, but they were compelled to yield to the wishes of the people, and give the women a hearing. Hortensia pleaded so well the cause of her sisters, who resolved that they would not voluntarily aid in a *civil war,* that the number of women taxed was reduced from 1400 to 400.

In the wars of the Guelphs and the Ghibbelines[22] the emperor Conrad refused all terms of capitulation to the garrison of Winnisberg, but he granted the request of the women to pass out in safety with such of their effects as they could carry themselves. Accordingly, they issued from the besieged city, each bearing on her shoulders a husband, son, father, or brother. They passed unmolested through the enemy's camp, which rung with acclamations of applause.

During our struggle for independence, the women were as exemplary as the men in various instances of self-denial: they refused every article of decoration for their persons; foreign elegances were laid aside, and they cheerfully abstained from luxuries for their tables.

English history presents many instances of women exercising prerogatives now denied them. In an action at law, it has been determined that an unmarried woman, having a freehold, might vote for members of Parliament; and it is recorded that lady Packington returned two. Lady Broughton

---

20. Hersilia was one of the Sabine women carried away by the Romans, and was given to Romulus as his wife. After his death she became a divinity, called Hora.
21. Brutus is the Roman considered to be the author of the great revolution that drove Tarquin the Proud from the throne, establishing consular government in Rome. He is most infamous for being an assassin of Julius Caesar. Portia, wife of Brutus and daughter of Cato, is reputed to have been among the most courageous women of her day.
22. The Guelphs and the Ghibbelines were rival political factions in medieval Germany and Italy, feuding from 1125 until the fourteenth century.

was keeper of the gatehouse prison. And in a much later period, a woman was appointed governor of the house of correction at Chelmsford, by order of the court. In the reign of George II. the minister of Clerkenwell was chosen by a majority of women. The office of grand chamberlain in 1822 was filled by two women; and that of clerk of the crown, in the court of king's bench, has been granted to a female. The celebrated Anne, countess of Pembroke, held the hereditary office of sheriff of Westmoreland, and exercised it in person, sitting on the bench with the judges.[23]

I need hardly advert to the names of Elizabeth of England, Maria Theresa of Germany, Catherine of Russia, and Isabella of Spain, to prove that women are capable of swaying the sceptre of royalty. The page of history proves incontestibly, not only that they are as well qualified to do so as men, but that there has been a comparatively greater proportion of good queens, than of good kings; women who have purchased their celebrity by individual strength of character.

I mention these women only to prove that intellect is not sexed; that strength of mind is not sexed; and that our views about the duties of men and the duties of women, the sphere of man and the sphere of woman, are mere arbitrary opinions, differing in different ages and countries, and dependent solely on the will and judgment of erring mortals.

As moral and responsible beings, men and women have the same sphere of action, and the same duties devolve upon both; but no one can doubt that the duties of each vary according to circumstances; that a father and a mother, a husband and a wife, have sacred obligations resting on them, which cannot possibly belong to those who do not sustain these relations. But these duties and responsibilities do not attach to them as men and as women, but as parents, husbands, and wives.

Thine in the bonds of womanhood,

Sarah M. Grimké

LETTER X

Intellect of Woman

Brookline, 8th Mo., 1837

My Dear Sister,
It will scarcely be denied, I presume, that, as a general rule, men do not desire the improvement of women. There are few instances of men who are

---

23. Anne Clifford, Countess of Dorset, Pembroke, and Montgomery (1590–1676) is renowned for her restoration of castles and founding of almshouses.

magnanimous enough to be entirely willing that women should know more than themselves, on any subjects except dress and cookery; and, indeed, this necessarily flows from their assumption of superiority. As *they* have determined that Jehovah has placed woman on a lower platform than man, they of course wish to keep her there; and hence the noble faculties of our minds are crushed, and our reasoning powers are almost wholly uncultivated.

A writer in the time of Charles I. says—"She that knoweth how to compound a pudding, is more desirable than she who skilfully compounded a poem. A female poet I mislike at all times." Within the last century, it has been gravely asserted that, "chemistry enough to keep the pot boiling, and geography enough to know the location of the different rooms in her house, is learning sufficient for a woman." Byron, who was too sensual to conceive of a pure and perfect companionship between the sexes, would limit a woman's library to a Bible and cookery book. I have myself heard men, who knew for themselves the value of intellectual culture, say they cared very little for a wife who could not make a pudding, and smile with contempt at the ardent thirst for knowledge exhibited by some women.

But all this is miserable wit and worse philosophy. It exhibits that passion for the gratification of a pampered appetite, which is beneath those who claim to be so far above us, and may justly be placed on a par with the policy of the slaveholder, who says that men will be better slaves, if they are not permitted to learn to read.

In spite, however, of the obstacles which impede the progress of women towards that state of high mental cultivation for which her Creator prepared her, the tendency towards the universal dissemination of knowledge has had its influence on their destinies; and in all ages, a few have surmounted every hindrance, and proved, beyond dispute, that they have talents equal to their brethren.

Cornelia, the daughter of Scipio Africanus, was distinguished for virtue, learning and good sense. She wrote and spoke with uncommon elegance and purity. Cicero and Quintilian bestow high praise upon her letters, and the eloquence of her children was attributed to her careful superintendence.[24] This reminds me of a remark made by my brother, Thomas S. Grimke, when speaking of the importance of women being well educated, that "educated men would never make educated women, but educated women would make educated men." I believe the sentiment is correct, because if the wealth of latent intellect among women was fully evolved and improved, they would rejoice to communicate to their sons all their own knowledge, and inspire them with desires to drink from the fountain of literature.

24. Cicero wrote of Cornelia, "We have read the letters of Cornelia, mother of the Gracchi; they make it plain that her sons were nursed not less by their mother's speech than at her breast." *Brutus* lviii.210.

I pass over many interesting proofs of the intellectual powers of women; but I must not omit glancing at the age of chivalry, which has been compared to a golden thread running through the dark ages. During this remarkable era, women who, before this period, had been subject to every species of oppression and neglect, were suddenly elevated into deities, and worshipped with a mad fanaticism. It is not improbable, however, that even the absurdities of chivalry were beneficial to women, as it raised them from that extreme degradation to which they had been condemned, and prepared the way for them to be permitted to enjoy some scattered rays from the sun of science and literature. As the age of knight-errantry declined, men began to take pride in learning, and women shared the advantages which this change produced. Women preached in public, supported controversies, published and defended theses, filled the chairs of philosophy and law, harangued the popes in Latin, wrote Greek and read Hebrew. Nuns wrote poetry, women of rank became divines, and young girls publicly exhorted Christian princes to take up arms for the recovery of the holy sepulchre. Hypatia,[25] daughter of Theon of Alexandria, succeeded her father in the government of the Platonic school, and filled with reputation a seat, where many celebrated philosophers had taught. The people regarded her as an oracle, and magistrates consulted her in all important cases. No reproach was ever uttered against the perfect purity of her manners. She was unembarrassed in large assemblies of men, because their admiration was tempered with the most scrupulous respect. In the 13th century, a young lady of Bologna pronounced a Latin oration at the age of twenty-three. At twenty-six, she took the degree of doctor of laws, and began publicly to expound Justinian. At thirty, she was elevated to a professor's chair, and taught the law to a crowd of scholars from all nations. Italy produced many learned and gifted women, among whom, perhaps none was more celebrated than Victoria Colonna, Marchioness of Pescara. In Spain, Isabella of Rosera converted Jews by her eloquent preaching; and in England the names of many women, from Lady Jane Gray[26] down to Harriet Martineau,[27] are familiar to every reader of history. Of the last mentioned authoress, Lord Brougham said that her writings on political economy were doing more good than those of any man in England. There is a contemporary of Harriet Martineau, who has recently rendered valuable services to her country. She presented a memorial to Parliament, stating the dangerous parts of the coast, where light-houses were needed, and at her

---

25. Hypatia was a Greek philosopher of the fifth century A.D.

26. Lady Jane Grey (1537–54) reigned as queen of England for nine days in an attempt to prevent the succession of Mary Tudor to the throne. She was distinguished for her learning and piety.

27. Harriet Martineau (1802–76) was a writer and social reformer known for her social reform stories, *Illustration of Political Economy, Poor Laws and Paupers, Illustrated,* and *Illustrations of Taxation.* She was best known in America for her commentaries on American life, *Society in America* (1837).

suggestion, several were erected. She keeps a life-boat and sailors in her pay, and has been the means of saving many lives. Although she has been deprived of the use of her limbs since early childhood, yet even when the storm is unusually severe, she goes herself on the beach in her carriage, that she may be sure her men perform their duty. She understands several languages, and is now engaged in writing a work on the Northern languages of Europe. "In Germany, the influence of women on literature is considerable, though less obvious than in some other countries. Literary families frequently meet at each others houses, and learned and intelligent women are often the brightest ornaments of these social circles." France has produced many distinguished women, whose names are familiar to every lover of literature. And I believe it is conceded universally, that Madame de Staël[28] was intellectually the greatest woman that ever lived. The United States have produced several female writers, some of whom have talents of the highest order. But women, even in this free republic, do not enjoy *all* the intellectual advantages of men, although there is a perceptible improvement within the last ten or twenty years; and I trust there is a desire awakened in my sisters for solid acquirements, which will elevate them to their "appropriate sphere," and enable them to "adorn the doctrine of God our Saviour in all things."

Thine in the bonds of womanhood,

Sarah M. Grimké

LETTER XI

Dress of Women

Brookline, 9th Mo., 1837

My Dear Sister,

When I view woman as an immortal being, travelling through this world to that city whose builder and maker is God,—when I contemplate her in all the sublimity of her spiritual existence, bearing the image and superscription of Jehovah, emanating from Him and partaking of his nature, and destined, if she fulfils her duty, to dwell with him through the endless ages of eternity,—I mourn that she has lived so far below her privileges and her obligations, as a rational and accountable creature; and I ardently long to behold

---

28. Madame de Staël (1766–1817), author and critic, was a prominent literary and political figure of her day, famous for her salons. She was author of, among other works, *Corinne ou l'Italie* and *De l'Allemagne*. She was an early champion of women's right to self-expression.

her occupying that sphere in which I believe her Creator designed her to move.

Woman, in all ages and countries, has been the scoff and the jest of her lordly master. If she attempted, like him, to improve her mind, she was ridiculed as pedantic, and driven from the temple of science and literature by coarse attacks and vulgar sarcasms. If she yielded to the pressure of circumstances, and sought relief from the monotony of existence by resorting to the theatre and the ball-room, by ornamenting her person with flowers and with jewels, while her mind was empty and her heart desolate; she was still the mark at which wit and satire and cruelty levelled their arrows.

"Woman," says Adam Clarke,[29] "has been invidiously defined, *an animal of dress.* How long will they permit themselves to be thus degraded?" I have been an attentive observer of my sex, and I am constrained to believe that the passion for dress, which so generally characterizes them, is one cause why there so is little of that solid improvement and weight of character which might be acquired under almost any circumstances, if the mind were not occupied by the love of admiration, and the desire to gratify personal vanity. I have already adduced some instances to prove the inordinate love of dress, which is exhibited by women in a state of heathenism; I shall, therefore, confine myself now to what are called Christian countries; only remarking that previous to the introduction of Christianity into the Roman empire, the extravagance of apparel had arisen to an unprecedented height. "Jewels, expensive embroidery, and delicious perfumes, were used in great profusion by those who could afford them." The holy religion of Jesus Christ came in at this period, and stript luxury and wealth of all their false attractions. "Women of the noblest and wealthiest families, surrounded by the seductive allurements of worldly pleasure, renounced them all. Undismayed by severe edicts against the new religion, they appeared before the magistrates, and by pronouncing the simple words, 'I am a Christian,' calmly resigned themselves to imprisonment, ignominy and death." Could such women have had their minds occupied by the foolish vanity of ornamental apparel? No! Christianity struck at the root of all sin, and consequently we find the early Christians could not fight, or swear, or wear costly clothing. Cave, in his work entitled "Primitive Christianity," has some interesting remarks on this subject, showing that simplicity of dress was not then esteemed an unimportant part of Christianity.

Very soon, however, when the fire of persecution was no longer blazing, pagan customs became interwoven with Christianity. The professors of the religion of a self-denying Lord, whose kingdom was not of this world, began to use the sword, to return railing for railing, to take oaths, to mingle heathen forms and ceremonies with Christian worship, to engraft on the

29. Adam Clarke (1762?–1832), an Irish Wesleyan minister, was most famous for his written commentary on the Bible, *Commentary on the Holy Scriptures.*

beautiful simplicity of piety, the feasts and observances which were usual at heathen festivals in honor of the gods, and to adorn their persons with rich and ornamental apparel. And now if we look at Christendom, there is scarcely a vestige of that religion, which the Redeemer of men came to promulgate. The Christian world is much in the situation of the Jewish nation, when the babe of Bethlehem was born, full of outside observances, which they substitute for mercy and love, for self-denial and good works, rigid in the performance of religious duties, but ready, if the Lord Jesus came amongst them and judged them by their fruits, as he did the Pharisees formerly, to crucify him as a slanderer. Indeed, I believe the remark of a late author is perfectly correct:

> Strange as it may seem, yet I do not hesitate to declare my belief that it is easier to make Pagan nations Christians, than to reform Christian communities and fashion them anew, after the pure and simple standard of the gospel. Cast your eye over Christian countries, and see what a multitude of causes combine to resist and impair the influence of Christian institutions. Behold the conformity of Christians to the world, in its prodigal pleasures and frivolous amusements, in its corrupt opinions and sentiments, of false honor. Behold the wide spread ignorance and degrading superstition; the power of prejudice and the authority of custom; the unchristian character of our systems of education; and the dread of the frowns and ridicule of the world, and we discover at once a host of more formidable enemies to the progress of *true religion* in Christian, than in heathen lands.

But I must proceed to examine what is the state of professing Christendom, as regards the subject of this letter. A few words will suffice. The habits and employments of fashionable circles are nearly the same throughout Christian communities. The fashion of dress, which varies more rapidly than the changing seasons, is still, as it has been from time immemorial, an all-absorbing object of interest. The simple cobbler of Agawam, who wrote in Massachusetts as early as 1647, speaking of women, says, "It is no marvel they wear drailes on the hinder part of their heads, having nothing, as it seems, in the fore part, but a few squirrels' brains to help them frisk from one fashion to another."

It must, however, be conceded, that although there are too many women who merit this severe reprehension, there is a numerous class whose improvement of mind and devotion to the cause of humanity justly entitle them to our respect and admiration. One of the most striking characteristics of modern times, is the tendency towards a universal dissemination of knowledge in all Protestant communities. But the character of woman has been elevated more by participating in the great moral enterprises of the day, than by anything else. It would astonish us if we could see at a glance all the labor, the patience, the industry, the fortitude which woman has exhibited, in carrying on the causes of Moral Reform, Anti-Slavery, &c. Still, even these noble and ennobling pursuits have not destroyed personal vanity. Many of those who are engaged in these great and glorious reformations, watch with eager interest, the ever varying freaks of the goddess of fashion, and are not exceeded by the butterflies of the ballroom in their love of curls, artificial flowers, embroidery and gay apparel. Many a woman will ply her needle with ceaseless industry, to obtain money to forward a favorite benevolent scheme, while at the same time she will expend on useless articles of dress, more than treble the sum which she procures by the employment of her needle, and which she might throw into the Lord's treasury, and leave herself leisure to cultivate her mind, and to mingle among the poor and the afflicted more than she can possibly do now.

I feel exceedingly solicitous to draw the attention of my sisters to this subject. I know that it is called trifling, and much is said about dressing fashionably, and elegantly, and becomingly, without thinking about it. This I do not believe can be done. If we indulge our fancy in the chameleon caprices of fashion, or in wearing ornamental and extravagant apparel, the mind must be in no small degree engaged in the gratification of personal vanity.

Lest any one may suppose from my being a Quaker, that I should like to see a uniform dress adopted, I will say, that I have no partiality for their peculiar costume, except so far as I find it simple and convenient; and I have not the remotest desire to see it worn, where one more commodious can be substituted. But I do believe one of the chief obstacles in the way of woman's elevation to the same platform of human rights, and moral dignity, and intellectual improvement, with her brother, on which God placed her, and where he designed her to act her part as an immortal creature, is her love of dress. "It has been observed," says Scott, "that foppery and extravagance as to dress *in men* are most emphatically condemned by the apostle's silence on the subject, for this intimated that surely *they* could be under no temptation to such a childish vanity." But even those men who are superior to such a childish vanity in themselves, are, nevertheless, ever ready to encourage it in women. They know that so long as we submit to be dressed like dolls, we never can rise to the stations of duty and usefulness from which they desire to exclude us; and they are willing to grant us paltry indulgences, which forward their own design of keeping us out of our appropriate sphere, while they deprive us of essential rights.

To me it appears beneath the dignity of woman to bedeck herself in gewgaws and trinkets, in ribbons and laces, to gratify the eye of man. I believe, furthermore, that we owe a solemn duty to the poor. Many a woman, in what is called humble life, spends nearly all her earnings in dress, because she wants to be as well attired as her employer. It is often argued that, as the birds and the flowers are gaily adorned by nature's hand, there can be no sin in woman's ornamenting her person. My reply is, God created me neither a bird nor a flower; and I aspire to something more than a resemblance to them. Besides, the gaudy colors in which birds and flowers are arrayed, create in them no feelings of vanity; but as human beings, we are susceptible of these passions, which are nurtured and strengthened by such adornments. "Well," I am often asked, "where is the limitation?" This it is not my business to decide. Every woman, as Judson remarks, can best settle this on her knees before God. He has commanded her not to be conformed to this world, but to be transformed by the renewing of her mind, that she may know what is the good and acceptable and perfect will of God. He made the dress of the Jewish women the subject of special denunciation by his prophet—Is. 3. 16–26; yet the chains and the bracelets, the rings and the ear-rings, and the changeable suits of apparel, are still worn by Christian women. He has commanded them, through his apostles, not to adorn themselves with broidered hair, or gold, or pearls, or costly array. Not to let their adorning be the "outward adorning of plaiting the hair, or of wearing of gold, or of putting on of apparel, but let it be the hidden man of the heart, in that which is not corruptible, even the ornament of a meek and quiet spirit, which is in the sight of God of great price" [1 Pet. 3:3]; yet we disregard these solemn admonitions. May we not form some correct estimate of dress, by asking ourselves how we should feel, if we saw ministers of the gospel rise to address an audience with ear-rings dangling from their ears, glittering rings on their fingers, and a wreath of artificial flowers on their brow, and the rest of their apparel in keeping? If it would be wrong for a minister, it is wrong for every professing Christian. God makes no distinction between the moral and religious duties of ministers and people. We are bound to be "a chosen generation, a royal priesthood, a peculiar people, a holy nation; that we should show forth the praises of him who hath called us out of darkness into his marvellous light" [1 Pet. 2:5].

Thine in the bonds of womanhood,

Sarah M. Grimké

LETTER XII

Legal Disabilities of Women

Concord, 9th Mo., 6th, 1837

My Dear Sister,

There are few things which present greater obstacles to the improvement and elevation of woman to her appropriate sphere of usefulness and duty, than the laws which have been enacted to destroy her independence, and crush her individuality; laws which, although they are framed for her government, she has had no voice in establishing, and which rob her of some of her *essential rights*. Woman has no political existence. With the single exception of presenting a petition to the legislative body, she is a cipher in the nation; or, if not actually so in representative governments, she is only counted, like the slaves of the South, to swell the number of law-makers who form decrees for her government, with little reference to her benefit, except so far as her good may promote their own. I am not sufficiently acquainted with the laws respecting women on the continent of Europe, to say anything about them. But Prof. Follen,[30] in his essay on "The Cause of Freedom in our Country," says, "Woman, though fully possessed of that rational and moral nature which is the foundation of all rights, enjoys amongst us fewer legal rights than under the civil law of continental Europe." I shall confine myself to the laws of our country. These laws bear with peculiar rigor on married women. Blackstone,[31] in the chapter entitled "Of husband and wife," says:—

> By marriage, the husband and wife are one person in law; that is, *the very being, or legal existence of the woman* is suspended during the marriage, or at least is incorporated and consolidated into that of the husband under whose wing, protection and cover she performs everything. For this reason, a man cannot grant anything to his wife, or enter into covenant with her; for the grant would be to suppose her separate existence, and to covenant with her would be to covenant with himself; and therefore it is also generally true, that all compacts made between husband and wife when single, are voided by the intermarriage. A woman indeed may be attorney for her husband, but that implies no separation from, but is rather a representation of, her love.

Here now, the very being of a woman, like that of a slave, is absorbed in her master. All contracts made with her, like those made with slaves by their owners, are a mere nullity. Our kind defenders have legislated away almost all our legal rights, and in the true spirit of such injustice and oppression, have kept us in ignorance of those very laws by which we are governed. They have persuaded us, that we have no right to investigate the laws, and that, if we did, we could not comprehend them; they alone are capable of

---

30. Charles Theodore Christian Follen (1796–1840) was a professor of German language and literature at Harvard University.
31. Sir William Blackstone, a jurist (1723–80). His *Commentaries on the Laws of England* were for many years the authority for the interpretation of both English and American common law. His doctrine of "coverture," in which the wife is covered and protected by and yet subject to her husband under the law, set the tone for many of the laws regarding the legal relationship of husbands and wives.

understanding the mysteries of Blackstone, &c. But they are not backward to make us feel the practical operation of their power over our actions.

> The husband is bound to provide his wife with necessaries by law, as much as himself; and if she contracts debts for them, he is obliged to pay for them; but for anything besides necessaries, he is not chargeable.

Yet a man may spend the property he has acquired by marriage at the ale-house, the gambling table, or in any other way that he pleases. Many instances of this kind have come to my knowledge; and women, who have brought their husbands handsome fortunes, have been left, in consequence of the wasteful and dissolute habits of their husbands, in straitened circumstances, and compelled to toil for the support of their families.

> If the wife be indebted before marriage, the husband is bound afterwards to pay the debt; for he has adopted her and her circumstances together.

The wife's property is, I believe, equally liable for her husband's debts contracted before marriage.

> If the wife be injured in her person or property, she can bring no action for redress without her husband's concurrence, and his name as well as her own: neither can she be sued, without making her husband a defendant.

This law that "a wife can bring no action," &c., is similar to the law respecting slaves. "A slave cannot bring a suit against his master, or any other person, for an injury—his master, must bring it." So if any damages are recovered for an injury committed on a wife, the husband pockets it; in the case of the slave, the master does the same.

> In criminal prosecutions, the wife may be indicted and punished separately, unless there be evidence of coercion from the fact that the offence was committed in the presence, or by the command of her husband. A wife is excused from punishment for theft committed in the presence, or by the command of her husband.

It would be difficult to frame a law better calculated to destroy the responsibility of woman as a moral being, or a free agent. Her husband is supposed to possess unlimited control over her; and if she can offer the flimsy excuse that he bade her steal, she may break the eighth commandment with impunity, as far as human laws are concerned.

> Our law, in general, considers man and wife as one person; yet there are some instances in which she is separately considered, as inferior to him and acting by his compulsion. Therefore, all deeds

executed, and acts done by her during her coverture (i.e., marriage,) are void, except it be a fine, or like matter of record, in which case she must be solely and secretly examined, to learn if her act be voluntary.

Such a law speaks volumes of the abuse of that power which men have vested in their own hands. Still the private examination of a wife, to know whether she accedes to the disposition of property made by her husband is, in most cases, a mere form; a wife dares not do what will be disagreeable to one who is, in his own estimation, her superior, and who makes her feel, in the privacy of domestic life, that she has thwarted him. With respect to the nullity of deeds or acts done by a wife, I will mention one circumstance. A respectable woman borrowed of a female friend a sum of money to relieve her son from some distressing pecuniary embarrassment. Her husband was from home, and she assured the lender, that as soon as he returned, he would gratefully discharge the debt. She gave her note, and the lender, entirely ignorant of the law that a man is not obliged to discharge such a debt, actually borrowed the money, and lent it to the distressed and weeping mother. The father returned home, refused to pay the debt, and the person who had loaned the money was obliged to pay both principal and interest to the friend who lent it to her. Women should certainly know the laws by which they are governed, and from which they frequently suffer; yet they are kept in ignorance, nearly as profound, of their legal rights, and of the legislative enactments which are to regulate their actions, as slaves.

The husband, by the old law, might give his wife moderate correction, as he is to answer for her misbehavior. The law thought it reasonable to entrust him with this power of restraining her by domestic chastisement. The courts of law will still permit a husband to restrain a wife of her liberty, in case of any gross misbehavior.

What a mortifying proof this law affords, of the estimation in which woman is held! She is placed completely in the hands of a being subject like herself to the outbursts of passion, and therefore unworthy to be trusted with power. Perhaps I may be told respecting this law, that it is a dead letter, as I am sometimes told about the slave laws; but this is not true in either case. The slaveholder does kill his slave by moderate correction, as the law allows; and many a husband, among the poor, exercises the right given him by the law, of degrading woman by personal chastisement. And among the higher ranks, if actual imprisonment is not resorted to, women are not unfrequently restrained of the liberty of going to places of worship by irreligious husbands, and of doing many other things about which, as moral and responsible beings, *they* should be the *sole* judges. Such laws remind me of the reply of some little girls at a children's meeting held recently at Ipswich. The lecturer told them that God had created four orders of beings with which he had made us acquainted through the Bible. The first was angels, the second was man, the third beasts; and now, children, what is the fourth? After a pause, several girls replied, "WOMEN."

> A woman's personal property by marriage becomes absolutely her husband's, which, at his death, he may leave entirely away from her.

And further, all the avails of her labor are absolutely in the power of her husband. All that she acquires by her industry is his; so that she cannot, with her own honest earnings, become the legal purchaser of any property. If she expends her money for articles of furniture, to contribute to the comfort of her family, they are liable to be seized for her husband's debts: and I know an instance of a woman, who by labor and economy had scraped together a little maintenance for herself and a do-little husband, who was left, at his death, by virtue of his last will and testament, to be supported by charity. I knew another woman, who by great industry had acquired a little money which she deposited in a bank for safe keeping. She had saved this pittance whilst able to work, in hopes that when age or sickness disqualified her for exertion, she might have something to render life comfortable, without being a burden to her friends. Her husband, a worthless, idle man, discovered this hid treasure, drew her little stock from the bank, and expended it all in extravagance and vicious indulgence. I know of another woman, who married without the least idea that she was surrendering her rights to all her personal property. Accordingly, she went to the bank as usual to draw her dividends, and the person who paid her the money, and to whom she was personally known as an owner of shares in that bank, remarking the change in her signature, withdrew the money, informing her that if she were married, she had no longer a right to draw her dividends without an order from her husband. It appeared that she intended having a little fund for private use, and had not even told her husband that she owned this stock, and she was not a little chagrined, when she found that it was not at her disposal. I think she was wrong to conceal the circumstances. The relation of husband and wife is too near and sacred to admit of secrecy about money matters, unless positive necessity demands it; and I can see no excuse for any woman entering into a marriage engagement with a design to keep her husband ignorant that she was possessed of property. If she was unwilling to give up her property to his disposal, she had infinitely better have remained single.

The laws above cited are not very unlike the slave laws of Louisiana.

> All that a slave possesses belongs to his master; he possesses nothing of his own, except what his master chooses he should possess.

By the marriage, the husband is absolutely master of the profits of the wife's lands during the coverture, and if he has had a living child, and survives the wife, he retains the whole of those lands, if they are estates of inheritance, during his life; but the wife is entitled only to one third if she survives, out of the husband's estates of inheritance. But this she has, whether she has had a child or not. With regard to the property of women, there is taxation without representation; for they pay taxes without having the liberty of voting for representatives.

And this taxation, without representation, be it remembered, was the cause of our Revolutionary war, a grievance so heavy, that it was thought necessary to purchase exemption from it at an immense expense of blood and treasure, yet the daughters of New England, as well as of all the other States of this free Republic, are suffering a similar injustice—but for one, I had rather we should suffer any injustice or oppression, than that my sex should have any voice in the political affairs of the nation.

The laws I have quoted, are, I believe, the laws of Massachusetts, and, with few exceptions, of all the States in this Union. "In Louisiana and Missouri, and possibly, in some other southern States, a woman not only has half her husband's property by right at his death, but may always be considered as possessed of half his gains during his life; having at all times power to bequeath that amount." That the laws which have generally been adopted in the United States, for the government of women, have been framed almost entirely for the exclusive benefit of men, and with a design to oppress women, by depriving them of all control over their property, is too manifest to be denied. Some liberal and enlightened men, I know, regret the existence of these laws; and I quote with pleasure an extract from Harriet Martineau's *Society in America* [1837] as a proof of the assertion. "A liberal minded lawyer of Boston, told me that his advice to testators always is to leave the largest possible amount to the widow, subject to the condition of her leaving it to the children; but that it is with shame that he reflects that any woman should owe that to his professional advice, which the law should have secured to her as a right." I have known a few instances where men have left their whole property to their wives, when they have died, leaving only minor children; but I have known more instances of "the friend and helper of many years, being portioned off like a salaried domestic," instead of having a comfortable independence secured to her, while the children were amply provided for.

As these abuses do exist, and women suffer intensely from them, our brethren are called upon in this enlightened age, by every sentiment of honor, religion and justice, to repeal these unjust and unequal laws, and restore to woman those rights which they have wrested from her. Such laws approximate too nearly to the laws enacted by slaveholders for the government of their slaves, and must tend to debase and depress the mind of that being, whom God created as a help meet for man, or "helper like unto himself," and designed to be his equal and his companion. Until such laws are annulled, woman never can occupy that exalted station for which she was intended by her Maker. And just in proportion as they are practically disregarded, which is the case to some extent, just so far is woman assuming that independence and nobility of character which she ought to exhibit.

The various laws which I have transcribed leave women very little more liberty, or power, in some respects, than the slave. "A slave," says the civil code of Louisiana, "is one who is in the power of a master, to whom he belongs. He can possess nothing, nor acquire anything, but what must belong to his master." I do not wish by any means to intimate that the condition of free women can be compared to that of slaves in suffering, or in degradation; still, I believe the laws which deprive married women of their rights and privileges, have a tendency to lessen them in their own estimation as moral and responsible beings, and that their being made by civil law inferior to their husbands, has a debasing and mischievous effect upon them, teaching them practically the fatal lesson to look unto man for protection and indulgence.

Ecclesiastical bodies, I believe, without exception, follow the example of legislative assemblies, in excluding woman from any participation in forming the discipline by which she is governed. The men frame the laws, and, with few exceptions, claim to execute them on both sexes. In ecclesiastical, as well as civil courts, woman is tried and condemned, not by a jury of her peers, but by beings, who regard themselves as her superiors in the scale of creation. Although looked upon as an inferior, when considered as an intellectual being, woman is punished with the same severity as man, when she is guilty of moral offences. Her condition resembles, in some measure, that of the slave, who, while he is denied the advantages of his more enlightened master, is treated with even greater rigor of the law. Hoping that in the various reformations of the day, women may be relieved from some of their legal disabilities, I remain,

Thine in the bonds of womanhood,

Sarah M. Grimké

LETTER XIII

Relation of Husband and Wife

Brookline, 9th Mo., 1837

My Dear Sister,

Perhaps some persons may wonder that I should attempt to throw out my views on the important subject of marriage, and may conclude that I am altogether disqualified for the task, because I lack experience. However, I shall not undertake to settle the specific duties of husbands and wives, but only to exhibit opinions based on the word of God, and formed from a little knowledge of human nature, and close observation of the working of generally received notions respecting the dominion of man over woman.

When Jehovah ushered into existence man, created in his own image, he instituted marriage as a part of paradisaical happiness: it was a *divine ordination*, not a civil contract. God established it, and man, except by special permission, has no right to annul it. There can be no doubt that the creation of Eve perfected the happiness of Adam; hence, our all-wise and merciful Father made her as he made Adam, in his own image after his likeness, crowned her with glory and honor, and placed in her hand, as well as in his, the sceptre of dominion over the whole lower creation. Where there was perfect equality, and the same ability to receive and comprehend divine truth, and to obey divine injunctions, there could be no superiority. If God had placed Eve under the guardianship of Adam, after having endowed her, as richly as him, with moral perceptions, intellectual faculties, and spiritual apprehensions, he would at once have interposed a fallible being between her and her Maker. He could not, in simple consistency with himself, have done this; for the Bible teems with instructions not to put any confidence in man.

The passage on which the generally received opinion, that husbands are invested by divine command with authority over their wives, as I have remarked in a previous letter [Letter V], is a prediction; and I am confirmed in this belief, because the same language is used to Cain respecting Abel [Gen. 5:2–15]. The text is obscure; but on a comparison of it with subsequent events, it appears to me that it was a prophecy of the dominion which Cain would usurp over his brother, and which issued in the murder of Abel. It could not allude to any thing but physical dominion, because Cain had already exhibited those evil passions which subsequently led him to become an assassin.

I have already shown, that man has exercised the most unlimited and brutal power over woman, in the peculiar character of husband,—a word in most countries synonymous with tyrant. I shall not, therefore, adduce any further proofs of the fulfilment of that prophecy. "He will rule over thee," from the history of heathen nations, but just glance at the condition of woman in the relation of wife in Christian countries.

"Previous to the introduction of the religion of Jesus Christ, the state of society was wretchedly diseased. The relation of the sexes to each other had become so gross in its manifested forms, that it was difficult to perceive the pure conservative principle in its inward essence." Christianity came in, at this juncture, with its hallowed influence, and has without doubt tended to lighten the yoke of bondage, to purify the manners, and give the spiritual in some degree an empire over the animal nature. Still, that state which was designed by God to increase the happiness of woman as well as man, often proves the means of lessening her comfort and degrading her into the mere machine of another's convenience and pleasure. Woman, instead of being elevated by her union with man, which might be expected from an alliance with a superior being, is in reality lowered. She generally loses her individuality, her independent character, her moral being. She becomes absorbed into him, and henceforth is looked at, and acts through the medium of her husband.

In the wealthy classes of society, and those who are in comfortable circumstances, women are exempt from great corporeal exertion, and are protected by public opinion, and by the genial influence of Christianity, from much physical ill treatment. Still, there is a vast amount of secret suffering endured, from the forced submission of women to the opinions and whims of their husbands. Hence they are frequently driven to use deception, to compass their ends. They are early taught that to appear to yield, is the only way to govern. Miserable sophism! I deprecate such sentiments, as being peculiarly hostile to the dignity of woman. If she submits, let her do it openly, honorably, not to gain her point, but as a matter of Christian duty. But let her beware how she permits her husband to be her conscience-keeper. On all moral and religious subjects, she is bound to think and to act for herself. Where confidence and love exist, a wife will naturally converse with her husband as with her dearest friend, on all that interests her heart, and there will be a perfectly free interchange of sentiment; but *she is no more bound to be governed by his judgment,* than he is by hers. They are standing on the same platform of human rights, are equally under the government of God, and accountable to him, and him alone.

I have sometimes been astonished and grieved at the servitude of women, and at the little idea many of them seem to have of their own moral existence and responsibilities. A woman who is asked to sign a petition for the abolition of slavery in the District of Columbia, or to join a society for the purpose of carrying forward the annihilation of American slavery, or any other great reformation, not unfrequently replies, "My husband does not approve of it." She merges her rights and her duties in her husband, and thus virtually chooses him for a savior and a king, and rejects Christ as her Ruler and Redeemer. I know some women are very glad of so convenient a pretext to shield themselves from the performance of duty; but there are others, who, under a mistaken view of their obligations as wives, submit conscientiously to this species of oppression, and go mourning on their way, for want of that holy fortitude, which would enable them to fulfil their duties as moral and responsible beings, without reference to poor fallen man. O that woman may arise in her dignity as an immortal creature, and speak, think and act as unto God, and not unto man!

There is, perhaps, less bondage of mind among the poorer classes, because their sphere of duty is more contracted, and they are deprived of the means of intellectual culture, and of the opportunity of exercising their judgment, on many moral subjects of deep interest and of vital importance. Authority is called into exercise by resistance, and hence there will be mental bondage only in proportion as the faculties of mind are evolved, and woman feels herself as a rational and intelligent being, on a footing with man. But women, among the lowest classes of society, so far as my observation has extended, suffer intensely from the brutality of their husbands. Duty as well as inclination has led me, for many years, into the abodes of poverty and sorrow, and I have been amazed at the treatment which women receive at the hands of those, who arrogate to themselves the epithet of *protectors*. Brute force, the law of violence, rules to a great extent in the poor man's domicil; and woman is little more than his drudge. They are less under the supervision of public opinion, less under the restraints of education, and unaided or unbiased by the refinements of polished society. Religion, wherever it exists, supplies the place of all these; but the real cause of woman's degradation and suffering in married life is to be found in the erroneous notion of her inferiority to man; and never will she be rightly regarded by herself, or others, until this opinion, so derogatory to the wisdom and mercy of God, is exploded, and woman arises in all the majesty of her womanhood, to claim those rights which are inseparable from her existence as an immortal, intelligent and responsible being.

Independent of the fact, that Jehovah could not, consistently with his character as the King, the Lawgiver, and the Judge of his people, give the reins of government over woman into the hands of man, I find that all his commands, all his moral laws, are addressed to women as well as to men. When he assembled Israel at the foot of Mount Sinai, to issue his commandments, we may reasonably suppose he gave all the precepts, which he considered necessary for the government of moral beings. Hence we find that God says,—"Honor thy father and thy mother," and he enforces this command by severe penalties upon those who transgress it: "He that smiteth his father, or his mother, shall surely be put to death"—"He that curseth his father, or his mother, shall surely be put to death"—Ex. 21:15, 17. But in the decalogue, there is no direction given to women to obey their husbands: both are commanded to have no other God but Jehovah, and not to bow down, or serve any other. When the Lord Jesus delivered his sermon on the Mount [Matt. 5–7], full of the practical precepts of religion, he did not issue any command to wives to obey their husbands. When he is speaking on the subject of divorce, Mark 16:11, 12, he places men and women on the same ground. And the Apostle, 1st Cor. 7:12, 13, speaking of the duties of the Corinthian wives and husbands, who had embraced Christianity, to their unconverted partners, points out the same path to both, although our translators have made a distinction. "Let him not put her away," 12—"Let her not leave him," 13—is precisely the same in the original. If man is constituted the governor of woman, he must be her God; and the sentiment expressed to me lately, by a married man, is perfectly correct: "In my opinion," said he, "the greatest excellence to which a married woman can attain, is to worship her husband." He was a professor of religion—his wife a lovely and intelligent woman. He only spoke out what thousands think and act. Women are indebted to Milton for giving to this false notion, "confirmation strong as proof of holy writ." His Eve is embellished with every personal grace, to gratify the eye of her admiring husband; but he seems to have furnished the mother of mankind with just intelligence enough to comprehend her supposed inferiority to Adam, and to yield unresisting submission to her lord and master. Milton[32] puts into Eve's mouth the following address to Adam:

> "My author and disposer, what thou bidst,
> Unargued I obey; so God ordains—
> God is thy law, thou mine: to know no more,
> Is woman's happiest knowledge and her praise."

This much admired sentimental nonsense is fraught with absurdity and wickedness. If it were true, the commandment of Jehovah should have run thus: Man shall have no other gods before ME, and woman shall have no other gods before MAN.

The principal support of the dogma of woman's inferiority, and consequent submission to her husband, is found in some passages of Paul's epistles. I shall proceed to examine those passages, premising 1st, that the antiquity of the opinions based on the false construction of those passages, has no weight with me: they are the opinions of interested judges, and I have no particular reverence for them, *merely* because they have been regarded with veneration from generation to generation. So far from this being the case, I examine any opinions of centuries standing, with as much freedom, and investigate them with as much care, as if they were of yesterday. I was educated to think for myself, and it is a privilege I shall always claim to exercise. 2d. Notwithstanding my full belief, that the apostle Paul's testimony, respecting himself, is true, "I was not a whit behind the chiefest of the apostles" [2 Cor. 11:5], yet I believe his mind was under the influence of Jewish prejudices respecting women, just as Peter's and the apostles were about the uncleanness of the Gentiles. "The Jews," says Clarke, "would not suffer a woman to read in the synagogue, although a servant, or even a child, had this permission." When I see Paul shaving his head for a vow, and offering sacrifices, and circumcising Timothy, to accommodate himself to the prepossessions of his countrymen, I do not conceive that I derogate in the least from his character as an inspired apostle, to suppose that he may have been imbued with the prevalent prejudices against women.

In 1st Cor. 11:3, after praising the Corinthian converts, because

---

32. John Milton (1608–74), author of *Paradise Lost*.

they kept the "ordinances," or "traditions," as the margin reads, the apostle says, "I would have you know, that the head of every man is Christ, and the head of the woman is the man; and the head of Christ is God." Eph. 5:23, is a parallel passage. "For the husband is the head of the wife, even as Christ is the head of the Church." The apostle closes his remarks on this subject, by observing, "This is a great mystery, but I speak concerning Christ and the Church" [Eph. 5:32]. I shall pass over this with simply remarking, that God and Christ are one. "I and my Father are one" [John 10:30], and there can be no inferiority where there is no divisibility. The commentaries on this and similar texts, afford a striking illustration of the ideas which men entertain of their own superiority, I shall subjoin Henry's[33] remarks on 1st Cor. 11:5, as a specimen: "To understand this text, it must be observed, that it was a signification either of shame, or subjection, for persons to be veiled, or covered in Eastern countries; contrary to the custom of ours, where the being bare-headed betokens subjection, and being covered superiority and dominion; and this will help us the better to understand the reason on which he grounds his reprehension, 'Every man praying, &c. dishonoreth his head,' i.e. Christ, the head of every man, by appearing in a habit unsuitable to the rank in which God had placed him. The woman, on the other hand, that prays, &c. dishonoreth her head, i.e. the man. She appears in the dress of her *superior,* and throws off the token of her subjection; she might with equal decency cut her hair short, or cut it off, the common dress of the man in that age. Another reason against this conduct was, that the man is the image and glory of God, the representative of that glorious dominion and headship which God has over the world. It is the man who is set at the head of this lower creation, and therein bears the resemblance of God. The woman, on the other hand, is the glory of the man: she is his representative. Not but she has dominion over the inferior creatures, and she is a partaker of human nature, and so far is God's representative too, but it is at second hand. She is the image of God, inasmuch as she is the image of the man. The man was first made, and made head of the creation here below, and therein the image of the divine dominion; and the woman was made out of the man, and shone with a *reflection of his glory,* being made superior to the other creatures here below, but in subjection to her husband, and deriving that *honor from him,* out of whom she was made. The woman was made for the man to be his help meet, and not the man for the woman. She was, naturally, therefore, made subject to him, because made for him, for HIS USE AND HELP AND COMFORT."

We see in the above quotation, what degrading views even good men entertain of women. Pity the Psalmist had not thrown a little light on this subject, when he was paraphrasing the account of man's creation. "Thou

---

33. Matthew Henry, biblical interpreter and author of *An Exposition of the Old and New Testament* (1829).

hast made him a little lower than the angels, and hast crowned him with glory and honor. Thou madest him to have dominion over the works of thy hands; thou hast put all things under his feet" [Ps. 8:5–6]. Surely if woman had been placed below man, and was to shine only by a lustre borrowed from him, we should have some clear evidence of it in the sacred volume. Henry puts her exactly on a level with the beasts; they were made for the use, help and comfort of man; and according to this commentator, this was the whole end and design of the creation of woman. The idea that man, as man, is superior to woman, involves an absurdity so gross, that I really wonder how any man of reflection can receive it as of divine origin; and I can only account for it, by that passion for supremacy, which characterizes man as a corrupt and fallen creature. If it be true that he is more excellent than she, as man, independent of his moral and intellectual powers, then every man is superior by virtue of his manship, to every woman. The man who sinks his moral capacities and spiritual powers in his sensual appetites, is still, as a man, simply by the conformation of his body, a more dignified being, than the woman whose intellectual powers are highly cultivated, and whose approximation to the character of Jesus Christ is exhibited in a blameless life and conversation.

But it is strenuously urged by those, who are anxious to maintain their usurped authority, that wives are, in various passages of the New Testament, commanded to obey their husbands. Let us examine these texts.

> Eph. 5:22. "Wives, submit yourselves unto your own husbands as unto the Lord." "As the church is subject unto Christ, so let the wives be to their own husbands in every thing."

> Col. 3:18. "Wives, submit yourselves unto your own husbands, as it is fit in the Lord."

> 1st Pet. 3:2. "Likewise ye wives, be in subjection to your own husbands; that if any obey not the word, they may also without the word be won by the conversation of the wives."

Accompanying all these directions to wives, are commands to husbands.

> Eph. 5:25. "Husbands, love your wives even as Christ loved the Church, and gave himself for it." "So ought men to love their wives as their own bodies. He that loveth his wife, loveth himself."

> Col. 3:19. "Husbands, love your wives, and be not bitter against them."

> 1st Pet. 3:7. "Likewise ye husbands, dwell with them according to knowledge, giving honor unto the wife as unto the weaker vessel, and as being heirs together of the grace of life."

I may just remark, in relation to the expression "weaker vessel," that the word in the original has no reference to intellect: it refers to physical weakness merely.

The apostles were writing to Christian converts, and laying down rules for their conduct towards their unconverted consorts. It no doubt frequently happened, that a husband or a wife would embrace Christianity, while their companions clung to heathenism, and husbands might be tempted to dislike and despise those, who pertinaciously adhered to their pagan superstitions. And wives who, when they were pagans, submitted as a matter of course to their heathen husbands, might be tempted knowing that they were superior as moral and religious characters, to assert that superiority, by paying less deference to them than heretofore. Let us examine the context of these passages, and see what are the grounds of the directions here given to husbands and wives. The whole epistle to the Ephesians breathes a spirit of love. The apostle beseeches the converts to walk worthy of the vocation wherewith they are called, with all lowliness and meekness, with long suffering, forbearing one another in love. The verse preceding 5:22, is "SUBMITTING YOURSELVES ONE TO ANOTHER IN THE FEAR OF GOD." Colossians 3, from 11 to 17, contains similar injunctions. The 17th verse says, "Whatsoever ye do in word, or in deed, do all in the name of the Lord Jesus." Peter, after drawing a most touching picture of Christ's sufferings for us, and reminding the Christians, that he had left us an example that we should follow his steps, "who did no sin, neither was guile found in his mouth" [1 Pet. 2:22], exhorts wives to be in subjection, &c.

From an attentive consideration of these passages, and of those in which the same words "submit," "subjection," are used, I cannot but believe that the apostles designed to recommend to wives, as they did to subjects and to servants, to carry out the holy principle laid down by Jesus Christ, "Resist not evil" [Matt. 5:39]. And this without in the least acknowledging the right of the governors, masters, or husbands, to exercise the authority they claimed. The recognition of the existence of evils does not involve approbation of them. God tells the Israelites, he gave them a king in his wrath, but nevertheless as they chose to have a king, he laid down directions for the conduct of that king, and had him anointed to reign over them. According to the generally received meaning of the passages I have quoted, they directly contravene the laws of God, as given in various parts of the Bible. Now I must understand the sacred Scriptures as harmonizing with themselves, or I cannot receive them as the word of God. The commentators on these passages exalt man to the station of a Deity in relation to woman. Clarke says, "As the Lord Christ is the head, or governor of the church, and the head of the man, so is the man the head, or governor of the woman. This is God's ordinance, and should not be transgressed. 'As unto the Lord.' The word church seems necessarily to be understood here: that is, act under the authority of your husbands, as the church acts under the authority of Christ.

As the church submits to the Lord, so let wives submit to their husbands."
Henry goes even further—"For the husband is the head of the wife. The
metaphor is taken from the head in the natural body, which being the seat
of reason, of wisdom and of knowledge, and the fountain of sense and
motion, is more excellent than the rest of the body." Now if God ordained
man the governor of woman, he must be able to save her, and to answer in
her stead for all those sins which she commits by his direction. Awful responsibility. Do husbands feel able and willing to bear it? And what becomes
of the solemn affirmation of Jehovah? "Hear this, all ye people, give ear all
ye inhabitants of the world, both low and high, rich and poor" [Ps. 49:1].
"None can by any means redeem his brother, or give to God a ransom for
him, for the redemption of the soul is precious, and man cannot accomplish
it" [Ps. 49:8].—*French Bible.*

  Thine in the bonds of womanhood,

                Sarah M. Grimké

LETTER XIV

Ministry of Women

                 Brookline, 9th Mo. 1837

My Dear Sister,
According to the principle which I have laid down, that man and woman
were created equal, and endowed by their beneficent Creator with the same
intellectual powers and the same moral responsibilities, and that consequently whatever is *morally* right for a man to do, is *morally* right for a
woman to do, it follows as a necessary corollary, that if it is the duty of man
to preach the unsearchable riches of Christ, it is the duty also of woman.

  I am aware, that I have the prejudices of education and custom to
combat, both in my own and the other sex, as well as "the traditions of
men," which are taught for the commandments of God. I feel that I have no
sectarian views to advance; for although among the Quakers, Methodists,
and Christians, women are permitted to preach the glad tidings of peace and
salvation, yet I know of no religious body, who entertain the Scripture doctrine of the perfect equality of man and woman, which is the fundamental
principle of my argument in favor of the ministry of women. I wish simply
to throw my views before thee. If they are based on the immutable foundation of truth, they cannot be overthrown by unkind insinuations, bitter
sarcasms, unchristian imputations, or contemptuous ridicule. These are
weapons which are unworthy of a good cause. If I am mistaken, as truth

only can prevail, my supposed errors will soon vanish before her beams; but I am persuaded that woman is not filling the high and holy station which God allotted to her, and that in consequence of her having been driven from her "appropriate sphere," both herself and her brethren have suffered an infinity of evils.

Before I proceed to prove that woman is bound to preach the gospel, I will examine the ministry under the Old Testament dispensation. Those who were called to this office were known under various names. Enoch, who prophesied, is designated as walking with God. Noah is called a preacher of righteousness. They were denominated men of God, seers, prophets, but they all had the same great work to perform, viz. to turn sinners from the error of their ways. This ministry existed previous to the institution of the Jewish priesthood, and continued after its abolition. *It has nothing to do with the priesthood.* It was rarely, as far as the Bible informs us, exercised by those of the tribe of Levi, and was common to all the people, women as well as men. It differed essentially from the priesthood, because there was no compensation received for calling the people to repentance. Such a thing as paying a prophet for preaching the truth of God is not even mentioned. They were called of Jehovah to go forth in his name, one from his plough, another from gathering of sycamore fruit, &c. &c. Let us for a moment imagine Jeremiah, when God says to him, "Gird up thy loins, and arise and speak unto the people all that I command thee" [Jer. 1:17], replying to Jehovah, "I will preach repentance to the people, if they will give me gold, but if they will not pay me for the truth, then let them perish in their sins." Now, this is virtually the language of the ministers of the present day; and I believe the secret of the exclusion of women from the ministerial office is, that that office has been converted into one of emolument, of honor, and of power. Any attentive observer cannot fail to perceive, that as far as possible, all such offices are reserved by men for themselves.

The common error that Christian ministers are the successors of the priests, is founded in mistake. In the particular directions given to Moses to consecrate Aaron and his sons to the office of the priesthood, their duties are clearly defined: see Ex. 28th, 29th and 30th chap. There is no commission to Aaron to preach to the people; his business was to offer sacrifice. Now why were sacrifices instituted? They were types of that one great sacrifice, which in the fulness of time was offered up through the eternal Spirit without spot to God. Christ assumed the office of priest; he "offered himself," and by so doing, abolished forever the order of the priesthood, as well as the sacrifices which the priests were ordained to offer.*

---

*I cannot enter fully into this part of my subject. It is, however, one of great importance, and I recommend those who wish to examine it, to read "The Book of the Priesthood," by an English Dissenter,[34] and Beverly's "View of the Present State of the Visible Church of Christ." They are both masterly productions.

34. Thomas Stratten, author of *Book of the Priesthood* (1830).

But it may be inquired, whether the priests were not to teach the people. As far as I can discover from the Bible, they were simply commanded to read the law to the people. There was no other copy that we know of, until the time of the kings, who were to write out a copy for their own use. As it was deposited in the ark, the priests were required, "When all Israel is come to appear before the Lord thy God in the place which he shall choose, thou shalt read this law before all Israel in their hearing. Gather the people together, men, women, and children, that they may hear," Deut. 31:9–33. See also Lev. 10:11, Deut. 33:10, 2d Chr. 17:7–9, and numerous other passages. When God is enumerating the means he has used to call his people to repentance, he never, as far as I can discover, speaks of sending his priests to warn them; but in various passages we find language similar to this: "Since the day that your fathers came forth out of the Land of Egypt unto this day, I have even sent unto you all my servants, the PROPHETS, daily rising up early and sending them. Yet they hearkened not unto me, nor inclined their ear, but hardened their neck; they did worse than their fathers." Jer. 7:25, 26. See also, 25:4, 2 Chr. 36:15, and parallel passages. God says, Is. 9:15, 16, "The prophet that teacheth lies, he is the tail; for the leaders of this people cause them to err." The distinction between priests and prophets is evident from their being mentioned as two classes. "The prophets prophesy falsely, and the priests bear rule by their means," Jer. 5:31. See also, Ch. 2:8, 8:1–10, and many others.

That women were called to the prophetic office, I believe is universally admitted. Miriam, Deborah, and Huldah were prophetesses.[35] The judgments of the Lord are denounced by Ezekiel on false prophetesses, as well as false prophets [Ezek. 13:17–18]. And if Christian ministers are, as I apprehend, successors of the prophets, and not of the priests, then of course, women are now called to that office as well as men, because God has no where withdrawn from them the privilege of doing what is the great business of preachers, viz. to point the penitent sinner to the Redeemer. "Behold the Lamb of God, which taketh away the sins of the world" [John 1:29].

It is often triumphantly inquired, why, if men and women are on an equality, are not women as conspicuous in the Bible as men? I do not intend to assign a reason, but I think one may readily be found in the fact, that from the days of Eve to the present time, the aim of man has been to crush her. He has accomplished this work in various ways; sometimes by brute force, sometimes by making her subservient to his worst passions, sometimes by treating her as a doll, and while he excluded from her mind the light of

---

35. Miriam (Exod. 2:4–10), sister of Moses, led women in song when they were crossing the Red Sea (Exod. 15:20–21). Deborah, a Hebrew prophetess and judge, was called the "Mother of Israel" (Judges 4:5). Huldah, the Hebrew prophetess to whom King Josiah sent his high priest for counsel, prophesied that Jerusalem would be destroyed, though Josiah would be spared (2 Kings 22:14; 2 Chron. 34:22).

knowledge, decked her person with gewgaws and frippery which he scorned for himself, thus endeavoring to render her like unto a painted sepulchre.

It is truly marvellous that any woman can rise above the pressure of circumstances which combine to crush her. Nothing can strengthen her to do this in the character of a preacher of righteousness, but a call from Jehovah himself. And when the voice of God penetrates the deep recesses of her heart, and commands her to go and cry in the ears of the people, she is ready to exclaim, "Ah, Lord God, behold I cannot speak, for I am a woman." I have known women in different religious societies, who have felt like the prophet. "His word was in my heart as a burning fire shut up in my bones, and I was weary with forbearing." But they have not dared to open their lips, and have endured all the intensity of suffering, produced by disobedience to God, rather than encounter heartless ridicule and injurious suspicions. I rejoice that we have been the oppressed, rather than the oppressors. God thus prepared his people for deliverance from outward bondage; and I hope our sorrows have prepared us to fulfil our high and holy duties, whether public or private, with humility and meekness; and that suffering has imparted fortitude to endure trials, which assuredly await us in the attempt to sunder those chains with which man has bound us, galling to the spirit, though unseen by the eye.

Surely there is nothing either astonishing or novel in the gifts of the Spirit being bestowed on woman: nothing astonishing, because there is no respect of persons with God; the soul of the woman in his sight is as the soul of the man, and both are alike capable of the influence of the Holy Spirit. Nothing novel, because, as has been already shown, in the sacred records there are found examples of women, as well as of men, exercising the gift of prophecy.

We attach to the word prophecy, the exclusive meaning of foretelling future events, but this is certainly a mistake; for the apostle Paul defines it to be "speaking to edification, exhortation and comfort." And there appears no possible reason, why women should not do this as well as men. At the time that the Bible was translated into English, the meaning of the word prophecy, was delivering a message from God, whether it was to predict future events, or to warn the people of the consequences of sin. Governor Winthrop, of Massachusetts, mentions in a letter, that the minister being absent, he went to,——to prophecy to the people.[36]

Before I proceed to prove that women, under the Christian dispensation, were anointed of the Holy Ghost to preach, or prophecy, I will mention Anna, the (last) prophetess under the Jewish dispensation. "She departed not from the temple, but served God with fasting and prayers night and day." And coming into the temple, while Simeon was yet speaking to Mary, with the infant Savior in his arms, "spake of Christ to all them that looked

36. John Winthrop (1638–1707), colonial governor of Connecticut.

for redemption in Jerusalem." Blackwall, a learned English critic, in his work entitled, "Sacred Classics,"[37] says, in reference to this passage, Luke 2:37— "According to the *original* reading, the sense will be, that the devout Anna, who attended in the temple, both night and day, spoke of the Messiah to all the inhabitants of that city, who constantly worshipped there, and who prepared themselves for the worthy reception of that divine person, whom they expected at this time. And 'tis certain, that other devout Jews, not inhabitants of Jerusalem, frequently repaired to the temple-worship, and might, at this remarkable time, and several others, hear this admirable woman discourse upon the blessed advent of the Redeemer. A various reading has Israel instead of Jerusalem, which expresses that religious Jews, from distant places, came thither to divine offices, and would with high pleasure hear the discourses of this great prophetess, so famed for her extraordinary piety and valuable talents, upon the most important and desirable subject."

I shall now examine the testimony of the Bible on this point, after the ascension of our Lord, beginning with the glorious effusion of the Holy Spirit on the day of Pentecost. I presume it will not be denied, that women, as well as men, were at that time filled with the Holy Ghost, because it is expressly stated, that women were among those who continued in prayer and supplication, waiting for the fulfilment of the promise, that they should be enbued with power from on high [All the following passages are from Acts 2]. "When the day of Pentecost was fully come, they were ALL with one accord in one place. And there appeared unto them cloven tongues like as of fire, and it sat upon each of them; and they were all filled with the Holy Ghost, and began to speak with other tongues as the Spirit gave them utterance." Peter says, in reference to this miracle, "this is that which was spoken by the prophet Joel. And it shall come to pass in the last days, said God, I will pour out my Spirit upon all flesh; and your sons and your daughters shall prophesy—and on my servants and on my hand-maidens, I will pour out in those days of my Spirit, and they shall prophesy." There is not the least intimation that this was a spasmodic influence which was soon to cease. The men and women are classed together; and if the power to preach the gospel was a supernatural and short-lived impulse in women, then it was equally so in men. But we are told, those were the days of miracles. I grant it; but the men, equally with the women, were the subjects of this marvellous fulfilment of prophecy, and of course, if women have lost the gift of prophesying, so have men. We are also gravely told, that if a woman pretends to inspiration, and thereupon grounds the right to plead the cause of a crucified Redeemer in public, she will be believed when she shows credentials from heaven, i.e. when she works a miracle. I reply, if this be

37. Anthony Blackwall (1674–1730), English critic and lecturer at Emmanuel College, Cambridge, was the author of *The Sacred Classics Defended and Illustrated; or an Essay humbly offered towards proving the purity, propriety and true eloquence of the Writers of the new Testament* (1725).

necessary to prove her right to preach the gospel, then I demand of my brethren to show me their credentials; else I cannot receive their ministry, by their own showing. John Newton[38] has justly said, that no power but that which created a world, can make a minister of the gospel; and man may task his ingenuity to the utmost, to prove that this power is not exercised on women as well as men. He cannot do it until he has first disclaimed that simple, but all comprehensive truth, "in Christ Jesus there is neither male nor female" [Gal. 3:28].

Women then, according to the Bible, were, under the New Testament dispensation, as well as the Old, the recipients of the gift of prophecy. That this is no sectarian view may be proved by the following extracts. The first I shall offer is from Stratton's "Book of the Priesthood."

> While they were assembled in the upper room to wait for the blessing, in number about one hundred and twenty, they received the miraculous gifts of the Holy Spirit's grace; they became the channels through which its more ordinary, but not less saving streams flowed to three thousand persons in one day. The whole company of the assembled disciples, male and female, young and old, were all filled with the Holy Ghost, and began to speak with other tongues as the Spirit gave them utterance. They all contributed in producing that impression upon the assembled multitude, which Peter was instrumental in advancing to its decisive results.

> Scott, in his commentary on this passage, says—

> At the same time, there appeared the form of tongues divided at the tip and resembling fire; one of which rested on each of the whole company." "They sat on every one present, as the original determines. At the time of these extraordinary appearances, the whole company were abundantly replenished with the gifts and graces of the Holy Spirit, so that they began to speak with other tongues."

> Henry in his notes confirms this:

> It seems evident to me that not the twelve apostles only, but all the one hundred and twenty disciples were filled with the Holy Ghost alike at this time,—all the seventy disciples, who were apostolical men and employed in the same work, and all the rest too that were to preach the gospel, for it is said expressly, Eph. 4:8–12: "When Christ ascended up on high, (which refers to this) he gave gifts unto men." The "all" here must refer to the all that were together.

38. John Newton (1725–1807), author and ordained minister. His collected works were edited by Richard Cecil in 1816.

I need hardly remark that man is a generic term, including both sexes.

Let us now examine whether women actually exercised the office of minister, under the gospel dispensation. Philip[39] had four daughters, who prophesied or preached. Paul calls Priscilla, as well as Aquila, his helpers;[40] or, as in the Greek, his fellow laborers* in Christ Jesus. Divers other passages might be adduced to prove that women continued to be preachers, and that *many* of them filled this dignified station.

We learn also from ecclesiastical history, that female ministers suffered martyrdom in the early ages of the Christian church. In ancient councils, mention is made of deaconesses; and in an edition of the New Testament, printed in 1574, a woman is spoken of as minister of a church. The same word, which, in our common translation, is now rendered a servant of the church, in speaking of Phebe, Rom. 16:1, is rendered minister, Eph. 6:21, when applied to Tychicus. A minister, with whom I had lately the pleasure of conversing, remarked, "My rule is to expound scripture by scripture, and I cannot deny the ministry of women, because the apostle says, 'help those women who labored with me IN THE GOSPEL.' He certainly meant something more than pouring out tea for him."

In the 11th Ch. of 1 Cor., Paul gives directions to women and men how they should appear when they prophesy, or pray in public assemblies. It is evident that the design of the apostle, in this and the three succeeding chapters, is to rectify certain abuses which had crept into the Christian church. He therefore admonishes women to pray with their heads covered, because, according to the fashion of that day, it was considered immodest and immoral to do otherwise. He says, "that were all one as if she were shaven"; and shaving the head was a disgraceful punishment that was inflicted on women of bad character.

> "These things," says Scott, "the apostle stated as decent and proper, but if any of the Corinthian teachers inclined to excite contention about them, he would only add, v. 16, that he and his brethren knew of no such custom as prevailed among them, nor was there any such in the churches of God which had been planted by the other apostles."

John Locke,[41] whilst engaged in writing his notes on the Epistles of St. Paul, was at a meeting where two women preached. After hearing them,

---

*Rom. 16:3, compare Gr. text of v. 21, 2. Cor. 8:23; Phil. 2:25; 1 Thes. 3:2.

39. Saint Philip the Evangelist was one of seven deacons of the early church which tended the Christians of Jerusalem (Acts 8).

40. Priscilla and her husband, Aquila, were early Christians and friends of Paul, risking their lives for him at one point (Romans 16:3).

41. John Locke (1632–1704), philosopher most noted for his *An Essay Concerning Human Understanding* and *Treatise of Civil Government and a Letter Concerning Toleration*.

he became convinced of their commission to publish the gospel, and thereupon altered his notes on the 11th Ch. 1 Cor. in favor of women's preaching. He says,—

> This about women seeming as difficult a passage as most in St. Paul's Epistles, I crave leave to premise some few considerations. It is plain that this covering the head in women is restrained to some peculiar actions which they performed in the assembly, expressed by the words praying, prophesying, which, whatever they signify, must have the same meaning applied to women in the 5th verse, that they have when applied to men in the 4th, &c. The next thing to be considered is, what is here to be understood by praying and prophesying. And that seems to me the performing of some public action in the assembly, by some one person which was for that time peculiar to that person, and whilst it lasted, the rest of the assembly silently assisted. As to prophesying, the apostle in express words tells us, Ch. 14:3, 12, that it was speaking in the assembly. The same is evident as to praying, that the apostle means by it publicly with an audible voice, ch. 14:19.

In a letter to these two women, Rebecca Collier and Rachel Bracken, which accompanied a little testimony of his regard, he says,

> I admire no converse like that of Christian freedom; and I fear no bondage like that of pride and prejudice. I now see that acquaintance by sight cannot reach the height of enjoyment, which acquaintance by knowledge arrives unto. Outward hearing may misguide us, but internal knowledge cannot err. . . . Women, indeed, had the honor of first publishing the resurrection of the God of love—why not again the resurrection of the spirit of love? And let all the disciples of Christ rejoice therein, as doth your partner, John Locke.

See "The Friend," a periodical published in Philadelphia.
Adam Clarke's comment on 1 Cor. 11:5, is similar to Locke's:

> Whatever be the meaning of praying and prophesying in respect to the man, they have precisely the same meaning in respect to the woman. So that some women at least, as well as some men, might speak to others to edification and exhortation and comfort. And this kind of prophesying, or teaching, was predicted by Joel 2:28, and referred to by Peter; and had there not been such gifts bestowed on women, the prophesy could not have had its fulfilment.

In the autobiography of Adam Clarke, there is an interesting account of his hearing Mary Sewall and another female minister preach, and he acknowledges that such was the power accompanying their ministry, that though he had been prejudiced against women's preaching, he could not but confess that these women were anointed for the office.

But there are certain passages in the Epistles of St. Paul, which seem to be of doubtful interpretation; at which we cannot much marvel, seeing that his brother Peter says, there are some things in them hard to be understood. Most commentators, having their minds preoccupied with the prejudices of education, afford little aid; they rather tend to darken the text by the multitude of words. One of these passages occurs in 1 Cor. 14. I have already remarked, that this chapter, with several of the preceding, was evidently designed to correct abuses which had crept into the assemblies of Christians in Corinth. Hence we find that the men were commanded to be silent, as well as the women, when they were guilty of any thing which deserved reprehension. The apostle says, "If there be no interpreter, let him keep silence in the church" [1 Cor. 14:28]. The men were doubtless in the practice of speaking in unknown tongues, when there was no interpreter present; and Paul reproves them, because this kind of preaching conveyed no instruction to the people. Again he says, "If any thing be revealed to another that sitteth by, let the first hold his peace" [1 Cor. 14:30]. We may infer from this, that two men sometimes attempted to speak at the same time, and the apostle rebukes them, and adds, "Ye may ALL prophesy one by one, for God is not the author of confusion, but of peace" [1 Cor. 14:31–33]. He then proceeds to notice the disorderly conduct of the women, who were guilty of other improprieties. They were probably in the habit of asking questions, on any points of doctrine which they wished more thoroughly explained. This custom was common among the men in the Jewish synagogues, after the pattern of which, the meetings of the early Christians were in all probability conducted. And the Christian women, presuming on the liberty which they enjoyed under the new religion, interrupted the assembly, by asking questions. The apostle disapproved of this, because it disturbed the solemnity of the meeting: he therefore admonishes the women to keep silence in the churches. That the apostle did not allude to preaching is manifest, because he tells them, "If they will *learn* any thing, let them ask their husbands at home" [1 Cor. 14:34]. Now a person endowed with a gift in the ministry, does not ask questions in the public exercise of that gift, for the purpose of gaining information: she is instructing others. Moreover, the apostle, in closing his remarks on this subject, says, "Wherefore, brethren (a generic term, applying equally to men and women), covet to prophesy, and forbid not to speak with tongues. Let all things be done decently and in order" [1 Cor. 14:39].

Clarke, on the passage, "Let women keep silence in the churches" [1 Cor. 14:34] says:

> This was a Jewish ordinance. Women were not permitted to teach in the assemblies, or even to ask questions. The rabbins taught that a woman should know nothing but the use of her distaff; and

the saying of Rabbi Eliezer is worthy of remark and execration: "Let the words of the law be burned, rather than that they should be delivered by women."

Are there not many of our Christian brethren, whose hostility to the ministry of women is as bitter as was that of Rabbi Eliezer, and who would rather let souls perish, than that the truths of the gospel should be delivered by women?

> "This," says Clarke, "was their condition till the time of the gospel, when, according to the prediction of Joel, the Spirit of God was to be poured out on the women as well as the men, that they might prophesy, that is, teach. And that they did prophesy, or teach, is evident from what the apostle says, ch. 11:5, where he lays down rules to regulate this part of their conduct while ministering in the church. But does not what the apostle says here, let your women keep silence in the churches, contradict that statement, and show that the words in ch. 11, should be understood in another sense? for here it is expressly said, that they should keep silence in the churches, for it was not permitted to a woman to speak. Both places seem perfectly consistent. It is evident from the context, that the apostle refers here to asking questions, and what we call dictating in the assemblies."

The other passage on which the opinion, that women are not called to the ministry, is founded, is 1 Tim. 2d ch. The apostle speaks of the duty of prayer and supplication, mentions his own ordination as a preacher, and then adds, "I will, therefore, that men pray everywhere, lifting up holy hands, without wrath and doubting. In like manner also, that women adorn themselves in modest apparel" [1 Tim. 2:8–9], &c. I shall here premise, that as the punctuation and division into chapters and verses is no part of the original arrangement, they cannot determine the sense of a passage. Indeed, every attentive reader of the Bible must observe, that the injudicious separation of sentences often destroys their meaning and their beauty. Joseph John Gurney,[42] whose skill as a biblical critic is well known in England, commenting on this passage, says,

> It is worded in a manner somewhat obscure; but appears to be best construed according to the opinion of various commentators (See Pool's Synopsis) as conveying an injunction, that women as well as men should pray everywhere, lifting up holy hands without wrath and doubting. 1 Tim. 2:8, 9. "I will therefore that men

---

42. Joseph John Gurney (1788–1847), a biblical critic and English Quaker philanthropist and reformer. He assisted his sister, Elizabeth Gurney Fry, in prison reform and was a critic of slavery in the United States.

pray everywhere, &c.; likewise also the women in a modest dress." (Compare 1 Cor. 11:5.) "I would have them adorn themselves with shamefacedness and sobriety."

I have no doubt this is the true meaning of the text, and that the translators would never have thought of altering it had they not been under the influence of educational prejudice. The apostle proceeds to exhort the women, who thus publicly made intercession to God, not to adorn themselves with braided hair, or gold, or pearls, or costly array, but (which becometh women professing godliness) with good works. The word in this verse translated "professing," would be more properly rendered preaching godliness, or enjoining piety to the gods, or conducting public worship. After describing the duty of female ministers about their apparel, the apostle proceeds to correct some improprieties which probably prevailed in the Ephesian church, similar to those which he had reproved among the Corinthian converts. He says, "Let the women LEARN in silence with all subjection; but I suffer not a woman to teach, nor to usurp authority over the man, but to be in silence" [1 Tim. 2:11], or quietness. Here again it is evident that the women, of whom he was speaking, were admonished to learn in silence, which could not refer to their public ministrations to others. The verb "to teach," verse 12 ["I permit no woman to teach or to have authority over men: she is to keep silent."] is one of very general import, and may in this place more properly be rendered dictate. It is highly probable that women who had long been in bondage, when set free by Christianity from the restraints imposed upon them by Jewish traditions and heathen customs, run into an extreme in their public assemblies, and interrupted the religious services by frequent interrogations, which they could have had answered as satisfactorily at home.

On a candid examination and comparison of the passages which I have endeavored to explain, viz., 1 Cor. chaps. 11 and 14, and 1 Tim. 2:8–12, I think we must be compelled to adopt one of two conclusions; either that the apostle grossly contradicts himself on a subject of great practical importance, and that the fulfilment of the prophecy of Joel was a shameful infringement of decency and order; or that the directions given to women, not to speak, or to teach in the congregations, had reference to some local and peculiar customs, which were then common in religious assemblies, and which the apostle thought inconsistent with the purpose for which they were met together. No one, I suppose, will hesitate which of these two conclusions to adopt. The subject is one of vital importance. That it may claim the calm and prayerful attention of Christians, is the desire of

Thine in the bonds of womanhood,

Sarah M. Grimké

LETTER XV

Man Equally Guilty with Woman in the Fall

Uxbridge, 10th Mo. 20th, 1837

My Dear Sister,

It is said that "modern Jewish women light a lamp every Friday evening, half an hour before sunset, which is the beginning of their Sabbath, in remembrance of their original mother, who first extinguished the lamp of righteousness,—to remind them of their obligation to rekindle it." I am one of those who always admit, to its fullest extent, the popular charge, that woman brought sin into the world. I accept it as a powerful reason, why woman is bound to labor with double diligence, for the regeneration of that world she has been intrumental in ruining.

But, although I do not repel the imputation, I shall notice some passages in the sacred Scriptures, where this transaction is mentioned, which prove, I think, the identity and equality of man and woman, and that there is no difference in their guilt in the view of that God who searcheth the heart and trieth the reins of the children of men. In Is. 43:27, we find the following passage—"Thy first father hath sinned, and thy teachers have transgressed against me"—which is synonymous with Rom. 5:12. "Wherefore, as by ONE MAN sin entered into the world, and death by sin, &c." Here man and woman are included under one term, and no distinction is made in their criminality. The circumstances of the fall are again referred to in 2 Cor. 11:3—"But I fear lest, by any means, as the serpent *beguiled* Eve through his subtility, so your mind should be beguiled from the simplicity that is in Christ." Again, 1st Tim. 2:14—"Adam *was not deceived*; but the woman being *deceived,* was in the transgression." Now, whether the fact, that Eve was beguiled and deceived, is a proof that her crime was of deeper dye than Adam's, who was not deceived, but was fully aware of the consequences of sharing in her transgression, I shall leave the candid reader to determine.

My present object is to show, that, as woman is charged with all the sin that exists in the world, it is her solemn duty to labor for its extinction; and that this she can never do effectually and extensively, until her mind is disenthralled of those shackles which have been riveted upon her by a "*corrupt public opinion, and a perverted interpretation of the holy Scriptures.*" Woman must feel that she is the equal, and is designed to be the fellow laborer of her brother, or she will be studying to find out the *imaginary* line which separates the sexes, and divides the duties of men and women into two distinct classes, a separation not even hinted at in the Bible, where we are expressly told, "there is neither male nor female, for ye are all one in Christ Jesus" [Gal. 3:28].

My views on this subject are so much better embodied in the language of a living author than I can express them, that I quote the passage entire: "Woman's rights and man's rights are *both* contained in the *same* charter, and held by the *same* tenure. *All rights* spring out of the *moral* nature: they are both the root and the offspring of *responsibilities*. The physical constitution is the mere *instrument* of the *moral* nature; sex is a mere *incident* of this constitution, a provision necessary to this *form* of existence; its *only* design, not to give, nor to take away, nor in any respect to modify or even *touch* rights or responsibilities in any sense, except so far as the peculiar offices of each sex may afford less or more *opportunity* and ability for the exercise of rights, and the discharge of responsibilities; but merely to continue and enlarge the human department of God's government. Consequently, I know nothing of *man's* rights, or *woman's* rights; *human* rights are all that I recognise. The doctrine, that the *sex of the body* presides over and administers upon the rights and responsibilities of the moral, immortal nature, is to my mind a doctrine kindred to blasphemy, *when seen in its intrinsic nature*. It breaks up utterly the *relations* of the two natures, and reverses their functions; exalting the animal nature into a monarch, and humbling the moral into a slave; making the former a proprietor, and the latter its property."

To perform our duties, we must comprehend our rights and responsibilities; and it is because we do not understand, that we now fall so far short in the discharge of our obligations. Unaccustomed to think for ourselves, and to search the sacred volume, to see how far we are living up to the design of Jehovah in our creation, we have rested satisfied with the sphere marked out for us by man, never detecting the fallacy of that reasoning which forbids woman to exercise some of her noblest faculties, and stamps with the reproach of indelicacy those actions by which women were formerly dignified and exalted in the church.

I should not mention this subject again, if it were not to point out to my sisters what seems to me an irresistible conclusion from the literal interpretation of St. Paul, without reference to the context, and the peculiar circumstances and abuses which drew forth the expressions, "I suffer not a woman to teach"—"Let your women keep silence in the church," [1 Cor. 14:34], i.e. congregation. It is manifest, that if the apostle meant what his words imply, when taken in the strictest sense, then women have no right to *teach* Sabbath or day schools, or to open their lips to sing in the assemblies of the people; yet young and delicate women are engaged in all these offices; they are expressly trained to exhibit themselves, and raise their voices to a high pitch in the choirs of our places of worship. I do not intend to sit in judgment on my sisters for doing these things; I only want them to see, that they are as really infringing a *supposed* divine command, by instructing their pupils in the Sabbath or day schools, and by singing in the congregation, as if they were engaged in preaching the unsearchable riches of Christ to a lost and perishing world. Why, then, are we permitted to break this injunction in some points, and so sedulously warned not to overstep the bounds set for us by our *brethren* in another? Simply, as I believe, because in the one case we subserve *their* views and *their* interests, and act *in subordination to them;* whilst in the other, we come in contact with their interests, and claim to be on an equality with them in the highest and most important trust ever committed to man, namely, the ministry of the world. It is manifest, that if women were permitted to be ministers of the gospel, as they unquestionably were in the primitive ages of the Christian church, it would interfere materially with the present organized system of spiritual power and ecclesiastical authority, which is now vested solely in the hands of men. It would either show that all the paraphernalia of theological seminaries, &c. &c. to prepare men to become evangelists, is wholly unnecessary, or it would create a necessity for similar institutions in order to prepare women for the same office; and this would be an encroachment on that learning, which our kind brethren have so ungenerously monopolized. I do not ask any one to believe my statements, or adopt my conclusions, because they are mine; but I do earnestly entreat my sisters to lay aside their prejudices, and examine these subjects *for themselves,* regardless of the "traditions of men," because they are intimately connected with their duty and their usefulness in the present important crisis.

All who know any thing of the present system of benevolent and religious operations, know that women are performing an important part in them, in *subserviency to men,* who guide our labors, and are often the recipients of those benefits of education we toil to confer, and which we rejoice they can enjoy, although it is their mandate which deprives us of the same advantages. Now, whether our brethren have defrauded us intentionally, or unintentionally, the wrong we suffer is equally the same. For years, they have been spurring us up to the performance of our duties. The immense usefulness and the vast influence of woman have been eulogized and called into exercise, and many a blessing has been lavished upon us, and many a prayer put up for us, because we have labored by day and by night to clothe and feed and educate young men, whilst our own bodies sometimes suffer for want of comfortable garments, and our minds are left in almost utter destitution of that improvement which we are toiling to bestow upon the brethren.

> Full many a gem of purest ray serene,
>   The dark unfathomed caves of ocean bear;
> Full many a flower is born to blush unseen
>   And waste its sweetness on the desert air.

If the sewing societies, the avails of whose industry are now expended in supporting and educating young men for the ministry, were to withdraw their contributions to these objects, and give them where they are *more needed,* to the advancement of their *own sex* in useful learning, the next generation might furnish sufficient proof, that in intelligence and ability to master the whole circle of sciences, woman is not inferior to man; and instead of a sensible woman being regarded as she now is, as a useless nature, they would be quite as common as sensible men. I confess, considering the high claim men in this country make to great politeness and deference to women, it does seem a little extraordinary that we should be urged to work for the brethren. I should suppose it would be more in character with "the generous promptings of chivalry, and the poetry of romantic gallantry," for which Catharine E. Beecher[43] gives them credit, for them to form societies to educate their sisters, seeing our inferior capacities require more cultivation to bring them into use, and qualify us to be helps meet for them. However, though I think this would be but a just return for all our past kindnesses in this way, I should be willing to balance our accounts, and begin a new course. Henceforth, let the benefit be reciprocated, or else let each sex provide for the education of their own poor, whose talents ought to be rescued from the oblivion of ignorance. Sure I am, the young men who are now benefitted by the handy work of their sisters, will not be less honorable if they occupy half their time in earning enough to pay for their own education, instead of depending on the industry of women, who not unfrequently deprive themselves of the means of purchasing valuable books which might enlarge their stock of useful knowledge, and perhaps prove a blessing to the family by furnishing them with instructive reading. If the minds of women were enlightened and improved, the domestic circle would be more frequently refreshed by intelligent conversation, a means of edification now deplorably neglected, for want of that cultivation which these intellectual advantages would confer.

DUTIES OF WOMEN.

One of the duties which devolve upon women in the present interesting crisis, is to prepare themselves for more extensive usefulness, by making use of those religious and literary privileges and advantages that are within their reach, if they will only stretch out their hands and possess them. By doing this, they will become better acquainted with their rights as moral beings, and with their responsibilities growing out of those rights; they will regard themselves, as they really are, FREE AGENTS, immortal beings, amenable to no tribunal but that of Jehovah, and bound not to submit to any restriction imposed for selfish purposes, or to gratify that love of power which has reigned in the heart of man from Adam down to the present time. In contemplating the great moral reformations of the day, and the part which they are bound to take in them, instead of puzzling themselves with the harassing, because unnecessary inquiry, how far they may go without overstepping the bounds of propriety, which separate male and female duties, they will only inquire, "Lord, what wilt thou have us to do?" They will be

43. Catharine E. Beecher (1800–78), American educator, was best known for her role in shaping the education of women. She emphasized women's domestic roles, especially in her book, *Domestic Economy for the Use of Young Ladies at Home and at School* (1841).

enabled to see the simple truth, that God has made no distinction between men and women as moral beings; that the distinction now so much insisted upon between male and female virtues is as absurd as it is unscriptural, and has been the fruitful source of much mischief—granting to man a license for the exhibition of brute force and conflict on the battle field; for sternness, selfishness, and the exercise of irresponsible power in the circle of home— and to woman a permit to rest on an arm of flesh, and to regard modesty and delicacy, and all the kindred virtues, as peculiarly appropriate to her. Now to me it is perfectly clear, that WHATSOEVER IT IS MORALLY RIGHT FOR A MAN TO DO, IT IS MORALLY RIGHT FOR A WOMAN TO DO; and that confusion must exist in the moral world, until woman takes her stand on the same plaform with man, and feels that she is clothed by her Maker with the *same rights,* and, of course, that upon her devolve the *same duties.*

It is not my intention, nor indeed do I think it is in my power, to point out the precise duties of women. To him who still teacheth by his Holy Spirit as never man taught, I refer my beloved sisters. There is a vast field of usefulness before them. The signs of the times give portentous evidence, that a day of deep trial is approaching; and I urge them, by every consideration of a Savior's dying love, by the millions of heathen in our midst, by the sufferings of woman in almost every portion of the world, by the fearful ravages which slavery, intemperance, licentiousness and other iniquities are making of the happiness of our fellow creatures, to come to the rescue of a ruined world, and to be found co-workers with Jesus Christ.

> Ho! to the rescue, ho!
>   Up every one that feels—
> 'Tis a sad and fearful cry of woe
>   From a guilty world that steals.
> Hark! hark! how the horror rolls,
>   Whence can this anguish be?
> 'Tis the groan of a trammel'd people's souls,
>   *Now bursting* to be free.

And here, with all due deference for the office of the ministry, which I believe was established by Jehovah himself, and designed by Him to be the means of spreading light and salvation through a crucified Savior to the ends of the earth, I would entreat my sisters not to *compel* the ministers of the present day to give their names to great moral reformations. The practice of making ministers life members, or officers of societies, when their hearts have not been touched with a live coal from the altar, and animated with love for the work we are engaged in, is highly injurious to them, as well as to the cause. They often satisfy their consciences in this way, without doing anything to promote the anti-slavery, or temperance, or other reformations; and we please ourselves with the idea, that we have done something to forward the cause of Christ, when, in effect, we have been sewing pillows like the false prophetesses of old under the arm-holes of our clerical brethren. Let us treat the ministers with all tenderness and respect, but let us be careful how we cherish in their hearts the idea that they are of more importance to a cause than other men. I rejoice when they take hold heartily. I love and honor some ministers with whom I have been associated in the anti-slavery ranks, but I do deeply deplore, for the sake of the cause, the prevalent notion, that the clergy must be had, either by persuasion or by bribery. They will not need persuasion or bribery, if their hearts are with us; if they are not, we are better without them. It is idle to suppose that the kingdom of heaven cannot come on earth, without their co-operation. It is the Lord's work, and it must go forward with or without their aid. As well might the converted Jews have despaired of the spread of Christianity, without the co-operation of Scribes and Pharisees.

Let us keep in mind, that no abolitionism is of any value, which is not accompanied with deep, heartfelt repentance; and that, whenever a minister sincerely repents of having, either by his apathy or his efforts, countenanced the fearful sin of slavery, he will need no inducement to come into our ranks; so far from it, he will abhor himself in dust and ashes, for his past blindness and indifference to the cause of God's poor and oppressed: and he will regard it as a privilege to be enabled to do something in the cause of human rights. I know the ministry exercise vast power; but I rejoice in the belief, that the spell is broken which encircled them, and rendered it all but blasphemy to expose their errors and their sins. We are beginning to understand that they are but men, and that their station should not shield them from merited reproof.

I have blushed for my sex when I have heard of their entreating ministers to attend their associations, and open them with prayer. The idea is inconceivable to me, that Christian women can be engaged in doing God's work, and yet cannot ask his blessing on their efforts, except through the lips of a man. I have known a whole town scoured to obtain a minister to open a female meeting, and their refusal to do so spoken of as quite a misfortune. Now, I am not glad that the ministers do wrong; but I am glad that my sisters have been sometimes compelled to act for themselves: it is exactly what they need to strengthen them, and prepare them to act independently. And to say the truth, there is something really ludicrous in seeing a minister enter the meeting, open it with prayer, and then take his departure. However, I only throw out these hints for the consideration of women. I believe there are solemn responsibilities resting upon us, and that in this day of light and knowledge, we cannot plead ignorance of duty. The great moral reformations now on the wheel are only practical Christianity; and if the ministry is not prepared to labor with us in these righteous causes, let us press forward, and they will follow on to know the Lord.

CONCLUSION.

I have now, my dear sister, completed my series of letters. I am aware, they contain some new views; but I believe they are based on the immutable truths of the Bible. All I ask for them is, the candid and prayerful consideration of Christians. If they strike at some of our bosom sins, our deep-rooted prejudices, our long cherished opinions, let us not condemn them on that account, but investigate them fearlessly and prayerfully, and not shrink from the examination; because, if they are true, they place heavy responsibilities upon women. In throwing them before the public, I have been actuated solely by the belief, that if they are acted upon, they will exalt the character and enlarge the usefulness of my own sex, and contribute greatly to the happiness and virtue of the other. That there is a root of bitterness continually springing up in families and troubling the repose of both men and women, must be manifest to even a superficial observer; and I believe it is the mistaken notion of the inequality of the sexes. As there is an assumption of superiority on the one part, which is not sanctioned by Jehovah, there is an incessant struggle on the other to rise to that degree of dignity, which God designed women to possess in common with men, and to maintain those rights and exercise those privileges which every woman's common sense, apart from the prejudices of education, tells her are inalienable; they are a part of her moral nature, and can only cease when her immortal mind is extinguished.

One word more. I feel that I am calling upon my sex to sacrifice what has been, what is still dear to their hearts, the adulation, the flattery, the attentions of trifling men. I am asking them to repel these insidious enemies whenever they approach them; to manifest by their conduct, that, although they value highly the society of pious and intelligent men, they have no taste for idle conversation, and for that silly preference which is manifested for their personal accommodation, often at the expense of great inconvenience to their male companions. As an illustration of what I mean, I will state a fact.

I was traveling lately in a stage coach. A gentleman, who was also a passenger, was made sick by riding with his back to the horses. I offered to exchange seats, assuring him it did not affect me at all unpleasantly; but he was too polite to permit a lady to run the risk of being discommoded. I am sure he meant to be very civil, but I really thought it was a foolish piece of civility. This kind of attention encourages selfishness in woman, and is only accorded as a sort of quietus, in exchange for those *rights* of which we are deprived. Men and women are equally bound to cultivate a spirit of accommodation; but I exceedingly deprecate her being treated like a spoiled child, and sacrifices made to her selfishness and vanity. In lieu of these flattering but injurious attentions, yielded to her as an inferior, as a mark of benevolence and courtesy, I want my sex to claim nothing from their brethren but what their brethren may justly claim from them, in their intercourse as

Christians. I am persuaded woman can do much in this way to elevate her own character. And that we may become duly sensible of the dignity of our nature, only a little lower than the angels, and bring forth fruit to the glory and honor of Emanuel's name, is the fervent prayer of
Thine in the bonds of womanhood,

Sarah M. Grimké

3.

The Education of Women

Sarah Grimké wrote "The Education of Women" at a time when education for women was not widely available, and when it was, was largely for the purpose of better preparing them for their domestic and maternal duties.

In colonial times, boys and girls received similar educations in basic skills and moral training. However, one of the effects of industrialization and urbanization was to split the economic and social worlds of women and men—women's sphere being the home and men's the competitive marketplace—and the education of females and males reflected these socioeconomic changes. Men's training in the classics, the sciences, mathematics, and history was to prepare them for leadership in business, the professions, and government; women's education in cooking, sewing, French, and embroidery prepared them for domesticity.

The views of prominent educators such as Jean-Jacques Rousseau and Benjamin Rush helped to reinforce the prevailing attitude that the purpose of educating women was to shape their characters to be better suited for their roles and their relationships with men. In 1787, Rush suggested three goals for women's education: to teach women (1) to exercise proper stewardship over their husband's property, (2) to raise their male children to be better citizens, and (3) to manage servants (Gordon and Buhle, 1976:282). Similarly, Rousseau's infamous plans for "Sophie's" education were to shape her nature vis à vis man's. He wrote in part: "The whole education of women ought to be relative to men. To please them, to be useful to them, to make themselves loved and honored by them, to educate them when young, to care for them when grown, to counsel them, to console them, and to make life sweet and agreeable to them—these are the duties of women at all times, and what should be taught them from infancy" (Rousseau, 1906:263). Thus it is not surprising, that in Grimké's day the few educational institutions for women that did exist were "ladies' seminaries" where young women were trained to be "good wives"—refined, submissive, domestic, genteel.

A few exceptions to this rule did exist. At Emma Willard's seminary in Troy, New York (1818), women received some training in the classics. Oberlin College in Ohio opened its doors to men and women in 1833, though women were taught separately from men and were given a shorter course. (It was believed that using the brain required a greater blood flow, which in women would come from their nervous system and reproductive organs. Thus, to require a full study load of women might result in their nervous collapse and possible sterility; Simmons, 1976:118). Established in 1837, Mount Holyoke, the oldest women's school in the country, provided young women with their first real opportunity to study the classics, history, geography, chemistry, philosophy, and other subjects of a standard liberal arts education.

Still, even these schools reflected the prevailing ambivalence toward educated women, and the curriculum shifted back and forth between training for women's special role and providing an education identical with men's (Simmons, 1976:124). It was not until the 1860s and 1870s that women could receive an education at a fully accredited university (Iowa, 1858; Wisconsin, 1863; Vassar, 1865; Smith, 1865; Wellesley, 1875; Michigan, 1875).

One reason for this ambivalence was the fact that there were few "acceptable" vocations for educated women. This is not to say that women did not work. By the 1850s, they comprised a quarter of the labor force, largely in textiles, clothing, and shoe manufacture. Women had also joined the professional ranks of ministers and doctors. However, at the time, a college education was not required for these professions. The only socially acceptable vocational outlets for an educated woman were to become either a teacher or a writer. Even into the twentieth century, the primary purpose of educating women was to enable them to be better wives and mothers.

In her essay, Grimké exhibits some of the prevailing ambivalent attitudes toward educating women. That women should be educated, and educated as rigorously as men, she has no doubt.

Nevertheless, she argues simultaneously that education would relieve women both from the vanities acquired in the pursuit of a husband and from the drudgeries of domesticity once the husband has been won, and that education would enable women to become better wives and mothers and fulfill their duties within "the sacred circle of Home." Yet, taken together, these two opposing views form a surprisingly consistent argument. The essay is as much about marriage reform as it is about educational reform.

Grimké writes that an education would allow women to develop their whole beings "symmetrically," at a time when "symmetry" was held up as an ideal by health reformers, moral reformers, and feminists.* It was widely believed and advocated that the emotional, intellectual, and physical harmony of each individual was the key to marital success and social order. In fact, reformers went so far as to suggest that only symmetrically developed men and women should be allowed to marry. Lack of symmetry, they argued, was the main cause of men's sexual excesses and the resultant sexual tyranny that women suffered in marriage. It was also the cause of social disorder. Sexual excess, they believed, had deep and lasting effects on the physical and mental organism, which could be transmitted to children. Not only did such excess result in diseased progeny, but it so shattered women's physical and emotional constitutions that they were incapable of being fit mothers. One of the main arguments for "voluntary motherhood" was simply that women should have fewer children so that they could be better mothers to the ones they did have (Gordon, 1973). At one time or another, Grimké raises all of these points in her essay.

Grimké does give many other reasons for women's education, among them that it would strengthen free institutions; enable women to develop their true natures and follow their moral and vocational callings; and, predating John Stuart Mill's argument in *The Subjection of Women* by several years, allow us to discover once and for all whether or not women are indeed intellectually inferior to men. Until it had been tried, no one could really say for certain. Grimké reveals a sophisticated view of Christianity when she argues that an education might have saved her and hopefully would spare other women from the perils and sufferings of evangelical religion. At the time she was writing, women were being drawn into evangelism, and Grimké hoped that education would enable them to experience a more rational Christianity. However, the bulk of her

---

*For an excellent discussion of the health reform movement, see William Leach, *Free Love and Perfect Union: The Feminist Reform of Sex and Society* (New York: Basic Books, 1980).

arguments center on the significance of women's symmetrical development and its resulting benefits for the home and for society at large. To educate women was to transform the nature of male-female relations; to allow for their physical, emotional, spiritual, and social health; to enable civilization to rise to its full height and power.

It is interesting to note that in Grimké's brief foray into education—her few years of running the Eagleswood School at Raritan Bay, New Jersey, with the Welds—she practiced what she preached. The school was coeducational and interracial. It strove for a balance between physical and intellectual labor, between school and life. Subjects included the standard history, English, French, chemistry, Greek, Latin, and mathematics, but included woodworking, agriculture, household skills, bookkeeping, art, music, and physical education as well. An observer noted that "young women were found educating their limbs in the gymnasium, rowing in boats, and making 'records' in swimming and high diving" (Quoted in Lerner, 1971:329). Students went on excursions into neighboring towns and the countryside, and were visited by some of the best and brightest minds of the day—Horace Greeley, Gerritt Smith, Henry David Thoreau. In general, students were taught with much affection and urged on to "noble" purposes in life (Birney, 1885).

One final note on the essay—in it Grimké reveals some of her characteristic ambivalence toward men. Like her contemporaries, Mary Wollstonecraft and Frances Wright, she largely addresses her arguments to men, urging them to "allow" women's education. In doing so, she is deferent, "gratefully accept[ing] [men's] sympathy and cooperation" and commending them for protecting women from the ravages of war. Yet she also unlooses her fury, accusing man of making woman "your slave, your bauble, the victim of your passions." In the grips of that fury, she calls, not on men to save women, but rather on women to "redeem ourselves." Her attitude fluctuates between that of a passive yet resentful supplicant to that of an angry yet affirmative rebel. However, that Grimké is moving from resentment to rebellion becomes apparent toward the end of the essay. She concludes that women who crave an education "are not stirred by envy, or jealousy, but are stimulated by an unsatiable desire for progress, by a deathless hope of usefulness." In seeking an education, women are seeking the affirmation of their beings.

The Education of Women

"Most of us come into the world and find the circuit of our thoughts traced out for us by routine and authority."

"The past and present meet and struggle with each other and slowly strive to attain an equilibrium and thereby to secure the peaceful extinction of the elder time."[1]

The approval of anything beyond ourselves "inspires a secret longing to assimilate our loves to the object of the love. Out of this longing the higher life gradually unfolds itself."

"Oh but could I unloose my soul. We are sepulchred alive and want more room."[2]

Ought women to enjoy equal advantages of education with Men?

"The one idea which history exhibits, as evermore developing itself into greater distinctions is the idea of *Humanity*—the noble endeavor to throw down the barriers erected by prejudice and one sided views, to regard the whole human race as one brotherhood, having one great object the free development of our spiritual nature."

"To regard any state of society as fixed is to regard it as the final good, the only healthy state. But there is nothing so revolutionary, because there is nothing so unnatural and convulsive as the strain to keep things stationary, when all the world is by the very law of its creation in external progress."[3]

There is rich instruction to be gained by "unrolling the scroll of history," by reviewing the past patiently, calmly, philosophically. It comes down to us to be catechized, and it is impossible to do honor to the present, to make the best use of all the advantages it offers, to appreciate all the facilities for improvement which cluster round us unless we are acquainted with the history of the Past. Nor can we otherwise know how large a debt of gratitude we owe to those who have preceded us in the conflict of ages,

1. Fichte [Grimké's note]. Johann Gottlieb Fichte (1762–1814), professor of philosophy at Jena, was a metaphysician and ethicist, a contemporary and colleague of Kant and Goethe. According to his philosophy of subjective idealism, the split between subject and object cannot be overcome through knowledge, but only through moral striving, expressed in his formula, "If I ought I can." He is the author of *The Science of Ethics as Based on the Science of Knowledge* (1789), *The Vocation of Man* (1800), *The Way Towards the Blessed Life* (1806), and other works.

2. Aurora Leigh [Grimké's note]. This is a reference to the narrative poem written by Elizabeth Barrett Browning entitled "Aurora Leigh."

3. Dr. Arnold [Grimké's note]. Doctor Thomas Arnold (1795–1842) was an educator in England well known for his educational reforms. He is said to have provided the model for English public schools and for boarding schools throughout the Western world. He was also interested in church and social reform.

who have made crooked paths straight, rough places smooth and prepared for us an easier ascent to that higher stage of development which we now occupy. To censure, or think lightly of the past were both insane and ungrateful. Let us rather study it reverently, lay it gently to rest, and profit by all its sufferings, its mistakes, and its experiences. Despise the past! as well might the gay and many tinted blossoms despise the sap from which they drew their nourishment, the gold and crimson fruits condemn the ephemeral flowers which preceded and without which they never could have been. Each generation is perfect in its day, fills up its measure of usefulness and then quietly yields its sceptre to the next. . . .

I have neither lamentation for the *Then* nor denunciation for the *Now*. All I feel is gratitude for the past, cheerful acquiescence in the present, bright hope for the future. In this spirit I come to the contemplation of a subject, so vast, that it baffles my powers of comprehension, yet so exacting and imperative that I dare not shrink from it. . . .

Knowledge has ever been the lever which has raised man to a higher state, from the moment when Jehovah proclaimed that man, by increasing his knowledge, has become more assimilated to the Divine. In all ages, through all the varied experience of individuals and nations, knowledge has been the power which has civilized, elevated and dignified humanity. In those countries where progress has been most rapid, the thirst for knowledge has been most intense. In his childhood man knew no better way to satisfy this thirst than by subduing his fellow man. He taxed his ingenuity to invent engines of destruction and thus strengthened his intellect and enlarged his capacity, not only to work evil, but to work good. The knowledge of evil is absolutely necessary to a growth in goodness; a state of innocence is not the highest state; man must pass through the varied experiences of temptation, sin, repentance and amendment, that he may gain strength by overcoming; learn thereby the blessedness of virtue, and enjoy the hallowed peace which is found in its possession. Good and evil, as we term them, are not antagonistic; they are ever found hand in hand. Humanity has never achieved a single conquest without the aid of both. Indeed how can she? What adds to moral strength, but a grappling with temptation? What gives intellect power, but a resolute will to overcome the obstacles interposed by ignorance, and by the difficulties, which in some way or other start up to impede our progress in knowledge? Difficulties [are] strewn much more thickly in the path of woman, than in that of man. If woman is ready to encounter these trials, to test her strength by conflict, shall she plead in vain for higher educational and industrial advantages? Give her the first, she will open for herself access to the second. Already there are thousands who are regarding the subject of Woman's Rights with earnest interest—thousands of generous hearts and liberal minds, whose sympathy strengthens her to press onward in the glorious work of Reformation. And she gratefully accepts the sympathy and cooperation of man, in this, her novel experience of individual yet conjoint existence and personal responsibility.[4] . . . We should neither be surprised nor daunted at the opposition made to giving woman the same educational advantages as men; it is but a few years since the same spirit rose in sterner rebellion against the laws providing for the education of the masses in some places. The ignorant were as well satisfied with their ignorance, as averse to be roused from their mental atrophy, or paralysis, as the women are to be roused from their present dependent state.

Nor is it the illiterate alone who so strenuously opposed the education of the poor. Hannah More's attempts to establish Sunday schools met with the most bitter hostility from both laity and clergy.[5] The persecution she met with is chronicled on the tablet of history. . . . "The brutal ignorance and degradation which at this period [a century ago] characterized the peasantry of England was shocking, but even these do not appear so utterly inhuman as the conduct of the rich farmer and particularly that of the clergy in opposing all reforms," Miss More says. "The opposition I have met with in endeavoring to establish schools would excite your astonishment, although I do not allow the poor to be taught to write as my object was not to make fanatics." Her principal adversary, a rich farmer, says, "The lower classes are fated to be wicked and ignorant and I cannot alter the decree." The success of her school was . . . great. . . . [Yet] so virulent was the feeling excited by these noble attempts to elevate and educate the poor that in one of the pamphlets issued respecting her it is asserted that her writings ought to be burnt by the hangmen. The grossest crimes were alleged against her and [to] her plan for their improvement were ascribed the most pernicious motives and the deepest hypocrisy. . . .

Nonetheless the law which furnished the means of improvement to the untaught,[6] has proved an incalculable blessing, has unfolded powers which would otherwise have lain dormant, and brought into activity a wealth of intelligence and virtue of more value than the mines of California. Indeed the loftiest flight of imagination must fail to picture the benefits that have accrued from the passage of that single law, or to portray the countless channels thereby opened, through which righteousness, prosperity, and happiness have flowed to the nation. "The most effectual way of raising the

4. The following has been moved from a later part of the manuscript.

5. Book of Araton Marshall P. 434 Sufferings of Woman [Grimké's note]. Hannah More (1745–1833) was a poet, playwright, and religious writer. She established a school with her sisters in the Mendip Hills, an ignorant and deprived mining region in England. The school met with opposition from both the landed class and the clergy.

6. Namely, the Massachusetts education laws. In 1642 the first general education law in America was passed in Massachusetts to remedy the intellectual deficiencies of children, requiring that they gain enough knowledge to read the Bible. Five years later, the Massachusetts Law of 1647 was passed by the General Court (legislature) and required every town of a hundred or more families to maintain a grammar school. This law is also known as the Old Deluder Satan Act.

intellectual condition of any class is to connect their interests closely with their improvement; that they may be eventually dependent on each other; to throw knowledge in the way of every one, that it may become of daily use and indispensable application." "*General* education imparts general freedom of thought. And this freedom of thought is the parent of vigorous exertion, of self reliance, of that thorough sense of responsibility, which causes every one to walk alertly and yet cautiously over the difficult paths of life."

> But woe to those who trample on the mind
> A deathless thing
> They know not what they do
> Nor what they deal with
> Man perchance may bind / raise the flower
> His step hath bruised
> Or light anew the touch he quenches
> Or to music wind the lyre string
> From his touch that flew.
> But for the mind "Oh tremble and beware
> Today rude hands on God's dominion / mystery there."

There are some faculties appertaining to the human species, which can never be smothered, much less extirpated. They are a part of man; without them he would no longer be distinguished from the brute: first, the religious sentiment; second, his intellectual nature. They constitute his capability of improvement. They preeminently call for cultivation. These make the most powerful appeal to our fellow beings for aid and cooperation, that they may have the best means of producing the highest results. We cannot alter the structure of the human mind, but we can assist in evolving its powers, or we can prevent their expansion by denying them the means adapted to their growth.[7] Women are gifted with the same powers and are as susceptible of cultivation as men. Why then should they not have the same facilities and the same inducements for improving their faculties?

Education in its most extensive sense is indissolubly connected with free institutions. Narrow, or circumscribe the limits of the one, and you inevitably cripple the other. The tendency of the mind is to progress and whatever widens the avenues of knowledge adds so much strength to our free institutions. . . . Our republic might be enlightened by the study of ancient history. In Egypt "trade was carried on by women, the sculptures represent them buying and selling in the market, and meeting with men at

---

7. Throughout the manuscript, editorial notes and comments are made by an E.J.C., most likely E. J. C. Cutler, who had come from Rome, New York, to be with the Weld's son Sody during his illness in 1860. Presumably, Grimké sought his advice on the manuscript. Here he writes, "would it not be better to make this more hypothetical and begin the sentence with if? . . . Seems like a begging of the question."

feasts apparently on terms of equality." Champollion[8] found on a doorway representations of Thoth[9] and a feminine divinity, who presided over arts, science and literature. Above their heads were "Lords of the Library" and "Lady of Letters." "In Persia the offices of the priesthood are hereditary among women, as well as men; both are treated with equal reverence." In Greece women were admitted to the priesthood, enjoyed its highest dignities and were regarded with great veneration; so were the vestal virgins of Rome, who were an order of priestesses. Among the Celtic tribes women were on the same level with men; "both sexes held consultation together in councils of state and fought in battle with equal bravery"—The Teutons were remarkable for the respect they showed to women. With them women were on an equality with men in church and state, and were habitually consulted by men in all important affairs, and were their only physicians. Tacitus[10] says "The Germans suppose some divine and prophetic quality in their women, and are careful neither to disregard their admonitions, nor neglect their answers."[11]

I do not cite these facts because I regard women as the recipients of the divine afflatus any more than men, but simply[12] to compare the solid advantages enjoyed by heathen women, in having the same opportunities for development and practical usefulness as their brethren, with the blighting system adopted in all Christian nations with respect to the education and practical usefulness of women. . . .

It is a remarkable fact that Christ made no distinctions between the responsibilities of men and women. He addressed to them the same precepts, required from them the same evidence of discipleship, and called upon them in the same language to fulfil their glorious destiny. Can they fulfil it? Can they develop symmetrically their whole being, when they are deprived of the advantages so lavishly bestowed by church and state upon their brethren?

How many millions are invested in colleges, universities, Theological Seminaries for the education and exaltation of *men* to prepare them to fill offices of honor, trust and emolument? Is there one million invested for such purposes for the benefit of women? Nay, they not only are not blest with such patronage, but are even deprived of property by legal enactments, so that they can do very little for themselves. Indeed such is the false estimation

8. Jean-François Champollion (1790–1832) devoted his life to deciphering Egyptian hieroglyphics.
9. Thoth is an ancient Egyptian god who was considered to be the inventor of writing and the patron of scribes.
10. Cornelius Tacitus (A.D. 56?–125?) was known as one of the greatest Roman historians. Little is known about his life except that he had a distinguished reputation as orator, lawyer, politician, writer, and especially historian.
11. Citing historical examples of women's importance was and continues to be a fairly typical means of dispelling myths of female inferiority.
12. This was moved from a later part of the manuscript.

of the needs of the sexes, that women are content to labor for the education of men, whilst they themselves sit down in *commendable* ignorance. How many girls have been united in sewing societies to educate young men for the ministry, nor dreamed that the intellectual feast prepared by their industry for others, was as well adapted to their own necessities, as really a need of their own minds, as of the minds of the other sex. I received a letter from Vermont in which the writer deplores the erroneous view which consigned herself and her sisters to comparative ignorance and poverty, while the sons of the family had college educations and were prospering in their several callings. The father's means being slender, his wife and daughters endured many privations that the young men might be supported at college, confidently believing that they would share the benefits conferred by their sufferings; but alas! the young men left college, married, set up for themselves and at the death of the father, the widow and daughters were compelled to toil on for a bare subsistence. Had they been educated, this would not have been so. Cases like this are numerous. Suffer me then to entreat that you will not close against woman the schools of learning and science thus shutting out the light from those whom God committed to your guardianship at the creation, by endowing you with superior physical strength. In the past you have nobly fulfilled your trust—you have shielded her in war; in seasons of peril you have thrown your bodies around her as a rampart, and sought safety for her at your own cost. But in the present how is it? The existing laws can answer that she is your slave, your bauble, the victim of your passions, the sharer willingly and unwillingly of your licentiousness. It is to save you, as well as her, from the gratification of unbridled desires, to open for you both a glorious path to happiness and usefulness, that I long to see her qualified to fill the station of wife and of mother.

Mother—Is aught so sacred? Is it strange that "the Hindoos regarded with holy reverence the great mystery of human birth? Were they impure thus to regard it? or are we impure that we do not so regard it? Let us not cavil at their tracing the Infinite Cause through all nature, lest by so doing we cast the shadow of *our own grossness* on their patriarchal simplicity." A reverence for the mystery of birth, a feeling, that the means by which this wonderful event is produced ought to be held sacred, would go far to inspire human beings with a love of chastity and to give to one sex self-control, to the other the proprietorship of her own person, and to bring into existence a race of beings who would be welcomed at their entrance into life with a mother's love and joy, and a father's blessing, and whose inheritance would be health of body, strength and elasticity of mind. How just and beautiful is that saying of the Parsees, "The power of evil is increased by a feeble and sluggish body." God is best worshipped when the body is fresh and vigorous as it renders the soul stronger to resist temptation.

In Hindustan the Devodesses, or women who are devoted to the service of the temple, are educated to prepare them for their duties. American women are devoted from their birth to serve in a holier temple even, the sanctuary of Home.

> Here woman reigns the mother, sister, wife,
> Strew with fresh flowers, the narrow way of life
> In the heaven of their delighted eyes
> An angel guard be
> Around their knees, domestic duties meet
> And fire side pleasures gambol at their feet.

Oh for a preparation to fit them for being a Shekinah in that holy of holies! A woman, such as education of the heart and the intellect would produce, would change the aspect of your homes. Such a woman would welcome you not only to the comforts of a well ordered household, but to a mental feast of intellectual companionship, and to that love which heart to heart and mind to mind, in sweetest sympathy can bind. Such a woman would be an ever present divinity, shedding around her a radiance and a calm, which can only be appreciated by those who have enjoyed the rare privilege of such a home, or who have virtue enough to idealize domestic happiness. . . .

Forgive me, if I intrude upon you a chapter of personal experience. With me learning was a passion, and under more propitious circumstances, the cultivation of my mind would have superseded every other desire. In vain I entreated permission to go hand in hand with my brothers through their studies. The only answer to my earnest pleadings was "You are a girl—what do you want with Latin and Greek etc.? You can never use them," accompanied sometimes by a smile, sometimes by a sneer. Had I received the education I coveted and been bred to the profession of the law, a dignity to which I secretly aspired, I might have been a useful member of society, and instead of myself and my property being taken care of I might have been a protector of the helpless and the unfortunate, a pleader for the poor and the dumb.

> "Back useless tears—back to your native spring"
> Your tributary drops might calm less bitter woes.
> But for an aimless life there is no balm

Every individual has some aim in life noble or ignoble. The reason why women effect so little and are so shallow is because their aims are low. Marriage is the prize for which they strive. If failed in that, they rarely rise above the disappointment. Their life blood is curdled and hence they become useless and maim. "Oh could I have unloosed my soul. I was sepulchred alive and wanted room."[13]

My nature thus denied her appropriate nutriment, her course coun-

---

13. Aurora [Grimké's note, see n. 2 above].

teracted, her aspirations crushed, found relief in another direction—painting, poetry, general reading, largely interspersed with words of imagination and tales of fiction occupied my time, but still I longed for an education which would prepare me for future usefulness. At gay fifteen I was ushered into fashionable life; there I fluttered a few brief years, my better nature all the while rising in insurrection against the course I was pursuing, teaching me to despise myself and those who surrounded me in this pageant existence. Ofttimes as I glittered in the ball room [was] my soul . . . awakened from its witching slumber by the solemn query "What doest thou; where are the talents committed to thy charge?" These intrusive thoughts were however soon silenced by the approach of some trifler, by the call to join the festive dance, and I drowned my remorse and my hopeless desires in thoughtless conversations and frivolity. But for my tutelary god, my idolized brother, my young passionate nature, stimulated by that love of admiration, which carries with terrific swiftness many a high and noble nature down the stream of folly to the whirlpool of an unhallowed marriage, I had rushed into this life long misery. I cannot even now look back to those wasted years without a blush of shame at this prostitution of my womanhood, without a feeling of agony at this utter perversion of the ends of my being.

Happily for me this butterfly life did not last long; my ardent nature had another channel opened through which it rushed with its wonted impetuosity. Yielding to the importunities of an elderly friend I went to hear Dr. Kollock[14] of Savannah preach; went, not to hear from his lips the glad tidings of salvation, but that my ear might be gratified with his ravishing eloquence. He described in his own touching, exquisite, powerful language the character of Christ, his tenderness, his yearning compassion, his surpassing love. My whole being was taken captive. I made a full and free surrender and vowed eternal fealty to Jesus. To manifest my sincerity, in my zeal I burnt my paintings, destroyed my little library of poetry and fiction and gave to the flames my gay apparel. I may not proceed with this sad history of the squandering of powers, which if rightly cultivated might have saved me on the one hand from vanity and folly, and on the other from superstitious terror and irrational fanaticism; might have made me worthy of the name of woman, a temple meet for divinity to dwell in. I might have been an intelligent Christian, not a blind and delirious devotee winding my agonized steps over a pathway of darkness and bitter experiences—experiences which almost dethroned reason, [and] made the benign and beneficent Creator, who openeth his hand and filleth all things living with plenteousness and joy, a cruel tyrant, and rendered life for many years one long, long task of suffering and penance, of voluntary, but insane sacrifices, to work out that salvation which consists in the cultivation of every part of our being, in

14. Dr. Henry Kollock (1778–1819) was pastor of the Independent Presbyterian Church of Savannah from 1806 until his death. He had a brilliant reputation as a preacher.

the ascendency of the higher, and the subjection of the lower nature. Again I say forgive me this brief notice of myself. I was tempted to give it, because I believe that my sorrows are not uncommon sorrows, that in those quiet chambers where woman hides her aspirations "never forgotten never removed, but sealed up in silence" I shall meet with many a deep response. Many a woman shudders as she takes a retrospect of life at the terrible eclipse of those intellectual powers, which in early life seemed prophetic of usefulness and happiness, hence the army of martyrs among married and unmarried women, who . . . not having cultivated a taste for science, art, or literature "form a corps of nervous patients who make fortunes for agreeable physicians and ideals of their clergymen."

The time has come for these secret breathings to be heard. The projection of the idea of Human Rights is only the irrepressible protest of reason through woman against her present position. What though the Tima of scorn should point his slow unmoving finger at her who dares to give them voice, let us not shrink. The prize is worth the suffering. Let us redeem ourselves from the degradation which has been the natural consequence of woman's having been regarded a mere instrument to be used for the gratification of passion, as the upper servant in the domestic relations of man to keep things comfortable for her lord, to prepare, or have prepared his food and clothing to produce a pair of slippers to put on when alas! he's weary and to nurse *his* babies. I may not say *hers,* for too often she has not been a willing partner to their birth, for she has felt that the rapid multiplication of children imposed upon her duties she was wholly unfit to perform. With shattered health and soured temper, and self control swept away by this over taxation of her physical powers, she has found it impossible to fill acceptably the station of wife and mother.[15] The uncongenial pair have been frequently held together because divorce under our existing laws, which often deprive a woman of her children, inflicts more agony. (The revelations I have heard from both sexes, would make your ears to tingle, your eyes to drop tears of blood over the ruined bliss of poor humanity.)

"The[16] present has been justly called the age of physical civilization. There never was a period when men were so much addicted to those pursuits, which minister to the comfort and enjoyment of life. There never was one when these were so widely diffused, and this very fact affords incontestable evidence of great intellectual exertion." Physical civilization lies at the foundation of all higher civilization. It constitutes the rudiments of moral and intellectual cultivation—and the immense progress in this direction offers a hope of redemption for women from those slavish and absorbing occupations which have devoured their time and stunted their intellect. Advanced minds among women are becoming wearied with the everlasting round of

15. This was moved from a later part of the manuscript.
16. This was moved from a later part of the manuscript.

domestic labor, and they hail with gratitude and joy every thing that promises to relieve them from constant revolution round the caldron and the kettle.

Does not the paucity of food for reflection in the pursuits of women in times past furnish us a sufficient answer to the query, Why are they inferior? They have been unable to bring into exercise their intellectual powers because they have had no field for the practical application of the knowledge they acquired. Hence the habit of reflection has been rarely and parsimoniously produced in them. Until[17] women are thoro'ly educated they stand in a false position to society and are a dead weight on the government under which they live. Nothing can render them otherwise, but the "full development of their intellectual, as well as active faculties. The first balances the mind and gives it a right direction; the second keeps it in motion." Open to them the avenues of education, usefulness and independence, free and unfettered they can enter the temple of science and enjoy the privileges of the other sex.

Inequalities and injustice in any government naturally produce dissatisfaction and suspicion. In a democracy, these feelings are greatly strengthened and increased by the superior intelligence of the people, for intelligence quickens the perception of wrong and greatly augments the suffering which arises from a sense of oppression. Perhaps there is no feeling which produces more disastrous effects than this, and whose corrosions are more seriously and inevitably blended with the whole social and domestic arrangements of society. Freedom and equality furnish a salutary discipline for the mind and open a vast field to intellectual effort. They enlarge, strengthen, and preserve the power, independence, acuteness, originality and elasticity of the mind, which can never become palsied, so long as it interests itself in Human Rights. Education furnishes the means for extensive information and widens the bounds of human experience, which embraces the past and the present.

It is doubtless the feeling of injury on the part of woman which has induced a few of us to claim the Rights so unjustly withheld. It is because we feel that we have powers which are crushed, responsibilities which we are not permitted to exercise, duties which we are not prepared to fulfil, rights vested in us as moral and intellectual beings, which are utterly ignored and trampled upon. It is because we feel this so keenly that we now demand an equal education with man, to qualify us to be coworkers with him in the great drama of human life. We come before him not in fear and trembling, as did Esther before Ahasuerus[18] crouching like a slave and ready to surrender her womanhood and even her life at his behest—nor like Scheherezade

17. This was moved from a later part of the manuscript.
18. This refers to the book of Esther in the Old Testament, where a Jewess married King Ahasuerus and became Queen Esther of Persia. Grimké invokes the incident where Esther appeals to her husband to intercede for her own people: "So I will go in unto the king, which is not according to the law: and if I perish, I perish" (Esther 4:16).

terror stricken before the Caliph,[19] trying to preserve her life by drawing from the rich stores of imagination those wonderful Arabian Nights' Entertainments, which kept her Lord entranced in wonder, and arrested his cruel and tyrannical decree. We come filled with a sense of the moral sublimity of our present position; not wreathed with the garlands of victory, or armed with the sceptre of command, but clothed in the panoply of *Truth* to demand as equals, in the name of Him who created us, our appropriate place in the scale of humanity. Marvel not that so few have joined our band. The mightiest river drops a little streamlet from the mountain's side, the most stupendous mountain is gathered grain by grain. The coral isles stretching a distance of 1000 miles and surrounding lakes 30 miles in diameter are the work of little insects thousands of which we might crush at every footstep. But two, or three were gathered together at the first meeting of our revolutionary fathers, but fifty six signed the Declaration of Independence. Nevertheless, the grand and glorious words had been uttered "Liberty or Death"—"Taxation and Representation" and they rang through the land with magic power. These works burst like a volcano from the depths of man's humanity, from the omnipotence within him and they were endowed with power from on high. Will it not be so with the words which woman utters? Rights, Equality, Education, Self-support, and Representation—their effect may be more gradual, because she appeals only to the highest nature of man, and that nature has not yet the ascendancy.

Can we marvel that woman does not immediately realize the dignity of her own nature, when we remember that she has been so long used as a means to an end, and that end the comfort and pleasure of man, regarded as *his* property, a being created for *his* benefit and living like a parasite on *his* vitality; when we remember how little her intellect has been taken into account in estimating her value in society, and that she received as truth the dogma of her inferiority.

From an account of the late embassy of Napoleon 3rd to Siam to negotiate a treaty of peace and commerce with the king I quote the following. "The Buddhism of the country inculcates the belief that the body of the king is sacred, as being the abode of a soul in the most advanced state of migration towards beatitude." Who can doubt that among civilized nations the prevalent idea of the superiority of man originated in some such superstitious idea combined with the awe and admiration produced by his physical prowess? His intellectual achievements—here let me bow in reverent gratitude for the labors of my brethren—the Thomas Aquinases,[20]—the Adam Clarkes,[21]

---

19. This refers to the story of the Arabian Nights. Scheherazade is the main character of the introductory story. Caliph refers to the supreme head of the worldwide Islamic community, who was also a character in the book.
20. Thomas Aquinas (1225?–1274) was an Italian scholar and theologian. He is most widely known as the systematizer of Catholic theology and as the father of moral philosophy.
21. Adam Clarke (1762?–1832). See chap. 2, n. 29.

the Jonathan Edwardses[22] and a host of others—have done a gigantic work for humanity. They have bridged rivers, levelled mountains and made a pathway through the deserts of science and literature, comparatively easy to tread and strewn with flowers on every side whose fragrance scents the zephyrs sing and whose prismatic hues charm the travellers' eye. Neither man nor woman will ever again expend their energies in trying to demonstrate how many seraphs could stand on the point of a needle, or in trying to prove that Satan assumed the form of an ape or an ourang outang instead of a serpent when he taunted Eve, or in settling the "Freedom of the Will," a subject entirely beyond the range of man's intellect. All these John Baptist labors were essential to the growth and vigor of the mind; without them man could not have attained his present attitude. But this era demands other efforts and woman pleads for an exalted culture that she may use her powers to promote the elevation and happiness of the Race—in conjunction with man.

The conflict of interests and opinions between the sexes cannot fail to create antagonistic feelings, and this will necessarily be felt in all their relations to each other. This conflict arises from withholding Rights on one side and the injury sustained from the injustice by the other. And perhaps there is nothing that will tend so rapidly and so powerfully to the equalization of the sexes as similar educational advantages. Education opens new theatres of action, furnishes new incentives to exertion. It gives the mind a just appreciation of itself, enables it to estimate its influence in society, and introduces it into new trains of reflection, and new habits of thought. True, education does not transform men or women into angels, but it goes farther than anything else to lessen vice, and is a constant counterpoise to idleness and frivolity. Who can imagine a company of intelligent and highly educated women bemoaning themselves that the Empress of France intended to lay aside hopes, because, if her royal highness imperial majesty did not give her countenance to this bewitching fashion it would be impossible to continue it, however beautiful and convenient it might be to continue to wear them; or spending an hour in settling which ribbon suited them best? Just as soon expect to hear Gerrit Smith[23] and Charles Sumner[24] gravely discussing the attitude most likely to attract attention in the ball room, or what mode of taking a pinch of snuff was most graceful and ravishing.

The fellow feeling which universal education produces among a peo-

22. Jonathan Edwards (1703–58) is said to have been one of the greatest preachers and theologians in American history. He was a colonial New England minister who combined the various philosophies of the Enlightenment to reinterpret man's relation to God.
23. Gerrit Smith (1797–1874) was an American philanthropist and reformer. He is widely known for his initiation of the radical-abolitionist Liberty party, as well as his interest in dress reform and women's suffrage, prison reform, and anti-tobacco and prohibition legislation.
24. Charles Sumner (1811–74) was an American senator well known for his opposition to slavery. He was the first prominent statesman to urge emancipation, and he worked for Negro rights legislation and reconstruction in the South.

ple is clearly discernible in America, and its influence in strengthening that sympathy is incalculable.[25] When learning in all its higher branches shall become the common property of both sexes; when the girl, as well as the boy, may anticipate with earnest delight the complete course of study, which will enable her to look forward to a life of continued culture, of independence and of the fulfilment of high and honorable trusts, the contemplation of such a future will raise her ideas of herself beyond the chameleon sphere of fashion, or the toilsome drudgery of that incessant manual labor, which is calculated in most cases to stultify intellect and which may be performed for a small compensation by those who have hands, but are nearly destitute of brains. It would be as wise to set an accomplished lawyer to saw wood as a business as to condemn an educated and sensible woman to spend all her time in boiling potatoes and patching old garments. Yet this is the lot of many a one, who incessantly stitches, and boils, and bakes, compelled to thrust back out of sight the aspirations which fill her soul. Think not because I thus speak, that I would withdraw woman from the duties of domestic life, far from it; let her fulfil in the circle of home all the obligations that rest upon her, but let her not waste her powers on inferior objects when higher and holier responsibilities demand her attention.

It is for the production of the highest civilization that my spirit yearns, but the highest civilization never can exist in all its beauty and fulness, unless the opportunities for education are the same for both sexes. Equality is the most powerful and the most efficient means of bringing mind to act upon mind, and this action and reaction stimulates and elevates, purifies and deepens thought power. "The observation and analysis of other minds is the foundation of much the greatest part of human philosophy, and the broader the field of vision, the more exact and comprehensive will be the result." Every reflecting mind must see what an immense as well as healthful influence would be brought to bear upon the interests of society by enlarging the field of observation and examination for woman.

The commencement of all great changes is seemingly unimportant, but their consequences are felt to the remotest generations. The common school system of education which was adopted in New England when the colony consisted of only a few thousands, is now established nearly all over the United States, and there can be no doubt that it has contributed, more than any single institution, to the advancement of the people in arts and manufactures, in commerce and literature, in morality and religion, and has been the prolific parent of innumerable blessings. Just in proportion as this system prevails and is carried out on the liberal principle of equality, just in that proportion will civilization increase.

25. This argument parallels that of Frances Wright twenty-five years earlier. She argued for equal education for all—male and female alike—partly because it would engender cooperation and community sympathy—"fellow feeling" (*Course of Popular Lectures*).

Among the most extraordinary and flagrant violations of the spirit of Republicanism is the exclusion of women from school committees, altho' the schools are composed of daughters, as well as sons.[26] It would be extremely difficult to repress the feeling of indignation at this ignoring of the feelings and rights of woman, if I did not clearly see that it originated from circumstances over which neither sex could exercise any control. In the early settlement of every country, the men greatly outnumber the women, school houses are often at a distance from most of the dwellings of the pupils' parents, the access to them is difficult, and women with families and few conveniences to aid in domestic labor are too busy and too much worn from fatigue to attend any thing but the immediate duties of home. This is now no longer the case. Women can afford the time, quite as well as men, and their judgment, their sympathy, their maternal care is needed in all such committees. That they have abundant leisure to attend to this important duty, is manifest from the fact that they devote so much time to benevolent associations, none of which have so strong a claim upon them as the sacred duty of examining and ascertaining the qualifications and character of those to whom is entrusted the care of their children, in the very spring time of life, when the seed that is sown ought to be of the finest quality, and nourished by the most genial influences. "But," said a gentleman, "you cannot find women fit to put on such committees." I shall not stop to disprove this assertion, but simply state, that I have known committee *men,* who certainly were more unfit for their business than any *women* who would be likely to be placed in that position, because unusual care would be taken in the selection of women, as is always the case in the introduction of any innovation. We have, moreover, an admirable safeguard in human nature, conservatism, which prevents changes from being brought about too rapidly. The love of old usages exercises a sort of guardianship over society, somewhat resembling the tutelage of a parent over a child. It is a salutary check to the headlong rush of youthful feeling. And as many parents find it difficult to recognize the manhood and womanhood of their children, albeit they are sometimes far ahead of them in clear sightedness as to what will be most conducive to their own benefit, so conservatism is very slow to acknowledge that any proposed amendment in the structure of society will be really beneficial.[27]

We cannot easily foresee what will be the result of placing men and women on an equality in education. One thing however is certain, it will be an unspeakable advantage to society. The community must increase in wis-

26. Grimké's suggestion of the value that women would bring to school boards is a predecessor of the social housekeeping views of the progressive era, in which women's political participation was justified as an extension of their maternal responsibilities.

27. Comment by E.J.C. (see n. 7 above): "I wish you would recast the form as to say all that is to be said of Education, at once, and that all of woman's wrongs, by itself. There is now some confusion. By a rearrangement of matter the value of the essay would be enhanced."

dom and strength, in proportion to the diffusion of learning, since there is
nothing more admirably calculated to strengthen individual character than
the unlimited extension of knowledge. In a popular government this is of
paramount importance, because intelligence and cultivation tend more than
any thing else, to qualify the elect to act with judgement and benevolence,
and the electors to judge of the fitness of those who are proposed as can-
didates for office, so that all the truly valuable institutions of the country
will rest upon a firmer basis. We appeal then to the States in which we live
to incorporate us among her citizens; to give us the same advantages she
gives to her sons; to open to us the portals of science, art and literature. We
ask them to extend to us the liberality they have so generously manifested
to our brethren. Judge and condemn us not, until you have placed within
our reach the intellectual advantages which those among the other sex, least
susceptible of improvement, can command at will; whilst we are compelled
to stand without and plead in vain for admission. But, it will be enquired,
why we desire an extended education, since we already have what is sufficient
for all the duties of woman's narrow sphere. What is the use of higher
educational privileges, when there is no field for the exercise of our powers,
after we have spent years in their cultivation. First, we ask education as a
means to an end; that end, is greater fitness to fulfil our duties in all the
domestic and social relations. There can be no attainment too high, no
learning too profound, not to be advantageously turned to account in the
sacred circle of Home. Second, we ask it, because we covet an enlarged sphere
of usefulness; we feel a thirst for improvement which can only be quenched
by drinking freely of the streams of knowledge. Third, we ask it, because
we feel as if the time had come, when God having awakened new desires
and stirred within us new aspirations, was calling upon us to aid with all
our powers in promoting the progress of the race. To God, to the cause of
Humanity, we desire to consecrate ourselves, and we ask your aid. Will you
give it us cheerfully, lovingly, as we have given ours to you? How many
toilsome hours have we spent to enable the poor, but aspiring youth, to
obtain an education? Our contributions have been small, but we have bestowed them rejoicingly, faithfully, to prepare some of our brethren for usefulness and duty. Yes, there are many men now filling stations of honor and
of profit, whose education and success have been purchased by the ceaseless
toil of their mothers, sisters and female friends. We speak not boastingly, we
simply state facts. Fourth, we ask an education, because we believe that it
will exalt and purify woman and will enlarge her means of happiness, and
because we know that there is a guarantee in woman's nature that she will
never forsake those duties and enjoyments in which are centered her supreme
felicity.

There is this surpassing blessing in knowledge that all may partake
to the utmost of their ability and desires, without depriving any one else of

the same privilege. Indeed, the greater the number of those who drink at the fountains of science and literature, the more abundant the waters become.

One[28] consideration I must place before the reader, viz:, the effect necessarily produced on girls and boys by the different prospects which their future presents. The boy, as soon as he is capable of thinking, feels that he has to be a worker, that he is to stand on his own feet and exercise his talents in some profitable business. His self-respect, his love of independence, are at once healthfully excited. He feels himself an individual being, draws in with every breath, at home, at school, in the social circle, the idea of self reliance and self-support. Hence, his efforts to prepare himself for this unavoidable business of life are powerfully stimulated. His studies, though often irksome and ill suited to his taste, are pursued as a means to an end, and thus he is constantly and urgently pushed onward in the career of learning. It is not so with girls. They study under the paralysing idea that their acquirements can never be brought into practical use; they may subserve the purposes of promoting individual pleasure, domestic and social enjoyment. But what are they in comparison with the grand stimulation of independence and self reliance and of the capability of contributing to the comfort and happiness of those whom they love as their own souls? Many a talented and highly educated girl feels no pleasure in looking beyond her school life, because she sees no bright and useful future beyond. Delighted as she is with the acquisition of knowledge, she yet sends forth the plaintive inquiry, What shall I do? My learning can purchase for me neither independence, nor the ability to minister to the wants of others. My food, my raiment are not the product of my own industry. Shall this touching appeal meet with no response in the heart of fathers, brothers, husbands and sons?

To institute a comparison between the sexes savors neither of justice nor common sense, because the advantages of the one have been, and are, so vastly superior to those of the other. If we wish to ascertain the capability of woman for improvement, let us compare the women of the present century with the women of two hundred years ago. The number of those who pursue science, literature and art are ten if not an hundred fold what they were during the later part of the 17th century. . . .

It is no longer a matter of speculation, but an established fact, that in proportion as education becomes the common property of a people, in that proportion crime lessens. The register of crimes testifies to this. If then the diffusion of the elements of education produces such blessed effects, is it not clear that to give to such women as desire it, and can devote themselves to literary and scientific pursuits, all the advantages enjoyed by men of the same class, will lessen essentially the number of thoughtless, idle, vain and frivolous women, and thus secure to society, the services of those who now

28. The following has been moved from a later part of the manuscript.

hang as dead weight on the family and the community? The number of these indeed is already lessened, for women have shared, to some extent, in the general diffusion of knowledge, through the common school system. . . . The multiplication of newspapers and periodicals, the rapid increase of which is one of the most remarkable features in the history of our country, has also greatly enlarged their means of information. We need not fear any change which is the result of a spirit of earnest enquiry, for this leads to the knowledge of great principles. Let us not suppose that an invariable adherence to any system of policy constitutes principle. This is only to be found where truth is the end aimed at, and is arrived at by gathering all the light that can be obtained by free and industrious investigation.

It is not from women who are reclining in the lap of opulence and splendor, and eating the bread of idleness, that we can expect aid; they have all they are capable of enjoying, nor ask a better lot. Reformers have almost universally arisen among what are termed the inferior classes of society. They are not so steeped in the enjoyment of material delights as to be unable to appreciate moral and intellectual pleasures. They are not prevented by luxury and selfish indulgence from casting their eyes over the condition of society and pondering the best means of advancing the happiness and prosperity of the race. Noble exceptions doubtless there are, but bold and novel opinions in advance of the age, I believe, have seldom had their origin among the titled and the rich. These do not feel the pressure of old and tyrannical customs, for wealth is their aegis of protection. But those who feel the daily calamity of unjust laws, the degradation of being in an inferior and abnormal position, whose souls are on fire because of oppression and imprisonment, these are the men and women who awaken public attention to the needed reformation. And altho' the first bursting forth of new opinions occasions a violent revulsion, a closer cleaving to the old lest the very foundation of society should be upheaved, yet they gradually insinuate themselves every where, are listened to, wondered at, condemned without examination by the unreflecting, but taken home and carefully weighed by the sober and the thoughtful. I am greatly mistaken if the time has not passed when women listened with astonishment to the wisdom of their brethren, and concluded that they alone were the repositories of knowledge, and the only part a woman had to perform was to listen in mute wonder to the gracious words which dropped from their lips. Women have conceived the bold design of scaling the heights of knowledge, and possessing themselves of the inestimable riches concealed behind the ramparts; riches, of which they have heard, but which they have been sedulously instructed were beyond their reach, and around which a flaming sword continually moved. They are not stirred by envy, or jealousy, but are stimulated by an insatiable desire for progress, by a deathless hope of usefulness, and it is by being elevated to the same level with man that they see the means of accomplishing these anticipations.

There is unquestionably in this day, more than at any preceding period, a willingness to hear and consider the various opinions now afloat touching the great interests of humanity; a stronger tendency to compare and analyze ideas of reform, to get light from every new source, and to form a judgment with calmness and impartiality, instead of idolizing one opinion and refusing a hearing to all others. Dissatisfaction with the state of society marks the present era. This feeling should never be disregarded for it is the daughter of Suffering, the mother of Reformation. Whatever may have given rise to it, it demands our sympathy and is entitled to a respectful hearing— rudely and unfeelingly, carelessly and sneeringly to thrust aside any who ask modestly and earnestly for a redress of grievances, is certainly unmanly and unchristian. To visit upon the petitioners the follies and the vices of a portion of the class with which they are identified is cruel. To deny them relief because they are dragging a tremendous weight of ignorance, idleness, fashion, helplessness and frivolity, is ungenerous. "Has not something living within us here found an utterance and that so powerful an utterance that it can never fall back into slumber? Is not one of our mightiest incentives the hope of redeeming these very persons from a state so fraught with misery? Those who penetrate [be]neath the surface of society discern that fickleness and frivolity are unerring signs that there is something gnawing within the heart from which we would willingly escape; and just on that account they are proofs that the noble nature they disguise is not wholly dead. He who can cast a searching glance into such souls must feel the deepest commiseration for their state, for they live in an atmosphere of dejection, while they would make all believe that they are happy."

The thought of the equality of the sexes is no man's invention, "but the rising of the general tide in the human soul." This idea is itself an epoch; that it is so fully accepted by a few individuals, as to stir them to remonstrance and to action, to union and natural communication of opinions, feelings and views is a commanding fact. "Revolutions go not backward. There is no good now enjoyed by society that was not once problematical." An idea built the wall of separation between the sexes, and an idea will crumble it to dust. . . .

4.

Condition of Women

This essay presents far from a coherent and finished argument. In the original manuscript, Grimké often crossed out words, even paragraphs, and indicated where certain paragraphs might be moved to a different section of the text. In editing it, I have tried to maintain the essentials of her argument and have remained as close to her final version as possible.

Here Grimké is making a case for the granting of full civil and political rights to women, with guarantees of equal education and employment. In doing so, she develops several arguments: that the nation will be better served by the inclusion of women; that since the franchise has been extended to black men and ignorant men without harm, it should also be extended to women; that women have been prepared in the school of suffering to be contributing members of society. She adopts the "moral superiority" argument typically advanced by her feminist contemporaries and suggests that, not only are women equally capable as men of serving in civil and political offices, but are indeed more capable because of their affectional and moral training as mothers. Like so many of her contemporaries, Grimké used the very cult of domesticity which confined women to the narrow sphere of home and family as the justification for women's political participation* However, curiously,

*For a good discussion of this phenomenon, see Nancy F. Cott, *The Bonds of Womanhood: Woman's Sphere in New England, 1780–1835* (New Haven: Yale University Press, 1977).

and typical of Grimké's tendency to contradict herself—or at least to cover all bases—she also argues that once women have been given the opportunity to work and to take part in the civil and political affairs of the nation, their womanly natures will improve. According to her, it is women's idleness, sense of inferiority, and lack of purpose which render them vain and frivolous. Given rights and occupations, women will both improve and be improved by society.

This contradiction in Grimké's thought is also apparent in her reflections on class in this essay. She shows strong sympathies for poor and working-class women, arguing that they, rather than vain upper-class women, are the ones "who are worthy of freedom and will use it worthily." Yet, Grimké shows strong nativist assumptions in the condescending tone she adopts in writing of women who, bending to their husbands' wills, refused to sign antislavery petitions, as well as in her belief, expressed later in the essay, that middle-class women will be most powerful in bringing about reform in society.

Finally, the main point of this essay, that women be granted full political rights and opportunities, contradicts Grimké's earlier sentiments, expressed in the *Letters,* that women should avoid the political arena altogether. This is a significant change in her thought. In part, it reflects her movement away from perfectionism and "come-outerism" and their "no-government" stance. But it also reflects Grimké's ever-widening views of women's sphere and capabilities.

Condition of Women

Every cycle of time brings about its appropriate changes in society. The philosopher looks on at the passing generation and in the occlusion of his study sees the concatenations of events which produce those changes. He sees how the actors work to bring about the very result they deprecate and notes the events which will produce that alteration in public sentiment which will destroy old usages and adopt new ones as the heralds of future benefits. Hence no one can be an earnest observer of men and manners who does not see that a great revolution is going on respecting the present position and rights of woman and her future destiny, and that to give her the longest liberty, to place her as a human being on the same platform with man will aid in her development, and strengthen and give a foundation to her character, and enable her with ease and naturalness to fall into the niche prepared to receive her. The transition will be easy to new duties, and new responsibilities (and new aspirations), and the improvement in the whole structure of our social organization will be noiseless though perceptible. It cannot be said that there is more difference in the capabilities of men and women than there is between men and men—why then impose educational, social, civil and political disabilities on woman? Education, human rights are hers by the imprescriptible decree which created her a moral and intellectual being. To obstruct the highest development, to render it difficult or useless for her to acquire property, to crush her industry, eclipse by stern behests her talents, coerce her activity and her energy is to commit an infinite wrong on society. For men to persist in occupying the whole field of lucrative employments of civil and political office deprives them of that softening influence which would tend to render their virtues more effective and be a stimulus to moderation. It surely never was designed that women should always be the mere instrument of man's gratification. Was she not rather designed to act as a controlling power upon him and he upon her, each to correct in the other those propensities which when unbridled plunge us into confusion and disaster? There is a worm gnawing at the root of the tree of social life. Into whatever department you look, the withering blight is on the leaf and must be there until the two halves of the human family stand beside each other as equals. It is with society as it is with individuals; that man or woman has the most perfect character who leaves no part of their nature uncultivated, and the most perfect social system can only be attained where the laws which govern the sexes are based on justice, and equality asserts its rightful influence.

The acquaintance which women naturally acquire of the workings of the human heart, of the unfoldings and operations of the passions, of the affectional nature, by virtue of their office as mothers renders them peculiarly fit to select those who are to represent and watch over the interests and legislate for a Christian Community. As society is deprived of the political, civil and ecclesiastical labors of woman, it is unquestionably defrauded of a purifying influence which could not but be felt in every department of government. Let the moral character of the women of the U.S. bear testimony to their power of self-government, power more essential than any other to qualify . . . women to reside in our halls of legislation.[1] True, I once heard a person in the House of Representatives in Washington declare that morality and law were divorced, that an attempt to govern political movements by moral right was an absurdity, but however this may have been the case I am

---

1. "As society . . . halls of legislation." is moved from a different manuscript, "Education of Women No. 2, Section 2," which appears to be a rough draft both of this manuscript and "Education of Women."

persuaded that as the race progresses the principle will become practically true that law and religion are a unit, and that the only stable foundation on which government can rest is morality. If this be true is it not manifest that that portion of the race which possesses most religion must form an element in government perfectly organized? . . .

The high moral ground taken at the time when the fabric of our constitution was commenced has doubtless been a great blessing to our country, not withstanding our monstrous departures from its spirit. It was greatly in advance of the age. It moved the scorn and the pity of European statesmen and thousands predicted our speedy failure, but half a century passed by and the nation who had dared to proclaim the right of all men to life, liberty and the pursuit of happiness . . . was standing in its grandeur. How sublime an example of the truth it promulgated America [would] have been had she lived out her principles. . . . We came here that we might be free and freedom could not but grow, although sometimes an attempt has been made to hinder it by the outburst of sectarianism and bigotry.

Perhaps nothing fortifies the human mind more than suffering, unless it has been so excessive as to paralyze or dethrone reason; and the severe trials incident to the settlement of a new country, combined with the fact that a long period must elapse before grievances could be redressed, or rulers changed, and the feeling that they had no choice in the choices of redress induced habits of reflection, humility and patience admirably calculated to prepare them for the noble tho' arduous task of self-government. I believe this is true of women; they have been undergoing a moral training in the school of affliction which will qualify them for the deep earnest work of life. Do not judge us by the butterflies of the ball room, by the extravagancies of fashionable life, by the women who watch with eager gazes the change in the costume of the French Empress and are the weathercocks of her caprices or her fancies. There are a multitude of women, thoughtful, intelligent, willing to bear the obloquy, contempt, reproach which assail them in consequence of their efforts to elevate the sex above the paltry pursuits of vanity. There are in the poorer classes many strong honest hearts, weary of being slaves and tools, who are worthy of freedom and who will use it worthily. There are women who are developed and developing, whose far sightedness, philanthropy and fortitude will enable them to labor with ceaseless industry until a balance is struck between the rights of the sexes. Since the legislative body is the medium of communication between the government and the various classes of society, it would seem but justice that women who form one half of every class should be participators in it, otherwise the government cannot open a healthy channel of reciprocal intercourse with one half the persons over whom it claims to exercise authority and for whom it enacts laws. Hence it seems self-evident that until women share the burdens and responsibilities of government it never can arrive at that perfection of which it is capable, or maintain an equipoise between the sexes. It is as true of government as of the marriage relation. God designs to unite the sexes. Let us beware how we put them asunder.

It is a subject worthy of earnest consideration whether granting the electoral franchise to women would do more violence to public opinion than did the extension of the privileges to all foreigners after the lapse of six months, a measure which opened the ballot box to an immense crowd of ignorant and debased foreigners, [or] as than the extension of the right to vote to colored men in the state of New York. Nor can it be doubted by any careful observer that political privileges [and] equal laws are among the most efficient means of elevating and developing [and] unfolding the latent powers of the human race. . . .

The[2] various associations which exist in America have . . . performed two important services for women—they have opened a wider field for the exercise of her moral and intellectual faculties and by this very exercise have increased their power and given birth to the movement which impels them to claim their rights as human beings.[3] It was when my soul was deeply moved at wrongs of the slave that I first perceived distinctly the subject condition of women. Often when I would ask a sister's signature to an anti-slavery petition, the reply was, I should be rejoiced to sign it, but my husband has forbidden me to have anything to do with it, or Mr. will not like it, or he will be displeased, or I cannot do it without his consent. I knew that women deferred greatly to the opinions of men, but I had no idea that they were expected to sacrifice their sympathies and their consciences to the opinions of their husbands, fathers and brothers [to] preserve domestic tranquility. . . . It requires but little thought to see that the condition of women and that of slaves are in many respects parallel. . . .

May we not compare the condition of women in every civilized country to that of younger sons in Italy. There the law of primogeniture prevails and, says an able writer, "The younger sons being disinherited, feel little or no incentive to exertion, and live as they can upon the pittance doled out to them by the oldest brother. Hence the number of idle persons is much greater in Italy than in France" where the law of primogeniture is abolished and consequently every man feels as if he had his right so far as property is concerned. The Italians, like the women, feel that they are wronged and degraded by the unjust laws which deprive them of property, and the natural consequence is inefficiency and unwillingness to exertion. There is no incen-

2. The following section had been moved from a later part of the manuscript.
3. Grimké is referring here to women's widespread involvement in benevolent societies and moral reform. She is making the argument, since advanced by historians—that women developed interests and skills in these societies which often led to their involvement in feminist activities. See, for example, Barbara Berg, *The Remembered Gate: Origins of American Feminism: The Woman and the City, 1800–1860* (New York: Oxford University Press, 1978), and Nancy Cott, *The Bonds of Womanhood: Woman's Sphere in New England, 1780–1835* (New Haven: Yale University Press, 1977).

tive to effort so great as equality. Any observer of human nature in family, in school, in society must have remarked the baneful influence which a sense of inferiority exerts, how it paralyses the hand and sickens the heart. This Upas is incessantly spreading its poisonous branches over woman, and until the rights of human beings are accorded to her, her powers never can be unfolded, or her faculties fully developed. The government of one portion of a community by forcible despotic and unjust laws is an indication that society is not in a healthful condition. It stimulates the lower nature of those who thus exercise injustice and cripples the powers of those upon whom it is exercised. The very fact that a class of individuals is elevated to the rights of humanity has a direct tendency to purify the whole community, because the act of equity performed by one party and received by another raises the tone of morality and religion. Who doubts for a moment that the amelioration of the penal codes of the United States, Great Britain, and parts of Europe [have] tended to humanize the race? Women are placed, as criminals used to be, without the pale of human rights; like them she will improve as soon as the laws which debase her as a moral and intellectual being are repealed. If the change in the penal code of England has had the wonderful effect stated by an eminent writer who says, "In England criminals were executed by thousands, where they now are by dozens," believe me, if woman stood on the high platform occupied by man, where there are thousands of silly women, there would be only dozens. Dr. Chalmers,[4] in his defense of the laws of primogeniture maintains that government ought to provide employment for younger sons in order to save them from idleness and vice. If our government had to make provision for all the idle and trifling women who are a burden to our social structure, the necessity of rescinding those laws which cripple our activities, stultify our faculties, and render us helpless and dependent would become imperative and the restoration of our rights be resorted to save the public treasure, but as long as the support of women is wrung out of the bone and sinew, the sweat and toil of the other sex as individuals, it is not felt politically, and the social canker has so long gangrened the social body that it is borne as a matter of course. . . .

Prussia has in many respects an admirable system of popular instruction, but when the Prussian youth emerge from their academies and schools they find themselves fettered in thought, word and action. The divine right of the king, the authority of a lonely aristocracy curbs the freedom of the mind, paralyses the physical powers and renders the being who was full of force and activity as a boy but half a man. The same educational advantages combined with the free institutions of America would bring forth fruit an hundred fold. It is precisely so with women; the advantages of education

4. Thomas Chalmers (1780–1847). A Scottish church reformer and theologian, he was a central figure in the 1843 succession of the Free Church from the Presbyterian establishment. Dr. Chalmers was a professor of moral philosophy at Saint Andrews.

which they enjoy, limited as they are, yield but half the benefit they might for want of freedom to exercise the knowledge they have acquired—women are literally ostracised by their brethren from most departments of honorable and remunerative employment.

There is nothing which strikes an observing mind more forcibly than that progress is the characteristic which distinguishes a man from the inorganic world as well as from the vegetable and animal creation—so far as we know the sun has revolved round on its axis, and the laws of centripetal and centrifugal forces have maintained the planets in their orbits since first they were rolled from the hand of omnipotence. The beaver continues to build his residence with the same neatness and skill and apparent foresight as he did when he first arrested the attention of man, the inhabitants of the air and the water still follow out their several instincts as they did at their creation. They do not possess the capability of improvement, but man was no sooner born than his power of reflection began to evolve and slowly but incessantly his faculties have been unfolded until he has been transformed from the ancient Gaul and Briton dressed in skins into the high-souled, intellectual Englishman, Frenchman, and American.

How shocked we should be at the revival in France of "corporate bodies of tradesmen endowed with exclusive privileges"[5] and any attempt to introduce such a system into our government would be repelled with indignation if not with violence, yet precisely such a system, sustained by the all-controlling power of public opinion, exists in our government and has spread like a leprosy through all our social structure, by the disfranchisement of women and their being excluded from offices of emolument and dignity.

The existence of a controlling middle class is one of the most important and commanding facts in the history of the United States. Neither the monied aristocracy, nor the laboring classes form the bulk of the population in the United States. The middle ranks hold the reins of government and administer it in a general fact in all its departments. The women of the class have risen in importance in proportion to their brethren. They exercise more sway over popular sentiment than either those above, or below them, and if they are true to themselves then will they produce a revolution such as the world has never yet witnessed. It is only because the majority of women are too undeveloped intellectually . . . to see the full and glorious bearing of the "Woman's Movement" that men hesitate to grant us the rights we claim and to acknowledge us as their equals as human beings. That the relative position which men have occupied has been a legitimate and a necessary position is held to be as self-evident as that kings and emperors once held rightful sway over the people, but as soon as the illusion is dispelled which

5. This passage refers to the Cobden-Chevalier Commercial Treaty (1853–60). During the Second Empire, Napoleon III repealed the severe protective legislation enacted after the fall of Napoleon I. It seems that in this act the interest of the consumers was subordinate to the opinion of the iron masters, cotton spinners, and agriculturists.

clothes them with imaginary superiority, the foundation on which their power and their authority rests crumbles away and a new form of society is demanded to meet the exigencies of the age.

5.

Essay on the Laws Respecting Women

In some ways, this brief essay would be more appropriate as two pieces rather than one. In the first theme, Grimké argues that since women are creatures endowed with reason, all legislation that proscribes their moral, legal, and political autonomy should be repealed. In the second, she suggests that the world has outgrown war and is moving steadily toward peace. If there is a link between the two themes, it is that as the world is becoming more reasonable and learning the error of its past ways, so should the nation recognize its error in legislating against women's autonomy and correct it.

Grimké had links with the peace reform movement in this country both through Garrisonian abolitionists who advocated pacifism and nonresistance* and, more significantly, through her brother Thomas, who was active in the American Peace Society. The American Peace Society opposed capital punishment, the penal code, aggression, and aggressive war. Thomas Grimké went even further and expressed opposition to defensive wars as well, arguing that since each side always considers the war it is waging to be defensive, only opposition to all wars can stop war. Sarah was very interested in her brother's ideas and edited them for publication. Undoubtedly many of those ideas are reflected here.

*For a good discussion of the connections between pacifism and Garrisonian abolition, see Lewis Perry, *Radical Abolitionism* (Ithaca, N.Y.: Cornell University Press, 1973).

This essay is significant in the development of Sarah Grimké's feminist thought in that it shows the evolution in her views regarding the basis of women's autonomy. In the *Letters,* she argued for women's autonomy on the grounds that women are creatures of God and require their full moral and legal autonomy to fulfill God's will. In this essay, while still invoking God's sanction, Grimké argued for women's autonomy on the basis of their capacity to reason and to discuss the truth for themselves, and concludes that women should be subject to no one's arbitrary will, not even God's.

Essay on the Laws Respecting Women

"There must be deficiencies in heaven to leave room for progression in bliss. A realm of unqualified *best* were a stagnant pool of being—And the circle of absolute perfection of the abstract cypher of indolence."

"Of law," says Hooker,[1] "there can be no less acknowledgment than that her seat is the bosom of God, her voice the harmony of the world, all things on heaven and earth do her homage the very *least* in feeling her care, angels and men with uniform consent admiring her as the mother of their peace and joy." With what delight has this beautiful quotation been read by thousands, by thousands too, whose attention never has been turned to the laws by which they are governed, laws which blight and stultify their being and render them comparatively useless members of Society. Law, in order to be what is here asserted of it, must be in accordance with reason, but reason abhors injustice; she cannot accept a foreign yoke. Her own is easy and light and she rejoices in wearing it. Place upon her tyrannical restraints and she renounces the authority which would thus coerce her into obedience to laws she can neither respect, nor love. This is clearly discernible even in children. I have never known a school in which the reason of the scholars was appealed to in the regulations established for their government, where a hearty response was not given. They may transgress the laws, but they do it with a totally different feeling from that with which they disobey an unreasonable demand. In one case they go counter to their highest instincts, in the other to the will of the teacher, and the will *of any being* ought not to be assigned

1. Richard Hooker (1554?–1600), Anglican divine, was best known for his *Laws of Ecclesiastical Polity,* which supplied a theological basis for the newly created Church of England.

as a rule of conduct for a rational creature. Truth should be the only standard of Right, and Truth stands alone, independent even of the will of Jehovah. I speak reverently but I speak confidently—God never designed to make his arbitrary will the standard of our actions. He endowed us with reason and in those oracles received as his revelation to man he says, "Come now let us reason together saith the Lord" [Isa. 1:18]. And Christ appealing to the Jews says, "Why judge ye not of yourselves what is right" [Luke 12:57]. Paul affirms the same thing when he says that the "heathen are a law unto themselves" [Rom. 2:14–15].

It is this awakening of our long slumbering reason that gives to woman the present impulse, that rouses her to an effort to obtain a repeal of the unrighteous laws which, not being in harmony with her reason, gall and chagrin, mortify and dwindle her, as the unjust decrees of Parliament harassed and fretted our forefathers and finally wrought them up to decided action. Let me again state that I have no censure for the past, no wailing for the present. "It is the sweetest reward of philosophy, that looking upon all things in their mutual dependence and upon nothing as isolated and alone; she finds *all* to be necessary and therefore good, and accepts that which is, *as it is,* because it is subservient to a higher end." And it seems to me unwomanly to waste that time in lamentation, or in satire which is so deeply needed to examine the causes of our grievances and endeavor to suggest the appropriate remedy.

Having glanced at the past and the present it now remains to decide at what point the race is standing—whether war has not nearly finished its sanguinary work between civilized nations, and is not rapidly beating swords into plough shares, spears into pruning hooks, exchanging the gory forms of slaughtered millions and the serried ranks of embattled foes, for the waving harvest and the luxuriant orchard. America has given to the world the first great lesson in peace; she, more than any other nation has cultivated agriculture, commerce, manufactures, all the arts which are essential to humanizing the race. Her independence secured, the portals of her temple of Jesus were closed for a period of nearly 70 years with one brief exception, while in Rome they were closed but once for 700 years and then only for a short time. The late war in Europe[2] is one of the many evidences that the spirit of Peace is becoming, not the eddy in the stream of human affairs, but the steady current sweeping onwards and sweeping away the currents of barbarism. What was the character of that war? . . . Not as formerly a mere game for glory, but a forced encounter for self preservation. How striking and prophetical was the fact that comparatively little was said of the military splendor of the achievements of the conquerors, but much was expressed and felt about the horrors of war, and the sufferings of the soldiery. . . . Florence Nightingale too has been born of that war, and the beneficial effects of that

2. The Crimean War (1853–56).

example, and of the schools established through her instrumentality, where women may study medicine and nursing, posterity only can estimate.[3]

The present may be stiled the era of conflicting worlds in which the past and the present have met in deadly antagonism, the present slowly struggling to attain the precedence and secure the peaceful dismission of the past. The great error which has pervaded society has been the idea that but one class of persons can exist, live, think and act for themselves, that in them is concentrated the thinking power of the age, whereas in truth they are but a part of the rays which converge to focus from the universal tho't.[4] The legislatures of the present day consult the chronicles of the elder time to obtain laws for the government of the people and in this way construct its political existence out of a confused patchwork, gathered from many ages long since dead, thereby acknowledging a consciousness of its own unfitness to legislate for its own era.[5] Common sense rises in insurrection at this violation. . . .

---

3. Florence Nightingale (1820–1910) organized a unit of thirty-eight women nurses to investigate and improve conditions in hospitals serving the British army in the Crimea, where medical supplies were lacking and hospitals were unsanitary and badly managed. It is said that her arrival marked a turning point in the fortunes of the British army in the Crimea.
4. This sentence from Fichte [Grimké's note].
5. This sentence from Fichte. See p. 19 1/4 [Grimké's note].

6.

Marriage

Another version of this essay was first edited by Gerda Lerner and published in her *The Female Experience: An American Documentary* (Indianapolis: Bobbs-Merrill, 1977, pp. 87–98).

The manuscript "Marriage" is written in Angelina's hand. The archivists at the Clements Library, University of Michigan, believe it to be Angelina's work. Lerner, however, believes it to be Sarah's, for two reasons: (1) many of the statements parallel statements in other writings known to be hers; and (2) it was common practice for Angelina to copy Sarah's work to make it more legible.*

The fact that this manuscript is in finished form, without crossed out words and indications of where portions of the text are to be moved, differentiates it from the other manuscripts in this collection. This, however, could just as easily indicate that Angelina had copied out Sarah's final version as suggest that Angelina wrote the essay herself.

Occasionally, the author reveals an intimate knowledge of marriage, as in her statement, "To me that embrace [sexual intercourse] is as spontaneous an expression of love in husband and wife *after* that [childbearing] period as before it. . . ." This would seem to suggest that Angelina, rather than Sarah, wrote the essay. How-

*These comments are written up and included with the unpublished manuscripts in the Clements Library.

ever, Sarah had intimate knowledge of her sister's marriage through the simple fact that she shared her and her husband's home for almost all of their married life. (Angelina's marriage was reputedly a happy one, though she suffered physically from complications in pregnancies and childbirth.) Also, in one of the other essays, Sarah alludes to the fact that many married women had confided in her concerning the intimate details of their marriages.

Sarah also had the confidence of her closest friend, Harriot Kezia Hunt who, through her medical practice, personally witnessed the physical and emotional sufferings of women resulting from forced intercourse, multiple pregnancies and childbirths, and abortions. Hunt was one of the first female doctors in this country. She opened her practice in 1835, mostly among women and children. In 1843 she organized the Ladies Physiological Society, which met for monthly talks on women's health issues. Certainly, many of the concerns raised in this essay were discussed in those meetings. It is also interesting to note that Hunt had many Shaker friends, which probably accounts for the reference to the Shakers in it.

What more than anything else points to this essay being Sarah's work is its thematic continuity with all the others. Here, as elsewhere, is the blending of arguments for economic and legal reform with those for sexual reform—a blending which Lerner, in discussing "Sisters of Charity," has called uniquely Sarah's (Lerner, 1985:815). The contrasting issues of forced maternity and the sacredness of marriage and motherhood certainly are not new in Grimké's work. This appears, rather, to be an elaboration of an already developed argument. Also expressed here is some of the antievangelistic sentiment that Sarah voiced in "The Education of Women," as well as the recurrent call that it is time for the past to yield to the present, which runs throughout these manuscripts. Especially given some of the arguments in "Education of Women," this essay might be viewed as the culmination of Sarah's writings on women—concluding that changes in women's education or employment or legal status were incumbent upon changes in the marital relation.

To place the essay in historical context, the *New York Times* article referred to in the beginning of the essay was a fairly typical statement of the view of mainstream Americans of the day (not unlike that of our contemporaries) that the women's movement was bringing about moral decay and the demise of the family. As previously discussed in the Introduction, the campaign for "voluntary motherhood" was being waged both by "Free Lovers" and by women's rights advocates. Both groups felt that women should have the right to determine when they become mothers. They disagreed, however, regarding marriage. "Free Lovers" believed the state had no right to impose itself on the private relations between women and men. Most women's rights advocates, on the other hand, believed strongly in the spiritual and legal institution of marriage and sought women's rights within that institution. (One major exception to this was Elizabeth Cady Stanton, who in the 1850s argued for liberalized divorce laws, and in a speech given in 1870 strongly criticized any type of regulation of men's and women's private affections [DuBois, 1975.]) Nevertheless, the two groups were often confused by their opponents, and women's rights advocates were often accused of advocating "free love."

The views that Grimké presents here are fairly typical of those of other feminists, health reformers, and moral reformers of her day.* These reformers advocated greater sexual restraint on the part of both men and women but, most significantly, they emphasized the right of women to refuse their husbands. Women had legitimate fears regarding sex. It brought with it pregnancy, childbirth, abortion, venereal disease, and often physical and emotional violation. According to health reformers, excessive sexual intercourse had degenerating effects, not only on the essential harmony between man and woman, but also on any children they might have. Certainly the argument that mothers overburdened with several children in close succession could provide them with neither the needed physical nor emotional nourishment was a reality.

This essay also reflects the prevailing view regarding prostitution: that prostitutes were "helpless young women who fell into illicit sex" (DuBois and Gordon, 1983:9). Feminists made this view central to their understanding of women's oppression (DuBois and Gordon, 1983:10). The solution in any case was the same—for men to restrain their sexual drives.

The other view advanced in this essay that is typical of nineteenth-century feminists is the reverence and awe with which marriage was regarded. It accentuates the point made by Gordon that "voluntary motherhood in this period remained almost exclusively a tool for women to strengthen their positions within conventional marriages and families, not to reject them" (Gordon, 1973:19).

---

*For excellent discussions of these views, see: Ellen Carol DuBois and Linda Gordon, "Seeking Ecstasy on the Battlefield: Danger and Pleasure in Nineteenth Century Feminist Sexual Thought," *Feminist Studies* 9, no. 1 (Spring 1983): 7–25; Nancy F. Cott, "Passionlessness: An Interpretation of Victorian Sexual Ideology, 1790–1850," *Signs* 4, no. 2 (Winter 1978): 219–36; and Linda Gordon, "Voluntary Motherhood, The Beginnings of Feminist Birth Control Ideas in the United States," *Feminist Studies* 1 (Winter/Spring 1973): 5–22.

Marriage

In the Summer of 1855, the *New York Times,* professing to give a history of the rise and progress of what is called "Free Love," identified it with the Woman's Rights movement. This writer says, "The Woman's Rights movement tends directly and rapidly, in the same direction, viz. to Free Love, that extreme section of it we mean which claims to rest upon the absolute and indefeasible right of woman to equality in all respects with man and to a complete sovereignty over her own person and conduct."[1]

This exposition of the *principles* of the Woman's Rights movement I heartily accept. We do claim the absolute and indefeasible right of Woman to an equality in all respects with man, and to a complete sovereignty over her own person and conduct. Human rights are *not* based upon sex, color, capacity or condition. They are universal, inalienable and eternal, and none but despots will deny woman that supreme sovereignty over her own person and conduct which Law concedes to man.

The conclusion which this writer draws from this equality of rights, viz., that this movement tends directly and rapidly to the principles of "Free Love," or that a claim for woman's rights "nullifies the very idea of marriage as anything more than a partnership at will," I utterly deny. Man is acknowledged to have rightfully supreme sovereignty over *his own* person and conduct, and yet who believed that this nullifies marriage, making it in his case, a mere partnership at will. Why then should it be so in the case of woman? Is she less worthy of being trusted with this right than he? Let the 20,000 prostitutes of New York whose virtue is too often bought by married men answer. Is her heart more inconstant and less penetrated than his by the love of children? Even if experience had not taught us otherwise, the nature of these two beings would determine the question. Merely from a careful analysis of the sexes, Philosophy would become Prophecy and unerringly predict the facts in the case. Is it not wonderful that Woman has endured so long and so patiently the hidden wrongs which Man has inflicted upon her in the marriage relation, and all because her heart so cleaves to her children and to home, and to *one* love, that she silently buries her sorrows and immolates herself, rather than surrender her heart's dearest treasures.

Let us examine these assertions calmly, reverently, for we are treading upon holy grounds: *all rights are holy.* Let us first look at the effect upon the marriage relation of the hitherto acknowledged principle that man had rights superior to woman. Has it not subordinated her to his passions? Has she not been continually forced into a motherhood which she abhorred, because she knew that her children were *not* the offspring of love but of lust. Has she not in unnumbered instances felt in the deepest recesses of her soul,

1. *New York Times,* September 8, 1855 (vol. 4, no. 120, p. 2).

that she was used to minister to Passion, not voluntarily to receive from her husband the chaste expression of his *love*? Has she not, too often, when thus compelled to receive the germ *she could not welcome,* refused to retain and nourish into life the babe, which she felt was not the fruit of a pure connubial love?[2]

Ponder well the effects upon woman of this *assumed superiority of rights* in the stronger sex, that sex too in which the constitutional element of sex has far greater strength. Look too at the effect upon children, who are the product of such *one sided rights*—puny, sickly, ill-organized and unbalanced—bearing about in body and mind the marks of their unholy origin.[3]

And yet the *Times* is horror struck at the idea of woman's claiming "a *supreme sovereignty over her own person and conduct.*" Is it not time that she should? Has not man proved himself unworthy of the power which he assumes over her person and conduct? How I ask has he protected and cherished her? Let her faded youth, her shattered constitution, her unharmonious offspring, her withered heart and *his* withered intellect answer these questions. Is it not time then that she asked for "a redress of grievances" and a recognition of that *equality of rights,* which alone can save her?

Let us now look at the results of such a recognition. A right on the part of woman to decide *when* she shall become a mother, how often and under what circumstances. Surely, as upon her alone devolves the necessity of nurturing into the fulness of life the being within her and, after it is born, of nursing and tending it thro' helpless infancy and capricious childhood, often under the pressure of miserable health, *she ought* to have the right of controlling all preliminaries. If man had all these burdens to bear, would not *he* declare that common sense and common justice confer this right upon him?

An eminent physician of Boston once remarked that if in the economy of nature, the sexes alternated in giving birth to children no family would ever have more than three, the husband bearing one and the wife two. But the *right* to decide this matter has been almost wholly denied to woman. How often is she forced into an untimely motherhood, which compels her to wean her babe, thus depriving it of that nutriment provided by nature as the most bland and fitting during the period of denlition? Thousands of

2. By the 1860s in the United States, new legislation had outlawed all abortions except those "necessary to save the life of the woman," and by the end of the 1870s virtually every state had a law forbidding abortions to women, even those whose lives were endangered by pregnancy.
3. This refers to the prevailing belief. "It is also a general conclusion among physiologists that repeated conjugal intimacy within a few hours is unprolific and a mere animal gratification. Abstinence for one or more days and tolerably good health are necessary to most individuals for procreation of healthful offspring." Michael Ryan, *The Philosophy of Marriage in Its Social, Moral, and Physical Relations* (reprint: Bala Cynwyd, Pa.: Ayer Publishing Company, 1974).

deaths from this cause, in infancy, are attributed by superstition and ignorance to the dispensations of Divine Providence. How many thousands too,
of miscarriages are forced upon woman, by the fact that man lives down
that law of his being which would protect her from such terrible consequences just as animal instinct protects the female among brutes? To save
woman from legalized licentiousness is then one of the reasons why we plead
for *equality of rights*.

No one can fail to see that this condition of things results from
several causes.—First, ignorance of those physical laws, which every man
and woman *ought* to know before marriage, the knowledge of which has
been withheld from the young, under a false and fatal idea of delicacy. Many
a man ruins his own health and that of his wife and his children too, thro'
ignorance. A diffusion of knowledge respecting these laws would greatly
lessen existing evils. Second, a false conception in man and woman of *his*
nature and necessities. The great truth that the most concentrated fluid of
the body has an office to perform in the production of *great* tho'ts and
original ideas, as well as in the reproduction of the species is known to few
and too little appreciated by all. The prodigal waste of this by legalized
licentiousness has dwarfed the intellect of man. Ignorance of this is a great
barrier to human progress, but the fiat "let there be light" has gone forth
and it will achieve a new creation wherein reason and righteousness will
reign triumphant over passion and selfishness. (I would recommend to all
inquirers an admirable work entitled *The Philosophy of Marriage* by Michael
Ryan MD.)[4] Third, the fact that many legal marriages are not love marriages.
In a pure, true relation between the sexes, no difficulties can ever arise, but
a willing recognition of each other's rights and mutual wants, naturally and
spontaneously resulting in voluntary motherhood, a joyful appreciation of
the blessedness of parentage, the birth of healthy, comely children and a
beautiful home.

But it may be asked, what is to be done in cases of uncongenial
marriages. Are not such men and women to follow their attractions outside
of the legal relation? I unhesitatingly answer no! Where two persons have
established a false marriage relation, they are bound to abide by *the consequences* of the mistake they have made. Perhaps they did love each other,
but a nearer intimacy has frozen this love or changed it into disgust. Or,
theirs may have been a marriage of *convenience,* or one *for the sake of
obtaining a home,* a fortune, a position in life: or it may have been a mere
act of obedience to parents, or of gratitude, or a means of canceling a monied
obligation. Multiform are the *unworthy* motives which seduce men and
women into this sacred relation. In all these cases, let them abide the con-

4. Michael Ryan, M.D., *The Philosophy of Marriage.* It was the general medical opinion at
the time that accumulation of seminal fluid, especially before the age of twenty-five, was
necessary for full mental development.

sequences of their own perversion of marriage, in exchanging personal chastity for the pride of life, vanity in dress, position or a house to live in, without that *love* which alone can make that house a *home*.

In some cases, it may be duty for the parties to separate, but let both keep themselves pure, so long as both are living. Let them accept the discipline thus afforded, and spiritual strength and growth will be their reward.

The Doctrine that human beings are to follow their attractions, which lies at the base of that miscalled "free love" system, is fraught with infinite danger. We are too low down to listen for one moment to its syren voice. Watchman what of the night echoes in thunder tones? How stand the hands of the dial plate of human progress and destiny? Let War and Slavery, Intemperance and Licentiousness, the multitudinous wrongs and outrages, the ignorance, animality and selfishness which encompass and involve us, point to the hour of our progress. We are then in the childhood of our moral development, however stalwart we may be as a Race, in animal passion and unmanly crime.

And this is according to the legitimate law of growth, first the animal nature unfolds itself, then the intellectual and moral. Man is an amalgam of these two natures, united for the education of the higher. As the material world has been created to call out bodily exertion, and develop physical strength and robust health, so the spirit has been bound to the animal, in order to call forth *its* powers of resistance, that it may unfold in beautiful proportions the glorious elements of its being. Purity and Truth are the magnet which attracts the soul—sensual indulgence is the physical lodestone. If we yield to the former it lifts us higher and higher, until we sway the sceptre of Reason over our lower nature. If to the latter, it drags us down victims and slaves.

Let me then exculpate "the woman's rights movement," from the charge of "tending directly" and rapidly to the Free love system, and nullifying the "very idea of Marriage as any thing more than a partnership at will." On the contrary, our great desire is to purify and exalt the marriage relation and destroy *all* licentiousness. To every unhappy couple we say again, bear in quiet home seclusion the heart withering consequences of your own mistakes. You owe this to yourselves, to your children, to society. Keep yourselves pure from that desecration of the marriage relation which brings children into the world who have not upon their brows the seals of love and chastity. If you cannot live thus purely together and separation become necessary, let no temporary or permanent relation be formed by either party during the life of the other.

In the present unsoundness of public opinion on this subject, offer yourselves up willing sacrifices for the good of others, and make your lives a public testimony *against* that miscalled "Free love," so fatal to Chastity, so disastrous to homes, so demoralizing to Society. This discipline of life, if regarded as a freewill offering on the altar of Purity and public weal, will be blessed to the individuals themselves, but, if legal and illegal connections be formed at will, the most terrible consequences must ensue. Men will put away their wives for every cause, as of old, and women their husbands, thus profaning the marriage relation, overthrowing all stability and whelming homes under a deluge of licentiousness.

In marriage is the origin of life. In the union of the sexes exists a creative energy which is found no where else. Human nature tends to the uses of all the faculties with which it is endowed, and desire is strong in proportion to the greatness of the result which flows from its exercise. Hence the creative is stronger than any other faculty, birth being *the* great fact of our existence here, and its *legitimate* exercise is the natural result of the purest and most unselfish love, the spontaneous giving away of onesself to the only loved one, and the receiving of that other to ourselves in return. Marriage is a necessity of our being, because of our halfness. Every man and woman feels a profound want, which no father nor mother, no sister nor brother can fill. An indescribable longing for, and yearning after a perfect absorbing of its interests, feeling and being itself into one kindred spirit: The man feels within him a lack of the feminine element, the woman the lack of the masculine, each professing enough of the other's nature to appreciate it and seek its fulness, each in the other. Each has a deep awareness of incompleteness without the other.

In brutes whose wants lie only upon the plane of the animal nature, any male can supply the wants of any female, but just in proportion as men and women develop above this low plane they feel that diversity of mind and heart and soul within them, and seek that divinity in her and in him with whom they would companion for life. This divinity is the only true basis of union, and of it alone grew these holy affinities which bind soul to soul, not only in a temporal relation but in an eternal marriage.

Full well do multitudes of human beings know in bitterness of soul, that the empty ceremony of a priest and connubial relations do not constitute marriage. Many a woman (I call her not *wife*) loathes the unhallowed connection she has formed, and would gladly welcome death as a deliverer from that polluted prison house, which the world *miscalls* her *home*. A revolting experience has forced upon her the humiliating conviction that she is a legal prostitute, a chattel personal, a tool that is used, a mere convenience—and too late does she learn that they who desecrate the marriage relation sin against their own bodies and their own souls, for no crime carries with it such physical suffering, or so deep a sense of *self* degradation.

So common has been this desecration, that many pure minds find it impossible to reconcile marriage with purity and love in their most exalted sense. Hence the Society of Shakers,[5] among whom are many noble men and

5. The Shakers were a Christian sect and religious community that evolved from Quakerism.

women. A friend[6] who visited them for the purpose of ascertaining upon what ground they repudiated marriage, was surprised to find that they regarded the connection of the sexes *the* vice for which Adam and Eve were expelled from Paradise, and regarding this as the cause of the fall of man. They believe that nothing but a universal abstaining from it can redeem the world. Their argument based upon this was easily answered by the fact that before they fell Adam and Eve were commanded to "multiply and replenish the earth" [Gen. 1:28]. In reply to this, they said Adam and Eve sinned against time. But of this there is no evidence, because they are introduced to us, *not* as children or youth, but in the fulness of manhood and womanhood, and this command was without any restriction as to time.

Would it not be folly in a Ruler to issue commands *ahead* of the development of his subjects? Ought not God to have waited until the fulness of time had come, especially as He knew that obedience to it, would involve the ruin of myriads, and as the Shakers believe, the consequent necessity of living down the deepest instinct and strongest impulse of his being? Does not such a belief charge God with folly and malignity too?

But, said the Shakers, look at the effect of the transgression; "they sewed fig leaves together and made themselves aprons" [Gen. 3:7]. True, was the reply, but it was a strong peculiarity among Eastern Nations to cover up and hide their *most sacred things,* and this part of the person was thus regarded by them. Look at the fact that among the early Hindoos, the organs of generation were looked upon as objects of worship. To their unsophisticated minds, birth was a great and glorious fact, and they very naturally transferred to the instruments of its production that reverence and religious veneration which they felt for the fact itself. Hence, to them, the emblems of the organs of generation were as *sacred* as was the sign of the cross to the early christian, and they wore their emblems in symbolic masks upon their foreheads, and hung them carved in gold and ivory around their necks, and often had them buried with them. So *sacred* in their eyes were these emblems that they deposited them in the innermost recesses of their temples, crowned them with flowers and surmounted them with golden stars, regarding them as the fittest emblems of *their* god and Creator Seva,[7] whose ceaseless fiat of production ever clothes the world with grandeur and beauty.

Now it is certain that the first effect produced upon Adam and Eve

---

(They were first known as the "Shaking Quakers" due to their violent shaking, dancing, and speaking in tongues during meetings.) The Shakers reached their peak between 1830 and 1850, having nearly six thousand members. Now they are dying out, partly because of their practice of celibacy. In 1770, one of the founders, Ann Lee, had a vision that the union of Adam and Eve had not been for procreation but was lustful self-indulgence; thus sex was sinful and must be avoided at all costs.

6. Sarah is undoubtedly referring here to Harriot Hunt.

7. Grimké is referring to the Hindu god Siva, the third deity in the great Hindu triad of gods. Siva represents destruction and reproduction (or creation).

was that their eyes were opened and they knew that they were naked. Did they not then arrive at the stage of development when they became conscious of nakedness, and that *that* part of their bodies were *sacred* and therefore should be hidden? Hence their anxiety to conceal it even from each other. The tree of which they had eaten was good to make one wise, and the knowledge it imparted was of *good* as well as of evil. Had mankind continued ever to regard the organs of generation as *sacred* to the high and holy office of creating immortal beings, endowed with the noblest faculties and crowned with glory and honor, humanity never would have sunk so low as it now is in our boasted civilization. It has been the total *perversion, prostitution* and *profanation* of these organs, which has degraded them in our eyes, and dragged down a perfectly natural and therefore God-ordained institution, into the slime and mire of sensuality and crime.

This was the light in which the Apostle regarded them, for in speaking of these members of the body he says: "And those members of the body, which we think to be less honorable, upon these we bestow *the more abundant honor*. For our comely parts have no need, but God hath temper'd the body together, having given more abundant honor to that part which lacked, that there should be no schism in the body, but that the members should have the same care one for another" [1 Cor. 12:23–25]. How natural then was the feeling of shame in Adam and Eve, when first waked to the consciousness of nakedness? A deep and innate sense of the *sacredness* of that part of their persons suggested the propriety of covering it. And who would not feel ashamed of its exposure far more than of all the body beside? Has not Nature taken especial pains thro'out the animal kingdom to conceal the organs of generation? In human beings alone are they exposed, and has not this exposure been compensated for by that deep innate shrinking from exposure, which thro' all time has induced concealment? No one has ever desecrated that part of his person, or ever unnecessarily exposed it, without doing violence to the deepest instincts of his being.

I see nothing then in the conduct of Adam and Eve but a natural instinct, working itself out, without any consciousness of sin, as soon as they reached the stage of *self-consciousness,* for it is not until then that they are presented to us. In infancy no child feels ashamed of exposure, because it is not self-conscious, but as soon as it becomes so, how studiously is exposure avoided. As it advances to maturity, how increasingly sacred are the feelings which protect from exposure and associate with the uses of these organs the greatest sensitiveness and the highest sense of honor. Hence when a woman has imparted to anyone but a husband this part of herself, she is stamped with infamy, and becomes an outcast from society. And man would share the same fate, had he not erected for himself a false standard of virtue, contravening that Revelation, which enacts but one law for both sexes. Who does not know that the most guilty has been the last condemned, and that the confiding and tempted one, has too often drunk the cup of bitterness to the dregs in poverty and shame, whilst her heartless tempter and betrayer has walked abroad unscathed by the world's dread scorn?

But to return, why has this extreme sensitiveness been interwoven with the very warp and woof of our being? Why have mankind in all ages and countries regarded chastity as the greatest of all virtues, had not Nature herself taught that the organs of generation are the *holy of holies* in the temple of the body, that part of us which was designed by God to be consecrated to our holiest and most unselfish love, yearning to be absorbed into each other, and become one by mutual incorporation. Wherever this strong deep affection, this indissoluble marriage of spirit with spirit, does not prompt to the union of the sexes, wherever a momentary physical excitement is all that is sought, then mutual pollution and self degradation is the consequence. In every true marriage, the husband and wife become one, by irrepressible affinities. This soul oneness finds its most natural, most sacred and intense outward expression in that mutual personal embrace, which in the order of God, constitutes them Creators, exercising divine functions and ushering into being immortal existence.

It is only when pure things are perverted to impure uses, that they become impure, and the altar is desecrated by the swine that is offered upon it. If Roman standards and Heathen Priests and sacrifices of swine could pollute the temple of God built of wood and stone, how much more do men and women pollute that infinitely holier temple, their own bodies, whenever they sacrifice the holiest instincts of their being to the brutal passion of Lust, whether it be *in* the external marriage relations or *out* of it. And they do this whenever they give themselves to each other with any other feeling than that of absorbing *love*. If we shrink with horror at Judas' betrayal of his master with a kiss, how much more should we recoil from that treason to the race which prostitutes our highest nature and betrays humanity by desecrating that holiest of all kisses which should be the seal of *true marriage alone,* the natural outbirth of the deepest and most sacred instincts of our being. For whenever sexual intercourse is *not* prompted by a felt indissoluble oneness of love, a mutual incorporation of spirit with spirit ever yearning more fully to pass into, to permeate and absorb each other's life, then hearts are deceived and betrayed, and affections are left mangled and bleeding upon the Altar of Lust.

What, I would ask is Chastity? Is it the entire absence of the sexual feeling? Then infants only are chaste. Does it consist in abstinence from the act of sexual intercourse? No! for "he who *looketh* upon a woman to lust after hath committed adultery already with her in his heart" [Mt. 5:28], and solitary vice is still more abominable and unnatural.

Is every married man and woman then destitute of Chastity? O no! What then is Chastity? Is it not that incorporation of soul with soul and heart with heart in two individuals, which consecrates to each other the holy of holies in the temple of the body, where divine creations are the sacred rites performed at the shrine of Love by souls exulting in a reverential appreciation of the ennobling Sacrament. The married are chaste when the soul rules over the body, and deepest yearnings after mutual incorporation of spirit life, seeks the aid of material organs, and finds in them a sacred expression of natural instincts.

In consonance with the idea that these parts are the holy of holies in the body, is the fact that that part of the spine which walls it in is called the Sacrum or Sacred bone, a name most appropriate, if these views are true, but wholly without meaning if they are false.

Some regard the termination of the childbearing period in woman as Nature's interdict upon sexual intercourse between man and woman. To me that embrace is as spontaneous an expression of love in husband and wife *after* that period as before it, and as natural and pure as the kisses press'd by the loving child upon its mothers lips, or that Mother's yearning pressure of her child to her bosom. If it be the outbirth of overflowing affection and spiritual affinity pervading each others' being with the aroma of faith in and love for the intrinsic qualities of character, then why repress this mode of manifestation which will never cease to be natural until disease or the infirmities of age have deadened all physical susceptibilities?

Married persons sometimes have no children, nor any hope of them. How then, can this fact render physical connection an inappropriate expression of *their* mutual love? For altho' the desire for children is a natural excitement to the sexual act, yet that is weak in comparison with that yearning for a mutual *absorption into each other,* which alone gives vitality to every true marriage, and the ceasing to have children does not and cannot destroy this deep abiding feeling.

And here I would say [a] few words on the artistic feeling which now exists with regard to naked statues and paintings. I have no doubt that in pure minds, no other feeling exists in viewing these, but admiration of their beauty and symmetry as a whole. But it is a serious question in my mind, whether it is best to allow our admiration of the beautiful, so far to ever master that instinctive shrinking from exposure, which is developed in every human being, as to enable us to look unmoved at that, in a statue or painting, from which we would turn away with holy horror in the living form, of which these are representations. For myself, I always shrink instinctively from such exhibitions of the human form, because to me *this part of the person is sacred*. A mysterious instinctive feeling calls for drapery for concealment in it just as in myself, and as it is the perfection of art to embody not the material only, but the tho'ts, emotions and sentiments of the spiritual being, so in veiling this part of statues and paintings this sacred feeling becomes embodied in the speaking marble and transfused into it. Drapery does homage to this universal instinct whilst nudity commonizes and profanes that which is consecrated to the expression our holiest laws.

Man seems to feel that Marriage gives him the control of Woman's person just as the Law gives him the control of her property. Thus are her most sacred rights destroyed by that very act which, under the laws of nature, should enlarge, establish and protect them. In marriage is the origin of life—in it woman finds herself endowed with a creative energy she never possessed before. In it, new aspirations take possession of her and indescribable longing after motherhood as the felt climax of her being. She joyfully gives herself away, that she may receive the germ of a new being, and true to Nature, would fain retire within herself and absorb and expend all her energies in the development of this precious germ. But alas! how few are permitted unmolested to pursue that end, which for the time being, has become the great object of life? How often is she compelled by various considerations to yield to the *unnatural* embraces of her husband, and thus to endanger the very existence of her embryo babe? How often is it sacrificed to the ungoverned passion of its own father and the health of the mother seriously impaired? Every *unnatural* process is deleterious, hence abortions are destructive to the constitution, and many women are broken down in the prime of life by them alone, and their haggard countenances too plainly reveal their secret sorrows. A lady once said to me I have but one child, but I have had twelve miscarriages—another had four children and fifteen abortions. And why I would ask this untimely casting of her fruit? Do the beasts of the field miscarry? Why not? They are governed by instinct. Are the *brutes* safe during the period of gestation whilst *woman* is not!!

But it may be said, in multitudes of instances abortion is not the result of sexual connection. True, but consequences even *worse* are constantly supervening; the vital forces of the embryo are deteriorated by such disturbing forces, and sickly constitutions are entailed upon multitudes of children. Many more grow up under the terrible effects of an inherited lechery, which is the hidden cause of abounding licentiousness. That inexorable law of inheritance by which are transferred not only physical peculiarities but moral characteristics, parents have yet to learn.

This Law has, in the unripeness of humanity, perpetuated and intensified the *lower* nature, but when appreciated it will offer to parents the most powerful motives to the cultivation of a fine, healthy physique, combined with the noblest mental and moral endowments. Water cannot rise higher than its head. Bitter fountains cannot send forth sweet waters. Let us then reverently obey the laws of our being, and then will our children be born blessings to the world. If in animals this non-interference is necessary to the production of a fine breed, how much *more necessary* must it be in the case of woman, who is divinely ordained to develop a vastly higher and more complicated form of life?

After her babe is born and nature's own nutriment is provided for it, how often is it robbed of this natural food, and consequently subjected to disease and death thro' the instrumentality of that father, whose sacred province it is, to guard it from all injury. Again look at the burdens imposed upon her by the care of many children following in quick succession. How can any mother do her duty to her family, if in eight years she have six children? Look at the unnatural tug upon her constitution, her night watches, her sore vexations and trials and causes nameless and numberless, that wear away her life. If men had to alternate with their wives, the duties of the nursery, fewer and further between would be its inmates. Children should be nursed thro' the *second* summer during denlition, at which period infantile diseases are most prevalent, and are fearfully increased by the fact of their being generally deprived of the *only* proper food at this critical time. Call not the death of thousands of our population every year in infancy, "a dispensation of Divine Providence." This destruction of infantile life is mainly chargeable to man *not* God. Give us a race of strong and healthy children, free from excessive predominance of the animal propensities, and a few generations will lift the Race from its low estate. It is absurd to expect sudden transformations. Nature's laws are as slow as they are sure. The Millennium is not coming to us thro' Revivals or any miraculous interposition, but by "due process of law" and man must and will work out his salvation from evil by the Divine energy of his own Nature, "God working in him to will and to do of his own good pleasure," for "his will is our sanctification" thro' individual conflict and conquest. As Christ was made perfect thro' suffering, so must all be made perfect. This is the Divine Law for the individual and the Race.

The perfection of spirit life is the sole object of Creation, and for that end all material creations are so arranged as to furnish the great School of the Universe, with all the fixtures, apparatus and conditions necessary to the unfolding and perfection of all souls here and elsewhere.

O! how many Women who have entered the marriage relation in all purity and innocence, expecting to realize in it the completion of their own halfness, the rounding out of their own being, the blending of their holiest instincts with those of a kindred spirit, have too soon discovered that they were unpaid housekeepers and nurses, and still worse, chattels personal to be used and abused at the will of a master, and all, in a cold matter of course, obey. O! the agony of realizing that personal and pecuniary independence are annihilated by that "Law which makes the husband and wife *one* and that one is the husband." How many so called wives, rise in the morning oppressed with a sense of degradation, from the fact that their chastity has been violated, their holiest instincts disregarded, and themselves humbled under an oppressive sense of their own pollution, and that too a thousand times harder to bear, because a so called husband has been the perpetrator of the unnatural crime.

O! how the soul sickens at the oppressions heaped upon woman *in* the marriage relation as well as *out* of it, because Marriage is misunderstood, perverted and desecrated. Then again, the almost impossibility of enlightening the world on this subject, sits like an incubus upon the spirit. Why speak pure words into impure ears, or breathe holy tho'ts into minds reeking with pollution? Will they not whelm them under the slime of their own corruption? Will they not trample the pearls of truth in the mire of sensuality and turn again and rend us?

Who does not see that Men must grow out of that non-development in which they now are, before they will have ears to hear or hearts to love the truth on this subject, and that to Woman must be conceded an *equality of rights* thro'out the circle of human relations, before she can be emancipated from that worst of all slaveries—slavery to the passions of man.

And this equality cannot, will not be conceded until she too grows out of that stratum of development in which she now is. Her imperfect education unfits her for acquiring that pecuniary independence which would lift her above the temptation to marry for a home. Dependence subjects her too often to be duped *in* the marriage relation as well as out of it. And the great work to be done now for woman by woman, is to impress her with the necessity of pecuniary independence, each working out that independence according to her taste and ability. Now they work under great disadvantages and can obtain a mere pittance. But be not discouraged sisters. Is not a dinner of herbs and simple apparel such as you can provide, infinitely better than sumptuous fare, costly attire, elegant furniture and equipage received in exchange for *freedom* and *personal purity*? They must yearn to be *women* rather than fine statues to be draped in satins and lawns, elegant automata grace[ing] a drawing room or pretty play things to be toyed with by respectable rakes or heartless dandies under the guise of lovers and husbands. You must repress your passion for display and clothe your persons so modestly yet tastefully as not to excite impure desires, and so demean yourself in private and in public as to force upon every man and woman a sense of your womanhood—a conviction of your incorruptibility.

In all great change thro' which Society passes in her upward progress, there seem to be periods of interregnum, when the old usage has died out before the new one was ready to be inaugurated in its place. The Present is forever doomed to stand around the death-bed of the Past, watching her dying struggles, whilst Hope, springing eternal in the bleeding breast, points triumphant to that blessed Resurrection which will give to the world the spirit of the dead Institution in some holier and brighter form. As the beech tree clings to its withered leaves until the new spring buds push them off, so let it be with the existing institution of Marriage. Let the old contract system remain, until that new and divine form of spirit union, shall have gently undermined its hold upon Society, pushing it gradually off, and taking its place in the hearts and lives of all who are prepared to welcome it in purity and love.

The bitter experiences, thro' which many married persons are now passing, will not be lost either to themselves or the Race. It is a sorrow, out of which many minds will learn the lessons of mutual forbearance, whilst at the same time every such marriage must cause the family and friends of the parties to reexamine the whole subject, bringing them to regard it in a very different light from that low ideal of the Past, which scarcely lifted it, among the masses, above mere convenience, worldly policy of selfish passion. Thus the crucified parent will in many instances become the Savior of his children, giving his heart's blood daily, to purchase for them an inheritance in the sacredness, spirituality and purity of true Marriage.

7.

Sisters of Charity

Another version of this essay was first edited by Gerda Lerner and published in *Signs* 1, no. 1 (Autumn 1975): 246–56. The title is taken from a work by British feminist Anna Jameson, *Sisters of Charity and the Communion of Labour: Two Lectures on the Social Employments of Women* (3d rev. ed.; London: Longman, Brown, and Green, 1859).* Grimké quotes at length from Jameson's book in this essay, though, as Lerner has noted, she also makes significant departures from it. Jameson's tone is that of a moderate liberal seeking political and educational reforms for women; Grimké's is still that of the impassioned moral reformer, and her statements about women's oppression and dignity are filled with anger and zeal. I agree wholeheartedly with Lerner's assessment that Grimké's statements go well beyond the moderate demands of the liberal reformer to reflect a sophisticated awareness of feminist consciousness and a separate women's culture (Lerner, 1983:812–13).

The title of this essay also refers to women's widespread involvement in benevolent and moral reform societies. As discussed

---

*Gerda Lerner discovered the Jameson connection and wrote about it in "Comment on Lerner's 'Sarah M. Grimké's 'Sisters of Charity,'" *Signs* 10, no. 4 (Summer 1985): 811–15. She provides an excellent comparative analysis of the Grimkés' and Jameson's writings, as well as other useful insights into Grimké's feminism. She seems particularly enthusiastic over the discovery of an Anglo-American feminist connection as early as the 1850s.

in the Introduction, at the time Grimké was writing, during the height of "the cult of domesticity," women plunged into active involvement in reform societies of all sorts—moral and health reform, temperance, abolition, women's rights. Women brought about reform in prisons, mental institutions, and hospitals.

In this essay, Grimké reiterates a familiar theme in her writing—that the laws respecting women, especially married women, are an abomination to the nation and to women's souls, and should be repealed. She uses many of the same arguments against these laws that she used in the *Letters*—that they deprive women of their intellectual and moral autonomy and their capacity to fulfill their true natures and God's purposes for them. These points are also similar to those advanced in the *Declaration of Sentiments,* written only a few years before the time when Grimké most likely wrote this essay.

The new argument here is Grimké's citing the work of "sisters of charity" as evidence of women's capabilities. Women have already shown themselves to be capable of reforming penal codes and emigration laws and whole systems of hospital administration. Certainly, then, she argues, they must be capable of legislating wisely regarding other important matters.

With regard to the development of Grimké's feminism, this essay is the most significant. She writes with passion and eloquence about women's essential dignity. She exhibits a sophisticated feminist awareness in her analysis of the antagonism between the sexes as one between "classes." She suggests the notion of consciousness-raising both in acknowledging that the female sex is largely "ignorant of its own powers" and in stating that "there is now awakened in her [woman] a consciousness that she is defrauded of her legitimate Rights." She reveals her growing sense of sorority, both in her acknowledgment that men can never truly enter the world and experiences of women and in her declaration that women must claim their own destinies. "Self-reliance only can create true and exalted women," she writes. True to her religious beliefs, she calls on woman to discover the "divinity within," "her own selfhood revealed to her by the spirit of God."

This essay, more than any of the others, is Sarah Grimké's affirmation of womanhood—both her own and that of all womankind. One can almost see Sarah rising up and standing tall as she declares, "Hitherto there has been at the root of her being darkness, inharmony, bondage and consequently the majesty of her being has been obscured, and the uprising of her nature is but the effort to give to her whole being the opportunity to expand into all its essential nobility."

Sisters of Charity

It cannot be denied that the present state of society needs reformation. Various expedients have been tried, but as a sensible writer remarks we have not yet tried the experiment of giving to Women the same political Rights as men and throwing open to them all civil and ecclesiastical office. "In our hospitals, prisons, almshouses, lunatic asylums, workhouses, reformatory schools, elementary schools, Houses of Refuge—every where we want efficient women." No one who has visited such institutions, where, by the way, we are admitted as a favor, none of these institutions requiring in their by-laws that women should be associated with men as overseers etc. etc., but must perceive the absolute need of women as coadjutors. Even those who feel the importance of this union of the masculine and feminine elements regard it as a dernier resort to be tried as an experiment rather than the carrying out of a law which has its foundation in the very nature of man, ignoring this fact vital to the best welfare of society that without union of labor between the sexes nothing can be well done, because there is nothing done which does not affect the interests of both. The apostle uttered a great truth applicable to all the work that has to be done for Humanity—"Neither is the woman without the man, neither the man without the woman" [1 Cor. 11:9].

"Women in the midst of all splendor of a luxurious Home have perished by a slow wasting disease of body and mind because they have nothing to do—no sphere of activity commensurate with the large mental powers or passionate energy of character with which God had endowed them. Send such a woman to her piano, her novels, or her cross stitch, she answers with despair."

It must be conceded that there is an absolute necessity for the industrial sphere of woman to be enlarged. Sewing machines are depriving thousands, if not millions of their daily bread. Bless the inventor of sewing machines, although present misery may be the result, as is the case in all changes however beneficial, yet this invention will do a grand work in elevating women; it will impose upon her the necessity of seeking other occupations, and whatever widens the sphere of usefulness adds to the intelligence of the class thus pushed onward and outward.

It is most unjust for any individual to make his feelings or his opinions a standard for others; it betrays a most lamentable narrow-mindedness and an utter want of interest in the welfare of the race—the question before one is vital to our progress and is worthy of the most thorough examination not on the ground of sentiment and prejudice, but on the ground of philosophy, common justice and humanity. Such persons close their eyes and ears to the fact that unless honest employment is found for women, they must be driven by starvation and despair to dishonest and unworthy if not infamous means to preserve life.

"Every injustice is a form of falsehood, every falsehood accepted and legalized, works in the social system like poison in the physical frame, and will taint the whole body politic through and through, ere we have learned in what quivering nerve, or delicate tissue to trace and detect its fatal presence. Human Laws which contravene the laws of God, are not laws but lies; and like all lies must perish. There is a saying that a lie believed in half an hour might cause a century of mischief. What then is likely to be the effect of these laws which have existed as part of our common law for centuries— laws which may well be called lies inasmuch as they suppose a state of things which has no real existence in the divine regulation of the world? Laws which during all that period have tended to degrade women in the eyes of man, interfered with the sacredness of the domestic relations, and infected the whole social system." "I regard these laws as one cause of prostitution, because in so far as they have lowered the social position of women, they have lowered the value of her labor, and have thus exposed her to want and temptation which would not otherwise have existed. Far beyond the palpable visible working of these laws, cruel as they are in individual cases, lies an infinitely greater mischief in their injurious effect on the manners of the people." "They permeate, and vitiate the relations of the two sexes throughout the whole community."[1]

"Is it not rather absurd to devise as an antidote to the working of these laws, another law, really as unjust in its way, which punishes a man for ill-treating the creature he has been authorized to regard as his inferior? Every act of legislation which takes for granted antagonism, not harmony, between the masculine and the feminine nature, hastened to create that antagonism." "When the creator endowed the two halves of the race with ever aspiring hopes, ever widening sympathies, ever progressive capacities—when He made them equal in the responsibilities which bind the conscience and in the temptations which mislead the will, He linked them inseparably in an ever extending sphere of duties, and an ever expanding communion of affections—thus in one simple, holy and beautiful ordinance, binding up at once the continuation of the species and its moral, social and physical progress."

"It is indisputable that the mutual influence of the two sexes—brain upon brain—life upon life—becomes more subtle and spiritual and complex,

1. Note—This is the opinion of a man of large experience, Mr. F. Hill, for many years inspector of prisons. He observes that the sin and misery alluded to would probably be greatly diminished if public opinion no longer upheld the exclusive spirit by which most of the lucrative employments are restricted to the male sex, whereby the difficulties with which females have to contend in earning an honest livelihood are greatly increased. "*Crime Its Amount, Causes and Remedies,* by F[rederick] Hill Inspector of Prisons" (London: John Murray, 1853), pp. 84–87 [Grimké's note].

more active and more intense in proportion as the human race is improved and developed. Physiologists know this well."

"I have the deepest conviction founded not merely on my own observation and experience, but on the testimony of some of the wisest and best men that to enlarge the working sphere of woman, to give her a more practical and authorized share in all social arrangements . . . is to elevate her in the social scale, and what ever renders womanhood respected and respectable in the estimation of the people tends to humanize and refine them."

Miss Nightingale had long studied all that fitted her for the great work she undertook and the soldiers at once recognized a master mind and bowed before it.[2] Her studies had been what our mothers and grandmothers might have called unfeminine, even masculine perhaps. Why this last was made a term of reproach we are at a loss to discover, but how great was the power she exercised in consequence.

Had not this great occasion been presented to her, that power of intellect and Christian benevolence which has now warmed the heart of thousands would never have had its full scope and we should still be twaddling about "the true sphere of woman."

In the Crimea "All bear witness to the salutary influence exercised by the lady-nurses over the men. In the most violent attacks of fever and delirium when the orderlies could not hold them down in their beds, the presence of one of these ladies, instead of being exciting had the effect of calming the spirits and subduing the most refractory. It is allowed that these ladies had the power to repress swearing and bad and coarse language; to prevent the smuggling of brandy into the wards; to open the hearts of the sullen and desperate to contrition and responsive kindness." As one of the nurses wrote: "Whether[3] in the strain of overwork, or the steady fulfilment of our arduous duty there was one bright ray ever shed over it—one thing that made labor light and sweet, and this was the respect, affection and gratitude of the men. No words can tell it rightly for it was unbounded and so long as we stayed among them it never changed. Familiar as we were become to them, in and out day and night, they never forgot the respect due to our sex and position. Standing by them in bitter agony where the force of habits is great, or by those in the glow of returning health, or walking up the wards among orderlies and sergeants, never did a word which could offend a woman's ear fall upon ours. Even in the barrack yard passing by the guard-room or entrance, where stood groups of soldiers smoking and idling, the moment we approached all coarseness was hushed; and this lasted not a week or a month but the whole of my twelve months residence and my experience is that of my companions."[4]

2. Florence Nightingale (1820–1910). See chap. 6, n. 3.
3. This section has been moved from a later part of the manuscript.
4. Eastern Hospitals v. 2, p. 178 [Grimké's note].

What is the natural inference to be drawn from these facts with regard to the influence of woman in political and civil life? I wish it to be understood that I only advocate intelligent etc. women as eligible to office just as I would about men.

Under the laws which ordained death as the punishment for witch-craft, says Mrs. Jameson,[5] "The women who perished by judicial condemnation for heresy in the days of the Inquisition did not equal the number of women condemned judicially as witches—hanged, tortured, burned, drowned like mad dogs in the first century of the Reformed Church and these horrors were enacted in the most civilized countries in Europe and by grave magistrates and ecclesiastics."

Do you doubt the capability of Elizabeth Fry[6] to frame laws for the better regulation of Prisons, and the Reform of the Criminal Code, or of Caroline Chisholm[7] to alter and amend these relating to Emigration or of Mary Carpenter[8] who has become an authority in all that concerns the treatment of juvenile delinquents? Each of these women was "assailed by the bitterest animosity, and the most vulgar abuse, by those who condemned them and would have put them down merely as women." They have outlived prejudice and jealousy.[9]

"Why are parents so careless of the instruction of their daughters in aught that is really useful, or lucrative, merely because the law says no married female shall enjoy the fruit of her labor, and because the social position of women in this country is so influenced by the tendency of our code to repress their active participation in affairs, that a girl is fenced round by a hedge of prejudice, which it requires a rare combination of circumstances to enable her to break through."

5. Mrs. Anna Jameson, author of *Sisters of Charity and the Communion of Labour: Two Lectures on the Social Employments of Women*, from which much of the material in this essay is quoted.
6. Elizabeth Fry (1780–1845) brought about reforms for women prisoners in London's Newgate Gaol. She established the Ladies Association for the Improvement of the Female Prisoners, which organized workshops, Bible classes, and a system of discipline monitored by the inmates. They insisted that prisons provide separate women's quarters with female attendants. They hired a matron and tried to aid female prisoners after their release. Fry's 1827 treatise, *Observations in Visiting, Superintendence and Government of Female Prisoners*, furnished the principles that would later dominate American women's prison reform.
7. Caroline Chisholm (1808–77) opened an office for the use of emigrants in Sydney, Australia, and promoted the emigration of families from England. She is the author of *The ABC of Colonization* and *Emigration and Transportation*.
8. Mary Carpenter (1807–77) opened several ragged schools and reformatories in England in the 1840s and 1850s, including a reformatory for girls. She is the author of *Our Convicts, How They Are Made and Should Be Treated*.
9. En. Wo. Journal—Employments of Wo. P. 8 Edu. Wo. Ad.
Sat. July 10
3rd Page—
West. Rev. Jan. 57 [Grimké's note].

"Woman's work is wherever there is a good work to be wrought; and for this she should be educated: a mind so fortified would be in no danger of falling into the follies which the stringent etiquettes of society have been invented to curb" "and should be emancipated from the eternal tutelage in which the law insists on holding her."

It is to the pale scholar over his midnight lamp, not to the successful general, that we look for the improvement of the human race, and when the leaders of the age are those whose physical frame is assimilated more especially to the feminine phase of life, why should idle prejudice any longer shut out women from taking their place wherever intellect rather than strength is required? It will not be till the business of the world is more equally distributed that either sex will thoro'ly fulfil its vocation in life, or that we can hope for that harmonious cooperation which can alone make any great undertaking successful. At present women are depressed by the laws, depressed by the prejudice of parents and guardians, till the greater part of the sex is ignorant of its own powers.

"Why have legislators all but recognized the necessity of tolerating an order of wretched women, who while ruining both in body and soul those who habitually consort with them, pay the penalty of their sin against the established laws of nature by a short and suffering life." "Our social system makes seduction easy; and we must note this as the first great fault, which can only be remedied by making women less dependent on men."

"Our present lack of accomplished statesmen and legislators may be traced to the unrepealed barbarism of ancestral laws which have retained the mothers of the nation in a degraded position." . . .

The laws respecting married women are one of the greatest outrages that has been perpetrated against God and humanity.[10] To couple the highest and holiest institution, an institution connected not merely with the perpetuation of the race, but with the most sacred instincts, the holiest affections, the noblest aspirations of our being, an institution designed above all others to bring the sexes into harmony, to educate not only the married pair but their offspring for a more exalted life—to couple such an institution on the one side with injustice and oppression and on the other with the loss of self-respect, independence and degradation is an insult to omnipotence and to the divinity He has conferred upon man which has no parallel. Unless marriage becomes a great and holy institution, unless birth be invested with the consecration of the Divine Presence, it is in vain to expect domestic felicity. There may be kindness on one side and subserviency on the other, but the snaky coil will still entwine itself around the hymened altar and the hiss of the reptiles be heard mingling with the voice of love. I have used strong language. I feel deeply, strongly because I have seen where the husbands did

10. At the time, legal battles for women's property rights were going on in New York and Mississippi.

all in their power to annul them. It was impossible not to feel that their rights were ignored and that they enjoyed the privileges they had, not by right, but by courtesy. The laws respecting women are a blasphemy against God; they invade His right to decide on the equality of Human Rights and charge him with surrendering the duties and obligations, the conscience and the will of half His intelligent creation to the caprice, selfishness and physical superiority of the other. "Can you wonder that poisonous reptiles nestle and harbor their scaly loathsomeness in the very bosom of the marriage contract and hiss and rattle and rear their hooded heads, and whet their venomed fangs securely there." These things must be, my brethren, until you teach women self respect and self reliance by giving her just and equal laws, by raising her from her present degraded and abnormal position. The law which gives woman the right before marriage to make the most important far reaching contract which a human being can make and then by legal enactment proclaims her incapable of the most common business contracts is too absurd to need any comment. Is there any thing to hope for the world under the existing laws? Why hold we to these dead symbols of barbarism? We need laws now inspired by the vitality of the present era—laws bounding with the life blood of advancing civilization, if we would go on from glory to glory as a nation. Let us not borrow or reenact the laws of a barbarous age, but give utterance to the present revelation of Jehovah and invest woman with the halo which omnipotence designs for her brow. What an unwise man said of books, viz. that it would be better for the world if every book were destroyed, may be said of the laws respecting woman. If every one of the enactments were obliterated the world would be the better for it. . . .

"Fossils" are elegantly termed "the medals of creation." Laws may with equal truth be called the medals of legislation. They are chronometers which tell the evolution through which the society has passed. They mark distinctly the march of mankind in that distant period when barely anything else remains to tell us what we have been. Laws characterize certain epochs. In some of them we see the rude and savage state of infant society, in others the attempts of some elevated minds to rise above the barbarism of the times. I have no fault to find with past legislation. I believe it was in every age adapted to the highest honor—when like the wild man of the wilds his reputation kept pace with the number of murders he committed, his laws were bloody as his sword. By slow and painful experiences he learned to be less hostile to his brother man and we see in the codes of all civilized nations a gradual amelioration of the Laws, and those which were once in force, like the footprints of birds in red sandstone, only exist to tell that they have been.

The trials and suffering of woman unnoticed and unknown have been accumulating for her a wisdom and a will which must be heard in the counsels of the nation. Like the microscopic crustaceous animals, a billion of which occupy, says Ehrenburg,[11] but a cubic inch which now form one third of the earth's surface, the experiences of woman have been consolidating into a firm foundation on which she can confidently stand and build a temple to freedom, happiness and humanity. . . .

"The legislators of the present day consult the chronicles of the past to get from thence the law of its own conduct and in this way constructs its political existence out of a confused patchwork gathered from many ages long since dead thereby openly displaying a clear consciousness of its own utter nothingness."[12]

Man never can legislate justly for woman because "he has never entered the world to which she belongs."

Woman seeks to give to our laws an inward security and strength and permanence which is infinitely more important than any outward restraint; in fact the former is the only firm and durable basis of the latter. It is self evident that inequality of Rights creates antagonism and the assumption that we must continue in this state is productive of nothing but evil, because the privileged and the oppressed stand in opposition to each other, the latter yielding unwillingly the distinctions which the former demand and the former shutting themselves up in the self made circle of their superiority, and scorning even to examine the claims of the dependent class. How shall these two classes harmonize? The answer is simple. "Establish Justice" which will insure "domestic tranquility, promote the general welfare and secure blessings of liberty,"[13] to woman and posterity. "Then the differences which exist between them in matters of small moment would readily disappear before their equality in those higher privileges on which they set supreme value." This state of things must be actualized; for it is impossible to lull the awakened soul into a belief that it is free when the galling fetters still clank around it. It is impossible for any woman of lofty purpose and pure morality to accept the dogma that woman was made to be subservient to man.

Thus far woman has struggled through life with bandaged eyes, accepting the dogma of her weakness and inability to take care of herself not only physically, but intellectually. She has held out a trembling hand and received gratefully the proffered aid. She has foregone her right to study, to know the laws and purposes of the government to which she is subject. But there is now awakened in her a consciousness that she is defrauded of her legitimate Rights and that she never can fulfil her mission until she is placed in that position to which she feels herself called by the divinity within. Hitherto she has surrendered her person and individuality to man, but she can no longer do this and not feel that she is outraging her nature and her

11. Christian Gottfried Ehrenburg (1795–1876), geologist and paleontologist, is most noted for his pioneering achievements in the study of single-celled marine and fossil animals. He discovered single-celled fossils that had built up a geological stratum.
12. Johann Gottlieb Fichte (1762–1814); see p. oo, n. 1.
13. Preamble to the United States Constitution.

God. There is now predominant in the minds of intelligent women to an extent never known before a struggling after freedom, an intense desire after a higher life. Let us not imagine that because superstition, blind faith in unexamined and untenable dogmas are losing their power over the mind of woman, that her religious nature will be swept away. Far from it; the religion which reason sanctions will stand the test of change and we shall see her exhibiting "elevated philanthropy, the charities of social life, sympathy, benevolence, domestic affections, the self sacrificing attachment" of wife and mother, of sister and daughter to a degree even superior to that she has already manifested. She can no longer receive the superstitions whose death warrant her reason has signed, but she is awakening to higher and clearer ideas of her own nature and capacities and responsibilities. The debasing and unsatisfying babble of representations through another, of the beauty of feminine delicacy and dependence, has had time to echo and reecho itself. She has listened to it, paid homage to it. She is weary of it. She feels its emptiness with reference to that inward life which is not yet utterly extinguished. The fact that woman has eaten the bitter fruits of slavery to the will and selfishness and passions of man has prepared her to receive the truth of her own selfhood revealed to her by the spirit of God. Hitherto there have been at the root of her being darkness, inharmony, bondage, and consequently the majesty of her being has been obscured, and the uprising of her nature is but the effort to give to her whole being the opportunity to expand into all its essential nobility.

Legislation can do much towards producing that harmonious co-operation of the sexes which by the establishment of equal rights to person and to property will release woman from the horrors of forced maternity and teach her partner to subject his passions to the control of reason. Oh how many mothers have I heard say, I did not want this child, I am unable to do my duty to so many children and this feeling is a gangrene to my happiness. Think ye parents what a welcome awaits the helpless hapless being, the offspring of lust, not of sanctified affection, who is thus ushered into existence. Do I plead for woman? No I plead for the race, because I see then our endless curse hangs over humanity so long as marriage is thus misunderstood and desecrated.

"Suffering" says Cousin,[14] "is the most excellent of all things." I am inclined to think the philosopher is right. But for the suffering thro' which woman has passed as the mother of the race, she would not now feel so keenly the wrongs inflicted upon her, nor estimate as she now does how

14. Victor Cousin (1792–1867) was a French educator and philosopher who reorganized the French primary school system and established the study of philosophy as a major intellectual pursuit of French secondary and higher schools. He is best known for his concept of "eclecticism," whereby the human mind can accept all carefully thought-out and moderate interpretations of the world, so that no system of thought is seen to be false, merely incomplete.

treasonable it would be to herself and humanity longer to keep silence. Woman by surrendering herself to the tutelage of man may in many cases live at her ease, but she will live the life of a slave. By asserting and claiming her natural Rights she assumes the prerogative which every free intelligence ought to assume, that she is the arbiter of her own destiny, and if her soul is filled with this godlike sentiment she will strive to reflect in her life the representation of all that is pure and noble. Self-reliance only can create true and exalted women.

Chemistry has invested a breath of air, a drop of water with such a glory that days, for aught I know weeks, or months have been spent in their examination. Is woman, the mother of the race less worthy of being studied and understood? Great truths that have hitherto been hidden are assuming the importance they merit and the equality of the sexes in all natural Rights is one that claims the attention of every reasoning mind.

Health depends upon the inhalation of pure atmospheric air and the health of society depends no less upon inhalation of truth. If human beings are pent up in a vitiated atmosphere we all know the terrible results, as exhibited in that horrible den of iniquity the slave ship. The body politic exhibits now the ghastly and disfigured features of those who die a loathsome death by breathing putrefied air. The laws which ages ago were good for the people are no longer so and the convulsions in society which are everywhere apparent are only the agonized throes of human beings who are dying for the want of fresh air and sunshine. Change characterizes organic and inorganic bodies and the highest creation of God, his intelligent beings, are as much and as necessarily the subjects of change as any other part of his Creation. Every age has its own spirit. It is only by incessant change that the granite rock is formed; or that the majestic boabab rears its trunk and spreads out its branches, for change is the parent of stability. Every moment millions of the constituent cells of our bodies are dying and new ones coming in their stead; death is but the cessation of this change.

The law of might makes right, a distrust in woman, gave birth to the old domestic policy; it has had its iron reign. Let us not censure it—let us even believe it did the best it could, that it designed and did bless humanity, but let not the past tyrannize over the present when the spirit has departed from it. Liberty is the breath of God; wherever it penetrates there is prosperity, happiness and progress, but while liberty confers power it also imposes restraint. It quickens the perceptions of right and gives a keener sense of duty and responsibility—"The kingdom of God can only be an eternal revelation whose code is love and whose ministers are passing ages." . . .

Sources

Bartlett, Elizabeth Ann. 1986. "Liberty, Equality, Sorority: Contradiction and Integrity in Feminist Thought and Practice." *Women's Studies International Forum* 9, nos. 5 and 6, pp. 521–29.

Berg, Barbara J. 1978. *The Remembered Gate: Origins of American Feminism: The Woman and the City, 1800–1860.* New York: Oxford University Press.

Birney, Catherine H. 1885. *The Grimké Sisters: Sarah and Angelina Grimké: The First American Women Advocates of Abolition and Woman's Rights.* New York: Lee and Shepard Publishers. Reprint. St. Clair Shores, Mich.: Scholarly Press, 1970.

Conrad, Susan Phinney. 1976. *Perish the Thought: Intellectual Women in Romantic America, 1830–1860.* New York: Oxford University Press.

Cooper, James L., and Cooper, Sheila McIsaac. 1973. *The Roots of American Feminist Thought.* Boston: Allyn and Bacon.

Cott, Nancy. 1977. *The Bonds of Womanhood: "Woman's Sphere" in New England, 1780–1835.* New Haven: Yale University Press.

———. 1978. "Passionlessness: An Interpretation of Victorian Sexual Ideology, 1790–1850." *Signs,* 4, no. 2, pp. 219–36.

Daly, Mary. 1985. *Beyond God the Father: Toward a Philosophy of Women's Liberation.* 2d rev. ed. Boston: Beacon Press.

———. 1985. *The Church and the Second Sex.* Boston: Beacon Press.

———. 1978. *Gyn/Ecology: The Metaethics of Radical Feminism.* Boston: Beacon Press.

Dietz, Mary. 1985. "Citizenship and Maternal Thinking: Citizenship with a Feminist Face: The Problem with Maternal Thinking." *Political Theory* (February), pp. 19–37.

DuBois, Ellen. 1979. "Women's Rights and Abolition: The Nature of the Connection." In Perry, L., and Freeman, M., eds., *Antislavery Reconsidered.* Baton Rouge: Louisiana State University Press.

———, ed. 1975. "On Labor and Free Love: Two Unpublished Speeches of Elizabeth Cady Stanton." *Signs* 1, no. 1, pp. 257–68.

DuBois, Ellen Carol, and Gordon, Linda. 1983. "Seeking Ecstasy on the Battlefield: Danger and Pleasure in Nineteenth-Century Feminist Sexual Thought." *Feminist Studies* 9, no. 1, pp. 7–25.

Eisenstein, Hester. 1983. *Contemporary Feminist Thought*. Boston: G. K. Hall and Company.

Eisenstein, Zillah. 1981. *The Radical Future of Liberal Feminism*. New York: Longman.

Elshtain, Jean Bethke. 1981. *Public Man, Private Woman: Women in Social and Political Thought*. Princeton: Princeton University Press.

Evans, Sara. 1980. *Personal Politics: The Roots of Women's Liberation in the Civil Rights Movement and the New Left*. New York: Random House.

Firestone, Shulamith. 1971. *The Dialectic of Sex: The Case for Feminist Revolution*. New York: Bantam.

Flexner, Eleanor. 1959. *Century of Struggle: The Woman's Rights Movement in the United States*. New York: Atheneum.

Freeman, Jo. 1975. *The Politics of Women's Liberation: A Case Study of an Emerging Social Movement and Its Relation to the Policy Process*. New York: David McKay Company.

Gay, Peter. 1966. *The Enlightenment: An Interpretation, The Rise of Modern Paganism*. New York: W. W. Norton and Company.

Gordon, Ann D., and Buhle, Mary Jo. 1976. "Sex and Class in Colonial and Nineteenth-Century America." In Carroll, Berenice A., ed. *Liberating Women's History: Theoretical and Critical Essays*. Urbana: University of Illinois Press.

Gordon, Linda. 1973. "Voluntary Motherhood: The Beginnings of Feminist Birth Control Ideas in the United States." *Feminist Studies* 1:5–22.

Griffin, Susan. 1978. *Woman and Nature: The Roaring Inside Her*. New York: Harper & Row.

Grimké, Sarah Moore. 1838. *Letters on the Equality of the Sexes and the Condition of Woman*. Boston: Isaac Knapp. Reprint. New York: Source Book Press, 1970.

Hartsock, Nancy. 1986. *Money, Sex, and Power: Toward a Feminist Historical Materialism*. Boston: Northeastern University Press.

Hersh, Blanche Glassman. 1978. *The Slavery of Sex: Feminist Abolitionists in America*. Urbana: University of Illinois Press.

Hewitt, Nancy A. 1986. "Feminist Friends: Agrarian Quakers and the Emergence of Woman's Rights in America." *Feminist Studies* 12, no. 1, pp. 27–49.

Leach, William. 1980. *Free Love and Perfect Union: The Feminist Reform of Sex and Society*. New York: Basic Books.

Lerner, Gerda. 1985. Comment on Lerner's "Sarah M. Grimké's 'Sisters of Charity.'" *Signs* 10, no. 4, pp. 811–15.

———. 1971. *The Grimké Sisters from South Carolina: Pioneers for Woman's Rights and Abolition*. New York: Schocken Books.

Lorde, Audre. 1984. *Sister Outsider: Essays and Speeches by Audre Lorde*. Freemansburg, N.Y.: The Crossing Press.

McFadden, Maggie. 1984. "Anatomy of Difference: Toward a Classification of Feminist Theory." *Women's Studies International Forum* 7, no. 6, pp. 495–504.

Nies, Judith. 1977. *Seven Women: Portraits from the American Radical Tradition*. New York: Viking Press.

Ochs, Carol. 1983. *Women and Spirituality*. Totowa, N.J.: Rowman and Allanheld.

Perry, Lewis. 1973. *Radical Abolitionism: Anarchy and the Government of God in Antislavery Thought*. Ithaca: Cornell University Press.

Reuther, Rosemary. 1975. *New Woman/New Earth: Sexist Ideologies and Human Liberation*. New York: Seabury Press.

Rich, Adrienne. 1976. *Of Woman Born: Motherhood as Experience and Institution*. New York: Norton.

Rossi, Alice S. 1973. *The Feminist Papers: From Adams to de Beauvoir*. New York: Columbia University Press.

Rousseau, Jean-Jacques. 1906. *L'Emile, or a Treatise on Education*. Ed. W. H. Payne. New York and London: n.p.

Simmons, Adele. 1976. "Education and Ideology in Nineteenth-Century America: The Response of Educational Institutions to the Changing Role of Women." In Carroll, Berenice A., ed., *Liberating Women's History: Theoretical and Critical Essays*. Urbana: University of Illinois Press.

Smith-Rosenberg, Carroll. 1975. "The Female World of Love and Ritual: Relations between Women in Nineteenth-Century America." *Signs* 1, no. 1, pp. 1–29.

Stanton, Elizabeth Cady; Anthony, Susan B.; and Gage, Matilda Joslyn. 1881. *History of Woman Suffrage*. 2 vols. New York: Fowler and Wells, Publishers. Reprint. New York: Arno Press and The New York Times, 1969.

Starhawk. 1982. *Dreaming the Dark: Magic, Sex, and Politics*. Boston: Beacon Press.

Taylor, William R., and Lasch, Christopher. 1963. "Two 'Kindred Spirits': Sorority and Family in New England: 1839–1846." *The New England Quarterly* 36, no. 1, pp. 23–41.

Trebilcot, Joyce, ed. 1983. *Mothering: Essays in Feminist Theory*. Totowa, N.J.: Rowman and Allanheld.

Welter, Barbara. 1966. "The Cult of True Womanhood: 1820–1860." *American Quarterly* 18: 151–74.

Wollstonecraft, Mary. 1965. *The Rights of Woman*. London: Dent, Everyman's Library.

Woolman, John. 1962. *Journal*. In *The Quaker Reader*. Selected and with an introduction by Jessamyn West. New York: The Viking Press.

Wright, Frances. 1834. *Course of Popular Lectures, with Three Addresses, On Various Public Occasions, and a Reply to the Charges Against the French Reformers of 1789 and Supplement Course of Lectures*. London: James Watson. Reprint. New York: Arno Press, 1972.

Index